IMPROVING MARKETING EFFECTIVENESS

IMPROVING MARKETING EFFECTIVENESS

Robert Shaw

THE ECONOMIST IN ASSOCIATION WITH
PROFILE BOOKS LTD

Published by Profile Books Ltd
58A Hatton Garden, London ECIN 8LX

Typeset in EcoType by MacGuru
macguru@pavilion.co.uk

Printed in Great Britain by The Bath Press

A CIP catalogue record for this book is available
from the British Library

ISBN 1 86197 054 4

Contents

To Edith Hilda Shaw

Acknowledgements

In the conception and creation of this book I am especially grateful to my friend, editor and constant adviser, Carolyn White, who more than any other person saw the point and scope of it from its origins and encouraged me through the dark days of its adolescence. My thanks also go to Stephen Brough, Tim Ambler, Hugh Davidson and David Wethey, who read the manuscript and provided a great deal of sensible advice, some of it too sensible for me.

Nor would it have been written without the encouragement of a few individuals, who were kind enough to listen, argue and help shape my thinking, recently and in the past. I am particularly appreciative of the following people: John Dixon and Mike Green who I first met at Cambridge University; Bruce Weston with whom I first worked on energy policy and scenario planning in the 1970s; Kent Brooks, Bob and Kate Kestnbaum, Rudi Oetting and Geri Gantman, and Colin Norton-Smith, colleagues in my database marketing days at Andersen Consulting; Merlin Stone, who first tempted me to leave Andersen and start an independent consultancy; Liz Montgomery whose research skills have saved the day on some extremely challenging global projects; Zona Stroy, Ellen Dulberger, Mike Daniels and Sam Palmisano for their support through some of the most paradoxical client challenges of my career; Tim Ambler for inviting me to join him on the Metrics project; and Andrew Ehrenberg and Philip Kotler for their thoughtful interest in my recent work on measurement.

For some years the seeds of ideas planted by these discussions had been developing, and Carolyn White's prescience in commissioning a report for the *Financial Times* group on Marketing Accountability influenced my first attempt to commit the ideas to paper. I then began teaching and incorporating the new measurement framework into my consulting work. Gradually, it became apparent that this measurement topic was even more important than I had realised, and yet it was almost virgin territory. Further urging and encouragement led me to write a book that would be more accessible, and further teaching and consultation helped me to simplify and shape the ideas that have gone into it. I have benefited enormously from the feedback and insights of these students and clients. Last, but not least, my heartfelt thanks go to Malcolm McDonald, who tempted me back to academia and to the visiting professorship at Cranfield School of Management.

Robert Shaw, October 1998

1 Introduction: time for fresh thinking

"LET me try and clarify some of this for you. BestCo supermarkets are not interested in selling wholesome foods, they are not worried about the nation's health. What is concerning them is that the nation appears to be getting worried about its health, and that is what's worrying BestCo. Because BestCo wants to go on selling them what it always has, ie white bread, baked beans, canned foods, and that suppurating, fat-squirting little heart-attack traditionally known as the British sausage. So, how can we help them with that?"

These are the opening words of a successful marketing executive, Dennis Bagley, played by Richard E. Grant in the film *How to get ahead in advertising*. Bagley fulfils a popular stereotype of the marketing type. He is greedy, rude, egotistic, disorganised, and yet ultimately successful. He also invents facts and figures about customers' habits, motivations and social psychology. Asked by a junior colleague about supporting research evidence, he retorts: "I don't need to look at the market research, I've lived with 13 and a half million housewives for 15 years and I know everything about them. She is 37 years old, she has 2.3 children, 1.6 of which will be girls. She uses 16 feet 6 inches of toilet tissue a week, and has sex no more than 4.2 times a month. She has seven radiators, and is worried about her weight."

Bagley is immensely unappealing. People's habits are often undignified, and by association Bagley, who studies them, is unappealing. People's habits in the kitchen, the bathroom and toilet, and in bed are put under the microscope by the marketer. As a result, Bagley faces a crisis. He feels unsuccessful, and he is rejected by many of his peers. Of course, Bagley is a fictional character. But his fictional portrait is a good one, for in reality, too, marketing is facing a mid-life crisis, for exactly the same reasons: its lack of precision, misrepresentation of "facts" and lack of real understanding of customer needs.

Over the past five years there has been a storm of criticism of marketing and widespread disappointment. In 1993 *The McKinsey Quarterly* published an article entitled "Marketing's Mid-Life Crisis", quoting one typical CEO as saying: "Marketing is like a millstone round my neck." A 1994 Coopers & Lybrand survey, *Marketing At The Crossroads*, quoted another executive as saying: "Marketing is increasingly living a lie in my organisation." Other articles predicted the death of the brand and the rejection of marketing by Wall Street and the City.

The work that marketing people do has variously been described as a profession, an art, a science, a sinister instrument of mass persuasion and a ludicrous waste of money. The term "marketing" is widely used in a pejorative sense in the media, and marketing types are frequently portrayed as false, immoral scoundrels. Nevertheless, marketing people still see themselves as professionals, giving consumers the products they want and practising a marketing science which creates the very lifeblood of business. According to John Stubbs, CEO of the UK Marketing Council, "marketing deserves to be valued as the stuff of heroes, it is the beating heart of business".

However, there is clearly a problem to be resolved. Research by the UK Marketing Council in 1997 revealed that over 75% of organisations are actively reviewing the future roles of their marketing people. John Stubbs commented: "I was taken aback by just how little reputation marketing actually has among other functions ... marketing and marketers are not respected by the people in their organisations for their contributions to business strategy, results or internal communication. We often don't know what or who is good or bad at marketing; our measurements are not seen as credible; our highest qualifications are not seen to have compatible status with other professions."

And the band played on

P&O's flagship, *Oriana*, is a striking monument to self-confidence, luxury and success. In mid-September 1997 it hosted the most prestigious event on the European marketing calendar: the Marketing Forum. With its gilt and marbled corridors, its opulent meeting rooms and all-pervasive sense of well-being, the ship was a perfect meeting place for 1,000 of the best-qualified and best-connected marketers in Europe.

These were strange surroundings to have chosen for two days of anguished soul searching. People flocked to research presentations that showed how poorly marketing was regarded by the City, by consumers and by colleagues. They attended workshops where they wallowed in feelings of shame and guilt about their lack of influence, and at the "fools clinic" they laughed at their own desperate problems. At night the marketers toasted themselves in vintage champagne, then disco'd till the early hours, while the ship sailed round in circles.

The research findings which created this particular ambience came from a number of sources. The organisers of the cruise, Richmond Events, had surveyed City analysts on their perceptions of marketing and marketing personnel. The analysts responded that they thought companies were unnecessarily secretive about marketing; that they would like more data on market share, more market growth forecasts, and information about brand values and brand awareness. However, few analysts thought marketing personnel were important enough to be essential on the main board. (A view borne out in a study of 100 of Europe's leading companies by Ashridge Strategic Management Centre, which found that marketing was present in under 20% of company headquarters.)

Other commentators see marketing as being increasingly isolated from broader consumer issues. *Marketing* magazine commented on July 24th 1997 that marketing "is in danger of becoming marginalised as companies switch emphasis from focusing on the brand to delivering total customer satisfaction". As Mr Stubbs admits: "Marketing is isolated, it has too little impact on business effectiveness, it is narrowly seen as advertising, promotion and bunting, and its professional status is not recognised."

Research by a consultancy, Synesis, investigated the opinions of other managers about their marketing colleagues. Marketing work was described as tactical rather than strategic by 84% of marketing managers and 76% of general managers. This reflected a waste of talent according to the marketing managers, 80% of whom said their strategic ideas were good to excellent. Marketing managers themselves complained that they and their departments lacked time and authority for strategic planning, and were overloaded by a plethora of tactical jobs, including many information-gathering tasks of dubious importance.

Performance monitoring by marketing managers was also marked down; 81% of general managers have a poor opinion of marketing's performance monitoring, complaining that marketing's performance measurement is just adequate or worse. Marketers have a slightly better opinion of themselves, but 58% still see their performance measurement as just adequate or worse. Market knowledge was rated as good to excellent by 77% of general managers and 78% of marketing managers, but as one respondent commented it was "divorced from the operational world".

Other typical comments from the Synesis research were:

- "Too much blue sky, not enough feet on the ground, need to get nearer the front line."
- "Low profile, little understanding of what the company does. Strategic thinking not aligned to reality. Alice in Wonderland mentality."

■ "Marketing so-called couldn't recognise real marketing if it hit them. They are a bunch of salesmen, some failed. The few real marketing people we once employed have all left."

The Marketing Society itself scored an own goal in 1997 when it commissioned NOP to ask 1,000 consumers on their views of how trustworthy marketing people are. The survey showed that marketers are seen by the public as only slightly more trustworthy than estate agents and politicians, and they enjoy less trust than lawyers, bank managers, teachers and doctors.

Yet at the end of the *Oriana* cruise, despite the harsh facts, there was no overwhelming drive for change. Steve Cuthbert, director-general of the Chartered Institute of Marketing, summarised the general mood: "We've had a few years of soul searching, so maybe we should let people finish this event on a high note, despite all the research evidence."

A short history of marketing

To understand where marketing is going, it helps to know where it has come from. America can justly claim to be the cradle of marketing's evolution. American companies had, and have, a huge homogeneous national market. In the 19th century, as transport improved, travelling salesmen crossed the continent laden with every known cure, stimulant, medicine or treatment. The medical quacks may have sold snake oil, but their contribution to the development of marketing cannot be overlooked. For the development of recognisable brands, first regionally and then nationally, provided the foundation for growth on a much greater scale. In the early years of the 20th century American management developed a vast array of techniques – premiums, free samples, catalogues and advertising – to support the lonely travelling salesman. And American consumers began to identify brands with quality.

In 1931 Procter & Gamble (P&G) introduced a new function in businesses: the brand manager. With brands such as Ivory and Camay bath soaps, P&G believed that the best way to organise itself would be to give responsibility for advertising, promotion and packaging to a single individual, the brand manager. By 1967, 84% of large manufacturers of consumer packaged goods in the United States had brand managers. They were self-confident about their ability to influence customers and to bring in the profits. Yet this confidence was misplaced, for they underestimated the growing power of consumers.

By the 1960s the consumer revolution was under way. Marketing became a target for criticism. In 1962 John F. Kennedy delivered his spe-

cial message on protecting consumer interests, which was implicitly critical of marketing's power. Ralph Nader, Rachel Carson and others quickly
followed. Marketing somehow got left behind, siding with its corporate
masters and remaining more interested in what it could do to consumers
rather than for them. It would not be until the 1990s that governments
and most boards and senior executives really took stock of the importance of the consumer issue.

Gradually, the American brand manager model took root in indige-
nous European companies, as they copied American marketing methods.
Despite this, a National Economic Development Office (NEDO) report on
industrial performance in the 1980s concluded that the single most
important constraint on British companies' domestic and overseas market shares was poor marketing. Part of the problem was that marketing
commonly developed in companies as an offshoot of sales. Nigel Piercy,
Professor of Marketing at Cardiff Business School, studied 300 marketing
departments in 1992 and found that, even then, sales management and
sales support were the most widespread responsibilities. Where marketing departments did have strategic responsibilities, they were often small
and inconsequential, mostly involved in packaging the board's preconceived strategies for wider presentation, using attractive, colourful
graphics.

Market research grew up alongside the sales and brand management
functions like some leprous outcast. "Boffins", "eggheads" and "bean-
counters" are among the disparaging terms widely applied to market
researchers by their marketing colleagues. Despite the lip-service paid by
marketers to the importance of measurement, those who do the measuring are often kept at arm's length from the real business of marketing.

The 1990s have seen marketing in metamorphosis. Companies have
even removed the word "marketing" in job titles and replaced it by "customer". Customer relationship managers, customer retention managers,
customer acquisition managers are just some of the titles that have been
introduced. Throughout the 1980s and 1990s marketing was, for many
companies, applied as a veneer to businesses. For some, renaming marketing as "customer management" will provide new strength. But for
many others the issue is more than skin deep. For them, there is a deep-
rooted cause for marketing's weakness, which is perceived to be the
poverty of marketing education, in terms of both quality and quantity.

A qualified profession?

The roots of marketing as a professional qualification, and as an area of academic study, can be found around the turn of the century in Mid-western American land-grant universities. The early emphasis was on economic behaviour of customers. Professors of marketing studied economic and social issues. This concern with social issues re-emerged half a century later in the guise of consumerism. However, by the early 1950s the emphasis was switching. Marketing professors began to study the jobs that marketers performed. The managerial approach fitted well with the growing importance of business schools, where the case study ruled supreme. Books by Wroe Alderson (1957), John Howard (1957), K.R. Davis (1961) and, most famous of all, Philip Kotler (1967) all took management practices as their focus.

This managerial focus was not readily accepted by everyone in marketing circles. Two of the most successful authors of the time, Theodore Beckman and William Davidson, who wrote the most widely used marketing textbook in the early 1960s, argued that an over-emphasis on marketing's institutions and establishments ran the risk of overlooking important social and economic issues. These early criticisms anticipated later critiques of marketing's self-absorption, its vulnerability on issues of customer satisfaction, and its isolation from developments in consumerism.

Nonetheless, the voices of the consumer-specialists were drowned out by the clamour of tens of thousands of sales representatives eager for a piece of paper that would qualify them for more lucrative management positions. They were joined by thousands of advertising executives, designers, direct marketers, corporate hospitality staff, exhibition staff, market research staff, public relations staff, sales promotion staff, sponsorship staff, and many more.

In the absence of any accepted standards, qualifications and certification are forthcoming from a crazy muddle of trade associations, business schools, private training companies and others. There are over 30 representative bodies for marketing and its subdisciplines, including, in the UK, the CIM, IDM and ISP, all of which provide diplomas; the IPA which runs courses; and the IPR with ambitions to run its own courses and become chartered. Indeed, knowledge of where and how to obtain training could warrant a course in its own right.

This plethora of marketing bodies offers advice to businesses via another army of intermediary advisers (in the UK, TECs, Business Links, Chambers of Commerce, and so on). Confusion reigns, particularly when these bodies give conflicting advice and sell themselves and their own services, rather than the concept of "marketing to improve your business".

Comparison of marketing textbooks with their accounting counterparts provides a salutary lesson. Kotler's *Marketing Management* is the current best-seller by a large margin. It is about 800 pages in paperback. Horngren, Sundem and Stratton is a comparable representative of accounting texts. It is also 800 pages long, but there the likeness ends.

The accounting text is full of tables of numbers, and is highly focused on tools and techniques for analysing the financial situation. There is a small core of essential techniques, upon which the others build. Knowledge of the fundamentals is vital to accounting. Progress from these fundamentals to an accounting qualification usually takes three years or more. It involves mastering the basic tools and techniques, and polishing basic skills through repetition of problem-solving, before moving on to more difficult tools and techniques. In many ways this resembles the training that a scientist or engineer would receive.

The marketing text is a complete contrast. It surveys a vast range of management practices, catering for members of each of marketing's disparate trade associations. There is something there for members of the AA, BLBA, CIM, DMA, EDMA, FEDCO, IDM, IOP, IPA, IPR, ISBA, ISMM, ISP, ITMA, IVCA, MOPA, MRS, MS, OAA, PHA, POPAI, PRCA, SCIF, SCIP, SPCA and SPS. In many ways the book resembles a reader that might be used in the arts and humanities. It contains few quantitative tables and descriptions of models and tools; in contrast to accounting, skill in the use of such tools is deemed "specialist" work.[1] This provides a good excuse for those training for a marketing qualification never to need to learn how to construct an attitude questionnaire, or to analyse the questionnaire data, or to interpret the confidence tests that accompany a statistician's analysis of the data. Unlike their accounting counterparts, marketers never need learn the basic analytical and numerical skills.

The result is that all of marketing's clever analysis and interpretation work is done by a small cadre of specialists, and many marketing bosses may never have used any of these techniques at any stage in their careers, not even during training. As a result, they are ill-qualified to tell whether this statistician, or that market researcher, is pulling the proverbial wool over their eyes. By contrast, the CFO or finance director has used most of the techniques that his juniors apply on his behalf, and knows what he is dealing with.

This ignorance of analytical tools, and even contempt for them, is typified by a marketing vice-president of a major credit card company, who proudly stated in *Marketing Business* in June 1997: "Ask me to handle more than two statistics and I'm about as useful as a chocolate fireguard." How did this vice-president make business decisions? He briefed the boffins.

In the UK the Chartered Institute of Marketing (CIM) has declared that it will professionalise marketing, and it has introduced a Continuing Professional Development (CPD) scheme to encourage marketers to read about and attend seminars on their subject. Yet when it was asked how much training marketers already have, no facts were available. "Are marketers mostly arts graduates? How many marketers have marketing degrees? Or other marketing qualifications?" – neither the CIM the nor the CPD had any answers. One spokesperson commented: "It might be a bit impertinent to be seen to be investigating people's qualifications."

Taking responsibility for marketing

Should marketing managers be required to earn appropriate qualifications, as do accountants, engineers and doctors, before they are let loose on a company's principal assets – customers? Would marketing resolve its crisis if it were to be accepted as one of the professions? Has the organisation of the marketing department added to the present troubles? Should marketing departments be split up and disseminated throughout the organisation? Can multidisciplinary teams offer a better answer?

Although business process re-engineering (BPR) is becoming widely discredited as a management panacea, one of its lessons is that tearing down the rigid walls between business functions is a powerful mechanism for change and transformation. "Or is it the case that the marketing fraternity has forfeited too much respect over the years ever to hope of enjoying the complete confidence of colleagues in other parts of the business. [Have there been] too many unfulfilled promises; too much brashness and bravado; too little science and method; too few facts and inconsistencies?" asks Sir George Bull, former chairman of Grand Metropolitan and current chairman of UK grocery retailer J. Sainsbury.[2]

Rentokil, a UK services giant, sees marketing as a key strategic responsibility of the CEO, too important to be devolved to one department or one director. Fifteen years ago, when it was a low-profile pest control and wood preservative specialist, Rentokil's leadership was taken over by Sir Clive Thompson, a marketing man who left Cadbury Schweppes to run his own company. Until 1998 he had kept his promise, through thick and thin, to keep boosting the company's annual pre-tax profit and earnings per share by 20%. This astonishing performance earned him a large fan club in the UK financial markets. Sir Clive puts the role of marketing this way: "I am more or less convinced that corporate and marketing strategy are more or less the same things. The chief executive has to be the chief marketer. If you delegate that responsibility you're not doing your job."

There has been a chorus of agreement with Sir Clive about the corporate nature of marketing's crisis. "General management and top marketing management have to reconceive how marketing can better contribute to overall business effectiveness" is how Sir Alistair Grant, governor designate of the Bank of Scotland and chairman of Scottish & Newcastle, sees the issue.[3] "The simple principle is that the company exists to serve its customers long into the future. Business leaders that act on this, and persuade all their people to believe in it, can transform ordinary companies into world beaters," says Sir Colin Marshall, chairman of British Airways.[4]

To try and raise the status of the marketing debate in the UK to board and even to government level, the UK's marketing knights are going into battle. Sir Colin Marshall, Sir George Bull, Sir Peter Davis, CEO of Prudential, Sir John Egan, CEO of BAA, Sir Alistair Grant, chairman of the Argyll Group, and Sir Michael Perry, former chairman of Unilever and currently chairman of Centrica (British Gas), have formed a new organisation, The Marketing Council, to work with the government and the CBI on marketing issues. Its members are in no doubt that a lack of knowledge and authority is at the root of the problem with marketing. They believe that conviction and commitment to resolve marketing issues can originate only at the highest level within a business.

What is marketing supposed to deliver?

Part of the problem for senior executives trying to take responsibility for marketing is agreeing on what marketing is really there to do. A 1997 Marketing Forum survey found that the commonest colloquial definition of what marketing was for was "satisfying customer needs profitably". Despite the many more complex and technical definitions that have been published, this is the definition that will be used in this book.

Taking consumerism on board in defining marketing is more radical than it seems at first sight. According to the consumers' definition, it means that failure to satisfy customers, failure to anticipate customer needs before the competition and failure to achieve expected profitability are all marketing problems. Yet the root of these problems usually lies outside the marketing department. Blaming the marketing department is not necessarily a useful starting point, although marketing departments must undoubtedly take their share of responsibility for the poor direction and accountability at board level.

Consumerist slogans colour the top-level debate. In research by the author on a sample of 130 senior executives from around the world, 90% said that "good customer satisfaction levels are more important than good brand positioning" and that "quality, service and value are more important than the traditional marketing mix". "Zero customer defections and 100% retention are vital business goals," concurred 72%. The white heat of technology is also seen as the consumer's salvation. "I like to be at the leading edge with new technology," agreed 78%.

But how much of this rhetoric reflects reality? "How many senior executives talk the marketing gospel, but almost never walk it? Too many, I fear," says Sir George Bull. "Sadly, practice does not always match theory."[5]

A few companies are still not committed to the consumer. "SWT receives 40,000 complaints a year," wrote Brian Souter, head of South West Trains (SWT), in *Railway Magazine*.[6] "A high proportion of them are from people who have nothing to do when they get into the office in the morning. They sit down and write to SWT. I feel like writing to their bosses and saying 'do you know this guy spends two hours a week writing to a train company?'." SWT, at the time of writing, was reportedly cancelling 39 trains a day, on average, owing to lack of staff, having laid off 71 train drivers to cut costs. Yet for every Brian Souter there are dozens of chief executives who stress the importance of customers and speak of their commitment. In survey after survey of CEOs customers come top of the list of commitments, followed by quality, innovation, value and IT, as the key items on most boardroom agendas.

Contrast the boardroom agenda with the daily concerns of the average marketing manager. Surveys such as the Coopers & Lybrand *Marketing at the Crossroads* report, listed in order of priority:

- development of advertising
- development and implementation of promotional strategy
- analysis of market trends
- analysis of competitive performance
- reporting on marketing performance to senior management
- development of new products
- development of pricing strategy
- sales planning
- setting and monitoring of customer standards
- negotiation with suppliers.

Little wonder, then, that marketing activities are commonly perceived as tactical rather than strategic. Marketing's involvement in the higher-level issues – customer satisfaction, quality, innovation, value and information technology – is usually indirect, as members of committees and steering groups, and often absentee members at that (a point noted the Coopers & Lybrand report).

Unlearning fads and fashions

As a consequence of marketing not having a significant input into strategic issues, the management consultancy industry has a free rein in the board-level debate about marketing. As noted earlier, according to Ashridge Strategic Management Centre, marketing is now represented in under 20% of corporate headquarters in major businesses. Malcolm McDonald, professor of marketing at Cranfield School of Management and a leading international authority, is unequivocal in his views on consultants' ideas: "Unless the quality-street gang, the re-engineers and the culture-club crowd have a deep understanding of customers needs and wants, they will lead companies humming their mantras into the abyss."

Fred Reichheld, consulting director at Bain & Co, provides a good example of a romantic view that many management gurus put forward about customers, which is not supported by the evidence about actual customer behaviour: "Some customers are inherently predictable and loyal, no matter what company they're doing business with. They simply prefer stable long-term relationships. Some customers are more profitable than others. They spend more money, pay their bills more promptly and require less service. Some customers will find your products and services more valuable than those of your competitors."

Of course, some customers are more predictable than others. Some spend more. Some prefer one brand, some prefer others. But it is often untrue that loyal customers enjoy their position or are profitable. Research by Harvard Business School found many loyal customers were actually trapped by poverty or some other barrier, and many would enjoy more choice; research by London Business School and others suggests that loyal customers often spend less and are poorer people. Nor is it true that high spenders pay bills more rapidly or, generally, require less service. Studies of customer profitability indicate that high spenders are often less profitable than medium spenders.

The popular myth that adding value is a winning strategy is widely contradicted by cost accounting audits. These show that many companies which have customised and micro-segmented their offerings have incurred punitive overhead costs and have not been rewarded by customers, who still prefer their old mass-market products and services, which they habitually buy. As a consequence of challenging conventional wisdom, companies such as Procter &Gamble have actively cut back on the product clutter resulting from the pursuit of "added-value" and "micro-segmentation" theories.

This book aims to separate the truths from the half-truths and untruths, and to dig a little deeper to discover the factors which really matter when addressing customer and competitive issues. The chapters in Part 1 address the five main items on most boardroom agendas and show how a little more understanding of basic marketing techniques and a little less management hype might be a surer route to commercial success.

Quality

The word quality has become prominent in management vocabulary. Yet there seems to be immense confusion about what quality really is. Many claim there must be total quality standards if you are to deliver what customers value more than what your competitors deliver. A widely recognised standard that supports this philosophy is iso 900, but it was originally developed to prevent bombs going off in factories and, despite being revised a number of times, still bears no relation to product quality.

The problem arises from the assumption that absolute quality exists in its own right, independent of the customer. The gaps between internal perceptions and customers' perceptions of quality are rarely measured, as Gerald Ratner, chief executive of Ratners, a low-priced jewellery retailer, found to his cost. Memorably, he described one of his company's low-cost products as "crap" in an after-dinner speech, failing to understand it had perceived value in the eyes of his customers. He lost his job in the furore that followed, and the company changed its name to distance it from the Ratner slur. A few firms are now profiting from his mistake and learning to measure customers perceptions of quality. Chapter 2 explains how they are doing it.

Customer satisfaction and loyalty

A mantra of modern-day management is: "Care passionately for your customers and then they will care for you." Most senior executives are committed to the concept, but few customers would recognise it. Customer satisfaction is now measured by most major businesses. Yet somehow most firms in any market have near-identical satisfaction scores. Dissatisfaction is common, but it is not recorded. In one company studied recently, the basis for customer care suggested by a sample of customers was almost totally dissociated from the set of measures used by the customer-care team, who were unaware of what customers truly cared about.

Loyalty is another favourite with the consultants, and a cause of costly confusion for many companies. Habit is what underlies most customers' loyalty, but habit is a less dignified motive than the ones the consultants often attribute to consumers. Studying customers' habits, however, can be far more illuminating and profitable than making assumptions about loyalty and its causes. Chapter 3 explains how.

Innovation

Despite the efforts of two professors, Gary Hamel and C.K. Prahalad, to encourage companies to innovate and develop their powers of insight and foresight, most continue to pump out new-product failure after failure. The arch enemy of most innovators is the customer, who somehow rejects the innovator's brilliance in favour of a safe old formula. Not surprisingly, the least successful innovators studied by the author felt they had little to learn from customers, whereas successful innovators such as Microsoft felt they had much to learn from customers. The problem with the less successful innovators was not that they did not do market research, but that the research was designed to reveal little that was surprising or insightful. Chapter 4 gets to the heart of the matter.

Value

"Techniques like total quality, re-engineering, activity-based costing and empowerment are all useful tools, but each appears to address somewhat different goals and only limited aspects of performance. Ideas are colliding, not connecting. A comprehensive and unifying management approach is needed that responds to the new business environment." These were the conclusions of a major study of the management accounting profession in 1994.[7]

"Managers need to identify and encourage value creation in all their processes. These are the real numbers. But accounting systems don't see these numbers – it's as if they exist in a different dimension," comments Tony Hope, professor of accounting at INSEAD.[8]

"Today's management accounting information, driven by the procedures and cycle of the organisation's financial reporting system, is too late, too aggregated and too distorted to be relevant for managers' planning and control decisions. When such distorted data represents the only available data on product costs, the danger exists for misguided decisions on product pricing, product sourcing, product mix and responses to rival products. Many firms seem to be falling victim to this danger." Thomas

Johnson and Robert Kaplan, professors of accounting at Portland State University and Harvard Business School respectively, reach this disturbing conclusion in their influential study, *Relevance Lost, The Rise and Fall of Management Accounting*. An exotic range of new accounting techniques has recently emerged, from ABC to zero-based budgeting, to say nothing of EVA, MVA and other asset valuation approaches. Many are claimed to help improve competitiveness and customer-focus. The evidence is examined in Chapter 5.

Information technology
All the companies studied by the author put a high degree of emphasis on having the latest information technology (IT). Their managers said that technology was needed to enable them to compete effectively and to channel information from customers. Yet evidence of a direct pay-off from pouring money into IT is rare. The problem with less successful companies was not that they did not accumulate data, but that little knowledge was gained from the data collected. The interface between IT and knowledge clearly needs more examination. Chapter 6 explains what IT can and cannot find out about customers and profitability.

A new approach to marketing
These five cherished myths about the basis of business success are all useful concepts, but their implementation does not usually bear analysis. So what is the alternative? One option is to review what traditional marketing has to offer, and rediscover tried and tested marketing tools and techniques that can help make the ideas work.

Many companies are finding that their current measurement systems offer little guidance on what customers need and want. Most reflect what products they already sell. Internal data usually show what products were sold, but say little about who bought them or why. Even market research tracks products rather than customers. Jonathan Baggott, marketing chief of Eastern Natural Gas, put it this way: "Last year there were 250,000 half-inch drills sold in this country. And that wasn't because 250,000 people wanted half-inch drills. What they wanted was half-inch holes. That's a blinding glimpse of the obvious but true. In our market, people don't want gas, they want hot food, hot water and a warm, comfortable house."

Most measurement systems track what the company was doing financially in the short term, reflecting their origins in reporting management stewardship of other people's money. Measures that reflect anything longer term are a rarity, as noted by David Norton, measurements expert and originator of the balanced scorecard: "By the beginning of the 1980s there was a growing recognition on the part of most people that companies relied excessively on financial measurements as the basis of their measurement systems, and that financial measurement was essentially a lag indicator of your strategy and that if you focused excessively on financial management it was going to create a short-term mentality and take your eye off the long-term ball."

Marketing abounds with failures associated with lack of measurement or failure to heed the results of measurement. In August 1992 Hoover launched its now infamous travel promotion in the UK stating that anyone buying more than £100-worth of Hoover products before the end of January 1993 would get two free return tickets to selected European destinations. For £250-worth of Hoover products, buyers could get two free return tickets to New York or Orlando. Hoover had accepted the advice of its advertising agency that fewer than 50,000 people would respond, and had attempted neither research nor testing of this forecast. But more than 200,000 responded and qualified for the free tickets. Not only was this unprofitable, but the administrative bottleneck resulted in 2,000 complaints per day, extensive bad publicity and long-term damage to Hoover's brand image and reputation.

On April 23rd 1985 Roberto C. Goizueta, chairman of Coca-Cola, made a momentous announcement: "The best has been made even better." After 99 years the Coca-Cola company had decided to abandon its original formula in favour of a sweeter variation which was named New Coke. The decision was made under competitive pressure from Pepsi, which kept winning so-called taste challenges, and was backed by over $4m-worth of market research. Within ten weeks public pressure forced the company to admit it had made a mistake and bring back the old Coke. With the benefit of hindsight it was seen that the market research had been flawed. The main research was designed to prove to Goizueta's management team that the new flavour was better. However, focus group research had also shown unfavourable reactions towards the withdrawal of the original Coke, and taste-test participants had received the impression that the new taste was an addition to the Coke range, not a replacement. These other research findings had been overlooked, until the post-mortem after the disaster.

Measuring up: never mind the quantity, mind the relevance

Most businesses are not short of data in terms of pure quantity. What they lack, or fail to collect, is information that is suitable for the tasks in hand.

Sir Clive Thompson sees measurement and accountability as crucial issues for the board. "Measurement is totally important. I cannot over-emphasise its importance. I believe strongly that you don't expect but inspect. The key question is what is essential to measure, because it can become difficult if you handle too many things."[9]

Sir Colin Marshall takes Thompson's views further, and sees account-ability and standards as a fundamental to the board's problems. "If you go around and ask chairmen and chief executives, they will say they are very good at marketing, but only a handful of businesses measure up," he says.[10]

The five following chapters in Part 1 show that traditional marketing measures can reveal much more about performance than is widely appre-ciated. Moreover, the use of the right measurement techniques would radically influence major investment decisions. Figure 1.1 summarises the key marketing measurement tools which are useful and relevant to each main item on the boardroom agenda. In Part 3 of this book each tool is explained in more detail.

Among those who recognise the strategic importance of marketing measurement is Sir George Bull, who has said: "You can't begin to com-pete until you know precisely what your customers want. Knowing that, you can then design a product that sells itself. Branded goods manufac-turers live by this credo already, but every type of business should take it to heart. It's the critical element".

Sir John Egan, chairman of BAA, shares similar views: "Start by mea-suring and meeting existing needs. Then drive up quality standards and cost effectiveness by continuous improvement. Standards of customer satisfaction, targeted and measurable, are the bedrock on which to create long-term wealth."

Sir Michael Perry is also unambiguous about the importance of real knowledge of customers: "To sustain competitive advantage requires a total commitment to your customers – to understand what they want now, and anticipating what they will do tomorrow – and to being there on cue, first choice, every time."[11]

Few boards have yet developed the yardsticks and measurement tools they need to tackle the big customer issues. For them, investment in cus-tomer satisfaction, loyalty or innovation is often something of a hit or miss affair.

Marketing managers seem far more interested in chasing the latest fads and fashions than getting a solid grounding in tried and tested mea-surement tools and methods. Research by the author highlighted this: 95%

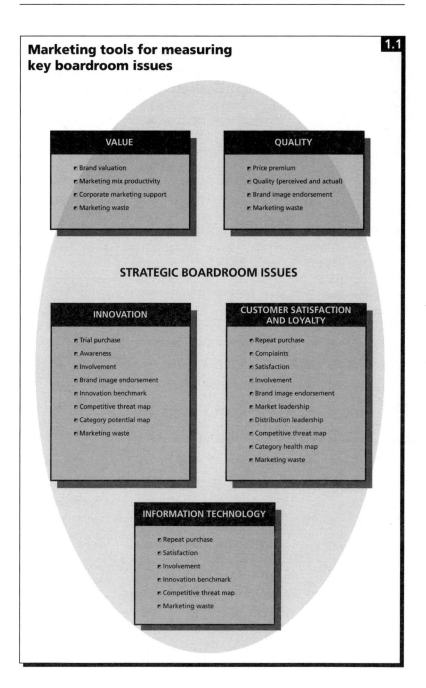

Marketing tools for measuring key boardroom issues 1.1

VALUE
- Brand valuation
- Marketing mix productivity
- Corporate marketing support
- Marketing waste

QUALITY
- Price premium
- Quality (perceived and actual)
- Brand image endorsement
- Marketing waste

STRATEGIC BOARDROOM ISSUES

INNOVATION
- Trial purchase
- Awareness
- Involvement
- Brand image endorsement
- Innovation benchmark
- Competitive threat map
- Category potential map
- Marketing waste

CUSTOMER SATISFACTION AND LOYALTY
- Repeat purchase
- Complaints
- Satisfaction
- Involvement
- Brand image endorsement
- Market leadership
- Distribution leadership
- Competitive threat map
- Category health map
- Marketing waste

INFORMATION TECHNOLOGY
- Repeat purchase
- Satisfaction
- Involvement
- Innovation benchmark
- Competitive threat map
- Marketing waste

of managers agreed that "Creative vision and foresight are very important when choosing new tools"; and 96% said "I like to keep delivering innovative improvements to the tools and techniques I use". Interestingly, only 40% agreed that "Using tried and trusted methods is more important than choosing the latest new methods", and 43% that "It is better to gain experience of using the same tools and techniques for many years". Rather predictably, there is a high rate of experimentation with new tools (over half of the 1,500 instances reported in the research were "pilots"), and almost as many tools are discarded as are adopted.

Today, saying that bricks and mortar represent only a fraction of the value of most companies has become almost a truism. Businesses are beginning to realise that their real competitive advantage comes from intellectual capital, knowledge, soft assets such as brands and customer relationships. Knowledge and intellectual capital are now at a high premium, but where will they come from?

The science side of marketing – customer science, knowing about satisfying customer needs profitably – has the capacity to create intellectual capital. The other side of marketing – the marketing imagination, creativity, the domain of the thousands of hopeful graduates who go into marketing – goes on in an atmosphere where knowledge is weak or absent. The so-called art of marketing is a pure gamble, based on pure optimism, and it is just as likely to destroy value as create it. "If marketing isn't yet a science, it needs to become more scientific" argues Peter Doyle, professor of marketing and strategic management at Warwick University. "The old reliance simply on the accumulation of 'experience' only equips marketers to answer yesterday's questions."

Frameworks for marketing measurement

Ask managers what help they crave to improve their performance, and many will call for a richer menu of tools and techniques. But they do not particularly want to find out about scarcely understandable methods such as correspondence mapping, logit models, negative binomial distributions, cluster analysis and other potions from the social statistician's storehouse. Their appetite is for manuals of techniques which are like manuals on motor maintenance: study the latter and the car will perform better; study the former and the business will perform better. But although servicing a car can be carried out by enthusiastic amateurs, many of the most valuable marketing tools and techniques cannot be left to such people. Nor can the technologies for implementing them.

Most organisations have lots of tools and techniques, too many perhaps, but they are collected and accumulated haphazardly. The collection of tools and techniques and the accumulation of facts and figures do not amount to intellectual capital or knowledge, or, much less, to wisdom. Chapter 7 outlines a number of different frameworks for sorting and organising marketing tools to suit business problems and strategies.

The trouble is that most marketing managers are trapped in a narrow specialism, such as advertising, sales promotion or packaging, and do not feel responsible for providing tools for the greater good of the business. Some marketing managers have also become so dependent on outsourcing to agencies and research firms that they are ill-equipped to advise their colleagues on best practices. Others show a distinct unwillingness to take on support roles, preferring the glamour of big-budget advertising to being labelled the corporate tool maker. Part 3 describes a range of traditional tools and techniques that should be more widely used in organisations.

The future of the marketing department

The time has come to shake up the marketing function, which in the words of Sir George Bull "bears all the hallmarks of abstract art – it costs an arm and a leg, it bears only a passing resemblance to real life and you're never quite sure what you've got at the end of it all". "Consider art as cunning, as deceit, as the root of words like artful, artificial and artifice, and as far as marketing's concerned it looks as if the smart money's on art," adds Nicola Foulston, chief executive of Brands Hatch Leisure.

The real problem is that the marketing function is in danger of being marginalised. Marketing had traditionally monopolised corporate thinking about customers and competition, but this tradition is being swept away. Customer and competitive strategies have become too big and complex to be addressed by one function alone. Marketing has become too big for the marketing department.

Organising for marketing is a major challenge. In particular, organising to ensure the creation and management of knowledge about customers and competition is causing businesses to develop hollow and virtual organisations, using information technology as an enabling tool. Change is difficult in itself. People resist change. Chapter 8 outlines a top-level approach to readdressing marketing measurement issues and tying them into the strategic planning process.

The dangers of benchmarking

The heart of customer and competitive programmes should be a sophisticated set of marketing tools and measurement techniques. Putting an end to the educated guess is all about having the best measures for consumers' thoughts and feelings about their needs, expectations, surprise, joy, frustration, value, excellence, relevance, fairness, trust, regret, fears and worries. Many such factors are potentially important. The right factors to track will be a small subset of these, chosen because they are relevant to an organisation's particular situation and practical to measure. Yet the reality is that most organisations are copying their neighbours. When one marketing manager was asked whether his organisation had learned from the mistakes of others, he quipped: "Yes we've learned all right, and we can repeat their mistakes perfectly."

Too many organisations are not measuring customers, but they are measuring other organisations. In the satisfaction area, benchmarking of other businesses has become all the rage. Such benchmarking leads to copying of the benchmarked processes, whether or not they are directly relevant to customers. It is easy to copy other firms, and benchmarking seems to guarantee big exciting budgets and huge disruptive change programmes.

Yet copying other organisations is highly questionable as a means of addressing the real issues for consumers. Banks are benchmarking McDonald's, but banks do not sell hamburgers. Telcos are benchmarking Xerox, but telcos are not into photocopiers. Retailers are benchmarking British Airways, but shopkeepers do not fly planes. As Gary Hamel, professor of strategy at London Business School, has commented: "The goal is simply not to benchmark a competitor's products and processes and imitate its methods, but to develop an independent point of view."[12]

Time for fresh thinking

A concern that many companies share is uncertainty about when to rethink their approach to marketing. As new opportunities develop, as new technology comes on stream, and as trials and pilots begin to show results, it is important to update your thinking.

Senior executives are interested in whether their organisations are doing the right marketing, and doing marketing right. How does your organisation measure up? To help you decide, use the checklist below. The more questions you are "unsure" about, the greater is your need to investigate. A significant number of "yes" answers suggests a clear need for fresh thinking.

Look around your own organisation. Look at the high-profile initiatives that have been launched recently. Look at the issues that are preoccupying senior management. Look at the budgets for projects that are deemed strategic. Look at the criteria by which success is being measured and ask yourself some questions:

- Do your senior managers have realistic solutions to the corporate issues?
- Are they driven more by fads and fashion than facts and figures?
- Are expectations grounded in realistic measures of what customers need and want?
- How good are you at choosing and using knowledge and measurement tools?
- Is your credibility at risk in the financial investment community?
- Do your executive managers feel out of touch?
- How effectively are you organised to respond to customers and competition?
- Is the marketing department isolated from the strategic issues and the operational needs of the business?
- What is driving changes to your organisation: costs, customers or competition?

Corporate issues

- Do you feel your quality management is out of touch from the needs and wants of external customers?
- Is your customer-care driven more by cost efficiencies than by customer needs and wants?
- Do you have trouble producing innovations that customers want?
- Are you unable to obtain above-average customer loyalty?
- Do IT projects burn up budgets without delivering the profitable competitive advantages that were promised?
- Have you experienced problems with your financial systems resulting in distortions to your marketing performance measures?

Knowledge and measurement tools

- Could your company lose credibility in the investment community because of inaccurate, incomplete or delayed market, customer and competitive information?
- Do you feel executive management are somewhat out of touch with your customers and competition?
- Do your marketing tools fail to reflect the business priorities you have established for your organisation?

◪ Are your competitors able to outmanoeuvre you because they have better or more timely information on market trends, customer needs and profitability?

◪ Do you have trouble pulling together the information you need for effective decision making?

Organisation

◪ Does your marketing department spend most of its time and effort on tactics rather than strategy?

◪ Are your marketing plans drafted towards the end of the budgeting process rather than at the beginning?

◪ Are new-product flops seen as a marketing department problem?

◪ Is marketing seen as an activity which should involve only the marketing manager?

These are not rhetorical questions. They are the themes of this book, which aims to help companies improve their marketing effectiveness.

PART 1

MODERN MYTHS

2 Quality

Not so long ago business had a new religion, quality, and a range of prizes, awards and certificates were devised to celebrate those who achieved the highest levels of devotion to the cause. There was the Deming Prize contest, the European Foundation for Quality Award and the Malcolm Baldridge Award, not to mention the more common ISO 9000.

The chances that devotion to pure quality will breed success remain slim, even for firms scoring highly against quality criteria such as Baldridge, or actually winning a quality award. The message is clear from companies such as General Motors, which have won Baldridge Quality Awards and yet have failed to produce what customers actually want to buy.[1] Yet some companies have benefited greatly from quality by linking it closely with marketing. Hewlett-Packard (HP) is ranked top in many quality surveys. For more than a decade its sales have grown by a steady 20% per year to over $32 billion, and its margins of 7–8% have made it a leading blue-chip company. HP has made a profit every quarter since it began trading. Its real secret, however, is the HP Way, a corporate philosophy defined in 1957 by its founders, Bill Hewlett and Dave Packard, which recognises that quality must be measured in terms of customers' perceptions as well as in relation to the company's competitors.

This chapter takes up the debate about quality and marketing.

Quality on trial

Quality came to the attention of western business in June 1980 as a result of an NBC television documentary, "If Japan Can, Why Can't We?". It fed off the racist stereotypes of the Japanese as clever little Asians producing ever smarter gadgets, backed by the fiendishly clever scientist Dr Deming. The day after the TV broadcast Deming's phone started ringing, and he spent the rest of his life until he died in 1993 being feted by western bosses and politicians.

Within two years of the NBC documentary new quality gurus emerged with rival claims about quality. Companies aligned themselves with their gurus. Ford, Dow, AT&T, Procter & Gamble, Kimberly-Clark and Campbell's Soup chose Deming; Apple Computer and Gillette chose Juran; and General Electric supported Feigenbaum. Within a decade faith in the quality movement was badly shaken. At IBM the CEO, John Akers, commented: "I'm sick and tired of visiting plants to hear nothing but great things about quality and cycle time, and then visiting customers who tell me of problems."[2] *Business Week* commented: "Every quality demigod boasts his own set of commandments, rituals and disciples. And within each approach, corporate managers are confronted by a numbing maze of acronyms and buzzwords."[3]

Internally focused standards such as ISO 9000 collected the most hostile criticism. A winner of the Baldridge Quality Award, Motorola, was particularly hostile to ISO 9000 and in June 1993 issued the following extraordinary statement: "We are critical of how ISO 9000 is being used and misrepresented. The unfortunate mandating of a static, partial quality system as a requirement to do business, which does not address the actual quality of product or service, sends the wrong message as to the real requirements and actions necessary to serve one's customers. Some recently certified companies, through advertisements, imply that a customer can be assured of high standards, reliable product and service as a result of ISO 9000 certification. This is false. ISO 9000 certification has no direct connection to a product or service."[4]

The British Institute of Management (BIM) became concerned with the poor track record of quality and, after interviewing 100 companies about their problems, issued a report called *Beyond Quality*. In it the BIM argued that quality managers "need to consider what lies beyond quality". It was the BIM team's discovery that: "Technical or product quality of itself may no longer differentiate between alternative suppliers. Many CEOS are looking beyond traditional or internal quality and towards attitudes and values, less tangible factors such as 'look or feel'."

Many quality managers seem to be seeking quality in the wrong places. As Malcolm McDonald, professor of marketing at Cranfield School of Management, puts it: "Quality people are obsessed with making crap, perfectly."[5]

What to do about quality

Faced with widespread criticism of quality management, there are three options: stick to the old approaches to quality; shut down the quality programmes; or somehow change the approach to quality.

Sticking to the old approaches

The old approaches to quality use hard measures of the cost of quality and aim for zero technical defects. For example, Canon has made major improvements by controlling what it called the nine waste categories:

- defective products
- slow new product run-up
- overdesign
- overskill
- idle machinery
- excess inventory
- inefficient movements
- high expenses
- excess indirect labour.

For some organisations the levels of faults, scrap and waste have been so high that such an approach paid dividends. However, the BIM study had this to say: "Companies relatively new to quality have significantly higher expectations about the potential benefits than those with years of the quality approach under their belt ... Many quality programmes seem to be running out of steam. After some initial improvements, diminishing returns appear to set in." Thus it would appear that most firms are not wasteful enough to gain great cost benefits.

Shutting down quality programmes
The second option is also unsatisfactory. Companies often have real quality problems – at least they do if you ask their customers or talk to their competitors. Perhaps the strongest evidence that quality is profitable comes from studies by Profit Impact of Market Strategy (PIMS), a consultancy spin-off from academia, set up to gather and analyse data on global company performance and its origins. Careful analysis of PIMS data has revealed that profitability is correlated with quality as perceived by the customer. Bradley Gale, who did the analysis, comments: "Businesses with superior market perceived quality average about 30% return on investment (ROI). Businesses with inferior perceived quality average a mere 10%."[6] Since there are PIMS data on more than 3,000 business units covering over a decade, the conclusion seems pretty solid.

Changing the approach
The third option is to change the approach to quality. The question is what to change and how. Quality people like to emphasise *kaizen*, the relentless search for small incremental improvements. Although these are at first imperceptible to consumers, when they do eventually become aware of them they are pleasantly surprised. Marketing people favour consumer awareness, and wish to flaunt their quality improvements.

Both approaches can work. American computer giants such as IBM and DEC pursued the technical quality route in the personal computer market, only to be soundly beaten by marketing specialists such as Dell. British high street banks, however, have been advertising their service quality heavily for almost a decade, but they have singularly failed to persuade bank customers.

Quality managers often underestimate the problem. Many of them claim to know that customers are important. But when it comes to analysing what is important to customers, most quality managers either do not know how to do customer measurements or they use flawed measures. Marketers are often not much better, preferring to focus on image and reputation rather than substance.

So who is right? In theory the customer should be asked. However, engineers and accountants as well as marketers have a real distrust of the answers. When engineers talk to customers they usually discuss defects, faults and complaints. When marketers canvass customer opinions they too bias their questions, focusing on what causes "customer delight" (most customers answer "getting a much better and much cheaper product") and what customers are aware of and unaware of (which can help with advertising and packaging).

Research tools which measure quality

There are, however, marketing tools and techniques derived from the social sciences which can shed some light on customers' perceptions of quality. Two areas need to be mapped: people's perceptions of relative quality; and people's perceptions of relative value.

Perceived relative quality

The first step is to find out how customers describe and categorise products or services, and then to discover the factors influencing people's perceptions of the relative quality of competing offerings. Older consumers generally have lower expectations; higher education is often associated with higher expectations; and men's expectations are usually met more easily than women's. There are also greater perceptions of quality when others make their perceptions of quality known. These perceptions of quality can be measured, and maps can be created setting out people's perceptions across a category.

Customers' categorisations of the products or services they want are critical. There is often a significant gap between the perceptions of customers and the assumptions made about customer perceptions by suppliers. Sometimes the whole supply side of the market misunderstands. In the IT services market, for example, suppliers often describe their products and services in jargon such as "multimedia FRADS", "PIX firewall", "systems integration", or "solutions", imagining that this terminology makes sense to their customers.

The author conducted a survey in this market where 1,200 services buyers, including CEOs, CFOs and CIOs, from 12 countries were interviewed. In total they had bought over 5,000 items. How did these fairly sophisticated customers talk about the products and services they needed? They talked about needing advice and help, and could specify precisely the quality of advice or help they needed. There was no talk of requiring systems integration or solutions.

The mismatches between the category definitions of customers and suppliers are acute in many markets. In a study of consumer perceptions of quality in the airline industry, John Ozment and Edward Morash found that consumers were sensitive to the level of congestion (percentage of aircraft seating capacity filled).[7] Yet no widely adopted measure of quality in the airline industry was related to this. Instead, airlines were widely found measuring quality in terms of useful but less important things such as on-time arrivals, problem-free baggage handling and minimal flight cancellations. They were dealing with the symptoms of congestion rather than trying to get rid of it. Underlying the conflict between the measures is a conflict between interests. Consumers desire less passenger congestion, but managers desire full loads. Since managers have an overriding say in defining quality, no wonder load-factor is not reported as a quality dimension, even though it is greatly desired by customers.

The strategic importance of perceived relative quality has been statistically confirmed in studies of the PIMS database. Bradley Gale, one of the founders of PIMS and author of *Managing Customer Value*, discovered that perceived relative quality was strongly correlated with bottom-line and shareholder value.

Perceived relative value
Research suggests that the price customers are prepared to pay for something depends on many factors. Some customers have a clear value-map. They talk of upmarket and downmarket and can place themselves on the map too. Value is a useful starting-point in thinking precisely about why people choose one item rather than another. One product is said to be better value than another if more people would buy it if the prices of the two products were the same.

Perdue Farms undertook a programme of research to learn about customers' perceptions of quality and value in chicken. According to the Southeast Egg and Poultry Association, two factors had dominated the poultry industry's view of quality: no pinfeathers or bruises; and freshness. (Pinfeathers are the little feathers that can remain in the meat if the plucking machine is not particularly efficient.)

Frank Perdue changed the quality standards in the chicken market by researching what consumers really expected of their chickens, and hence what influenced their purchasing. He discovered that consumers would pay more for yellower (corn-fed) and meatier birds. When he began his research he found that consumers did not all agree on a neat list of quality attributes. Some would refer to "yellow", some to "good colour" and others to "fresh looking" birds. Using this range of statements his researchers created a list of non-overlapping attributes and then asked customers how they ranked these attributes. From this work they developed a detailed understanding of the key points to be stressed when communicating with customers about the quality of their chickens.

Frank Perdue moved from a position where consumers saw all chickens as more or less equal to one where his brand was identified with meatier and yellower chickens. He invested in careful breeding and improved feed to give customers what his surveys showed they wanted. He even purchased a machine to blow-dry his chickens thoroughly just before they reached the torching station, so that their pinfeathers would be burnt off more effectively. Lastly, he invested heavily in advertising to tell customers what he had done. The result was a brand that now dominates a market for what had previously been a commodity.

Earning quality stripes

Quality is achieved by finding out about people's experiences of quality and how they affect their repeat purchases and recommendations. Yet there is more to it than just mounting another survey. Here are seven guidelines for success.

1 Do not ask customers if the quality specifications are right. This is an easy mistake to make, and it is widespread in the quality area. The market researcher has a firm's quality specifications in hand and asks: "Are these right: yes or no?" Customers routinely confirm specifications researchers give them. Why not? They are giving the question little thought or effort but they are not being dishonest. This is why most such surveys give a rating of about 8 or 9 out of 10 to almost any qual-

ity specification, even when declining sales show the item is not performing well compared with competitors' products.

2 Discard the old quality definitions. Despite the speed with which new quality specifications have emerged in automobiles, leisure and entertainment, computers, financial services, supermarkets or anything else, research programmes generally do not track these new quality factors until some considerable time afterwards. Redesigning research questionnaires is a lot of extra effort.

3 Search for the hidden need. Use open-ended questioning and careful probing to understand what customers really mean by quality. Talk to them in their language. It might reveal that quality is not what you thought at all – it is what they think (your customers, and your competitors' customers). BMW has obviously done this with its air-conditioning system that removes 97% of dust and other particles from the interior. In the past the air inside the car was not part of the quality equation.

4 Talk to your competitors' customers. It is all too common for firms to talk only to their own customers about quality. Thus Cadillac, a winner of the Baldridge Quality Award, scored highly on quality among its own customers. But in the marketplace as a whole its reputation for quality was eroded by Lexus, BMW, Mercedes and Acura. So Cadillac lost a great deal of market share, despite high-quality perception among its own customers.

5 Find new ways to bring more quality issues under your control. BMW learned that exhaust fumes from other vehicles was a concern to its customers. Most automobile manufacturers would have discounted this as a factor not under their control, but BMW found a way of bringing it under its control.

6 Ask: "Says who?" Often the salesforce is the source of ideas about quality. Firms that ask their salesforce how customers perceive quality commonly hear that price and value for money are problems, and then get a list of tangible factors. This is because any buyers, however happy with the quality, are likely to say to the salesperson that the price is too high and then list a series of objections, irrespective of whether they are really important objections. A salesperson talking to dozens of customers a week, year after year, who say the prices are too high and then list objections, will start to believe them. But this is obviously not true, because if it were the market leader in every market would be the cheapest, which is not the case. There are few markets where the salesforce provides a good guide to quality and value.

7 Spend more time with customers. Outside the sales team, customer interaction is rare. Even where there is interaction product issues are rarely addressed. By all means use analysis of market research, but also get more directly involved. If there have been focus groups or discussion groups, get a video recording. Review written correspondence with customers. Mike Jackson, CEO of Birmingham Midshires Building Society, which has won numerous quality awards, has his home telephone number on all customer correspondence and regularly gets customer calls at home.

Measuring relative perceived quality

AT&T has done more than almost any other company to turn customer quality analysis into a business science. In June 1993 it began to report quality measures from its operating units to its board of directors. The metrics the board now receives include relative perceived quality (that is, relative to its main competitors); price competitiveness; and relative perceived value (which combines quality and price measures).[8]

AT&T had originally measured customer satisfaction by monthly telephone surveys. Its General Business Systems (GBS) unit, for example, asked customers to rate its performance as excellent, good, fair or poor, on the following quality dimensions: equipment; installation; repair; billing; training; and sales. AT&T executives aimed to maximise the sum of good plus excellent figures. The total usually came close to 90%. They used these good plus excellent measures as the basis for recognition programmes, presenting awards to the regions with the highest scores. Regional managers focused more energy on beating internal competitors than external ones.

The change began in 1987 when some businesses were found to be making major losses, despite 90% satisfaction. AT&T discovered that repeat purchase rates were dramatically different for customers rating quality as excellent and those rating it as good. Two managers at the time commented: "Good and excellent are clearly different satisfaction values, implying significantly different levels of satisfaction. By combining these significantly different levels into a customer satisfaction index approaching 100%, an illusion is inevitably created that AT&T customer satisfaction is approaching the penultimate ... It is not surprising, therefore, that disappointment sets in as AT&T's market share erodes."[9]

Empirical research showed that scores of 95% were associated with scores in the low 80s on "worth what paid for". This was found to be associated with areas where AT&T charged a comparatively high price. Gradually, a model of repeat purchase was developed that took account of not only relative quality measures, but also relative price. AT&T mapped the attributes that counted towards customers' perceptions of better value (superior quality, lower price). Attributes such as equipment quality were analysed into subfactors and weighting, for example, reliability (40% weight), easy to use (20% weight) and features/functions (40% weight).

This analysis had enormous power as it could predict repeat purchase and market share. The GBS people formed cross-functional teams to deal with the problem factors and were able for the first time to focus their quality processes on factors that drove repeat sales and market share. Between 1987, when market share fell, and 1992 there were a number of targeted quality improvements. Meanwhile, in untenable parts of the value map, competitors dropped out. AT&T gained significant market share and high profits. Today it is well on its way to creating shareholder value through its new customer-driven focus on relative quality and value.

Putting your trust in marketing tools and techniques

Marketing tools and techniques can provide trustworthy measures of quality, but because of social science associations, many are widely distrusted by engineers and accountants. Four concerns are common, yet each may be eliminated, or at least significantly limited, by good research design and implementation.

1 The apparent differences in research techniques. There is widespread belief that different researchers and analysts introduce bias and so results cannot easily be repeated. Yet if research firms do their jobs well, then the analysis of quality by one researcher will be essentially the same as the analysis of quality by another. One firm may favour a five-point scale and another a four-point scale, but the difference in quality measures is really no more than, say, the difference between measurements in kilometres or miles. The distance is real and unchanging, even if the measurement tools are differently calibrated.
2 The apparent subjectivity of people's experience. Customers sometimes appear to say one thing about quality one moment and the complete opposite the next. However, different answers are usually a result of subtle differences in the wording of the research questions. The utmost care must be taken to ensure that the data-gathering uses appropriate wording, particularly when research covers multiple languages and geographies.
3 The multiple factors that influence quality. There seem to be too many factors. Two techniques can help. One is the use of powerful multi-

variate statistical tools, such as multiple regression. The other is the use of data on individual customers, rather than looking for effects in aggregate quality data.

4 The effect of external factors, also known as the boundary conditions problem. Competitor actions, government and regulatory factors, press coverage and TV all seem to obscure and confuse the picture of how quality affects customers. The main way of combating these effects is to look at long-term trends. This method is what John Leftwich, marketing vice-president at Microsoft, calls the video camera technique, as opposed to the snapshot or still camera.

Marrying quality and marketing

HP has one of the world's most envied quality records which has undoubtedly contributed to the company's commercial success. What is interesting about HP is that the quality managers have been using marketing tools without help from marketing specialists. David Gee, quality director, says: "It's really difficult to separate quality and marketing. Quality is the way that we run our business, and it's my responsibility as quality director to make sure that our management system delivers quality that customers need and want. If that means I have to help provide customer research, then that's what I will do."

HP's approach to quality reflects the views of its founders. "As important as they are," said Bill Hewlett, "marketing people must play a secondary role in the question of product definition."[10] HP's approach to new products is to reject opportunities when it feels that it cannot make enough of a technical contribution. Dave Packard has commented: "If a product isn't good enough to make an excellent gross margin in the first year, then it's not a product with a significant technical advantage and the Hewlett-Packard Company shouldn't be making it, period ... If I hear anyone talking about how big their share of the market is or what they're trying to do to increase their share of the market, I'm going to personally see that a black mark gets put in their personnel folder."[11] This tough, self-imposed standard led HP to bypass high-volume markets such as personal computers until it could figure out a way to enter with a technologically based quality leadership. It has paid off, and today HP has moved ahead of IBM in the personal computer market.

Marketing at HP is a traditional "marcom" function, with responsibility for marketing communications: advertising; direct marketing; literature fulfilment. It is HP's quality managers who help determine what customers need and want. However, the real power lies with the divisional technologists and engineers, and they turn to the quality managers to assist them in an internal consultancy role. If part of the business needs to get better information about customers' perceptions of quality, and quality relative to competitors, then it is the quality managers who will respond with customer surveys and measurements.

The majority of quality managers, like HP's people, seem to agree that what they need is marketing tools and techniques. What they do not need are usually unsupported opinions and marketing myths. Benson Shapiro, in a *Harvard Business Review* article provocatively entitled "What the hell is 'Market Oriented'?", comments: "To be of greatest use, customer information must move beyond the market research, sales and marketing functions and permeate every corporate function: the R&D scientists and engineers, the manufacturing people, the field-service specialists."

Diane H. Schmalensee, vice-president of the American Marketing Association, put it this way: "Quality improvement requires allowing the voice of the customer to guide the firm's activities, telling it where and how to use its resources. This means specifically that researchers cannot be content with merely describing what customers have said, but must interpret their answers with more sophistication than ever. For example, it is no longer enough to tell management that customers give the firm a B in its performance. Managers must know exactly what A performance looks like and what actions they must take to create this A performance. To assist in this throughout the firm, marketing must learn to speak the language of other functions and then help those other functions set priorities by determining where customers' need for quality improvement is greatest."[12]

Tools for measuring quality
Marketing tools covered in Part 3 that can help a quality manager are:

- Quality measures (perceived and actual conformance quality)
- Price premium
- Brand image endorsement
- Marketing waste

3 Customer satisfaction and loyalty

THE modern doctrines of customer satisfaction and customer loyalty have a seductive logic. Simply satisfy your customers, and they will love you. The more you satisfy them, the more profit they will give you. The more they love you, the better you must treat them. No idea has influenced management more, or for more years, than the concept of customers for life.

Loyal customers cost less to service than disloyal ones, according to Fred Reichheld, consulting director at Bain & Co and author of a best-selling book, *The Loyalty Effect*.[1] "Loyalty-based management is a Sunday school teacher's dream come true – an ethical approach to business that pays so well that it puts the unscrupulous approaches to shame ... we discovered that raising customer retention rates by five percentage points could increase the value of an average customer by 25–100%." And competitors will be kept at bay, according to Michael Porter, professor of competitive strategy at Harvard Business School, because loyalty "creates a barrier by forcing market entrants to spend heavily".[2]

Certainly the influence of such simple ideas can be found in the measurements and targets set by major corporations, the majority of which now circulate figures on customer satisfaction to board members, and some of which even tie executive rewards and bonuses to satisfaction. A survey carried out by the author (see Chapter 7) revealed that over 60% of the organisations studied measure customer satisfaction, making it one of the principal non-financial measurements in common use. There is also an overwhelming belief at board level in the importance of satisfaction, and thus the priority it should be given over branding and the traditional marketing mix. These practices have been supported for over a decade, and they are deeply entrenched in many businesses.

The Peters's Principle

"The customer is truly in partnership with effective companies," writes Tom Peters in *In Search Of Excellence*,[3] and adds in *Thriving On Chaos*,[4] "The well-served customer is an appreciating asset. Every small act on her or his behalf ups the odds for repeat business, add-on business, and priceless word-of-mouth referral."

Yet do customers in the real world really behave in the considered and considerate ways that this advice suggests? The basic theory probably has no fatal flaws in itself. If customers like a company's products and continue to buy them over a long period, then its profits probably will increase, provided it has its costs under control. But how is it done? Which investments in satisfaction will pay dividends, through increased loyalty, and which ones will waste investors' money? To answer these questions, it is important to understand more of the thinking behind the concepts of satisfaction and loyalty.

Where did these ideas come from?
In the 1950s behavioural studies found that customers generally bought one brand in a category more often than other brands. However, multibrand loyalty was also discovered to be the norm; customers bought a brand portfolio or brand repertoire within any category. This occurs for a number of reasons: some products have weak brand awareness (for example, paper towels); some buyers seek variety (for example, in confectionery); price promotions may temporarily attract purchasers; and a preferred brand may not be available.

From the early 1950s to the early 1990s the concept of brand power and loyalty came to be widely accepted. The market research industry turned towards the cognitive sciences, studying people's attitudes and perceptions, and away from the studies of how people actually behave. Research seemed to support the loyalty myth by asking not "What do you buy?" but "How do you feel?". The consumer backlash was slow to surface, but by the 1960s proposals were being made by John F. Kennedy, then American president, that consumer issues should receive research funding. He expressed distrust of marketers.

The term customer satisfaction was invented by Theodore C. Levitt in a 1960 *Harvard Business Review* article entitled "Marketing Myopia",[5] later expanded into a book, *The Marketing Imagination*.[6] "Industry is a customer satisfying process, not a goods producing process ... The sale merely consummates the courtship. Then the marriage begins." Eventually, consumer research was funded by the early management consultancies, and from the consultancies came measures of satisfaction, loyalty and competitive benchmarking. During this era marketing was uninvolved with consumerism.

Then in 1982 two non-marketers and McKinsey consultants, Tom Peters and Robert Waterman, published *In Search of Excellence*, a book that propelled the idea of caring for customers and customer satisfaction into a management religion. Up to this point most marketing ideas had been developed in connection with selling physical products such as toothpaste, cars, steel and equipment, and marketers were slow to grasp the growth of the rather more intangible consumerist concept. "Excellent companies are not only better on service, quality, reliability and finding a niche. They are also better listeners," wrote Peters and Waterman. "That is the other half of the close-to-the-customer equation. The fact that these companies are so strong on quality, service and the rest comes in large measure from paying attention to what customers want. From listening. From inviting the customer into the company. The customer is truly in partnership with the effective companies, and vice versa."

In the early 1990s the brand loyalty debate resurfaced, driven by the merger mania of the 1980s and the search for value in the newly created mega-conglomerates. In 1993, on "Marlboro Friday" as Wall Street called it, Philip Morris decided to cut the domestic American price of its Marlboro cigarette brand by 40 cents a pack. Procter & Gamble announced the launch of "everyday low prices". And Lehman Brothers published an analysts' report entitled *The End Of The Brand*, suggesting that consumer behaviour had changed dramatically, and that almost overnight consumers had stopped acting loyally towards heavily advertised brands.

This attack by Wall Street on the marketing industry was welcomed by the consulting industry. Most management consultants had been excluded from marketing work by the advertising agencies. Less than 5% of consultancy income came from marketing work. In quick succession, McKinsey, Bain and Coopers & Lybrand published reports attacking the traditional marketers with their advertising focus, who were vilified as being too tactical and peddlers of packaging. The consultants were only too happy to monopolise the board agenda on customer and competitive issues and portray marketing as being "at the crossroads" (Coopers & Lybrand), "unethical" (Bain) and suffering a "mid-life crisis" (McKinsey). They claimed the moral high ground, saying their consulting techniques would make customers loyal and "put unscrupulous approaches to shame", to quote Bain's Fred Reichheld.

Direct marketers also joined the fray. They had collected and analysed vast databases in order to understand consumer behaviour. Many direct marketers had come to hate the advertising industry, whose highly paid executives looked down on them. So they sided with the consultants and attacked the advertisers. "The old mass-marketing methods do not work well enough in the new world," claimed Angus Jenkinson, a direct marketing expert. "Studies by Boston Consulting Group, Bain & Co ... Manhattan Consulting group and others show that customer loyalty results in above average profits and growth".[7] Stan Rapp and Tom Collins in *The New Maximarketing*[8] proclaimed: "The erosion of advertised-brand loyalty in America is reaching new depths." They did not dismiss loyalty, however, claiming: "The right customer-care and customer-reward programs help you to retain the loyalty of your present customers despite the best efforts of your competitors to steal them away."

In place of marketing tools the consultants peddled an array of magic potions and aims: "Zero customer defections" (Earl Sasser of Harvard Business School); "total customer service" (William Davidow and Bro Uttal); "customers-for-life" (Terry Vavra); "customer intimacy" (Fred Wiersema); "customer-centered-growth" (Richard Whitely); "customer-engineering" (David Frigstad); "customer-inspired-quality" (James Shaw); "customer-one-to-one" (Don Peppers and Martha Rogers); "customer-value" (Bradley Gale); "the loyalty effect" (Fred Reichheld); "moments of truth" (Jan Carlzon); and many more.

These are the products of master storytellers who write extraordinary anecdotes about heroic managers and mythical companies. At conferences the storytellers move with ease among the audience, manipulating their emotions with the passions of a Baptist preacher. "We know. We've given our share of these presentations," say Earl Sasser, James Heskett and Leonard Schlesinger, three of the most vocal gurus.[9] They continue: "Who hasn't heard a Nordstrom story at one of these seminars? Most often it's the one about the Nordstrom store that accepts the return of a set of tire chains by someone claiming they have bought them there, even though Nordstrom doesn't sell tire chains." William Davidow and Bro Uttal tell the Nordstrom story in *Total Customer Service – The Ultimate Weapon,* except their version concerns a customer returning a pair of squeaky shoes.[10] Tom Peters tells a Nordstrom story, but his version concerns a business suit.[11] "The misguided moral is that by wowing the customer in that manner, Nordstrom will gain a new customer and possibly great word of mouth advertising."

What is perhaps most remarkable about the satisfaction gurus is how few cases are involved in their anecdote-based advice. Stories about AT&T Universal Card Services, A.G. Edwards, MBNA, SAS, Southwest Airlines, State Farm, Toyota/Lexus and United Parcel Service are repeated over and over again. But they seldom say that what is right for one firm will be wrong for others. Much of the advice is simplistic and offers no encouragement to go looking for supporting data.

There has undoubtedly been a surfeit of contradictions and a lack of clear thinking about customer loyalty and satisfaction. Vast chunks of corporate budgets have been wasted on ill-conceived schemes. Apart from distortion caused by the vested interests in the advertising, direct marketing and consulting industries, there is another reason for concern about this fuzzy thinking. Lack of hard evidence about actual customer behaviour has allowed romantic ideas to flourish. Theodore Levitt wrote "A Retrospective Commentary" some 15 years after the "Marketing Myopia" article appeared. In it he commented: "Marketing Myopia was not intended as an analysis or even a prescription; it was intended as a manifesto. It did not pretend to take a balanced position ... Not everything has been rosy. A lot of bizarre things have happened as a result of this article."[12]

Most marketers know that satisfaction gurus are mostly peddling fantasies about customers. Yet when companies begin spending millions on impossible dreams, how many marketers propose more realistic measures? Marketers do have the tools and know how, and their measurement techniques are potentially more appropriate than those of the consultants, yet marketers rarely get involved in customer care. Most customer satisfaction studies are sponsored from outside the marketing department, and often the tools and techniques used are poor.

The marketing tools that exist for providing information to improve satisfaction and profitability are often ignored and even denigrated by the gurus. For example, Jan Carlzon, who credits himself in *Moments of Truth*[13] with turning around the ailing airline sas, advocates the total abolition of market research in favour of frontline employees taking responsibility for monitoring customer care. But it is extremely difficult for even keen and committed frontline employees to do anything other than collect data. The planning and organisation of such data collection and its subsequent analysis are the stuff of traditional market research tools and techniques.

Relationship marketers are guided by the frequency and cost of contact. They listen to employees' opinions about customer satisfaction, but employees rarely register factors such as trust, fairness and privacy. In recent years customer service managers have learned how to survey something they call customer satisfaction. They get sales clerks and service engineers to hound customers with questions every time they "interface" with them. They analyse the surveys and introduce a galaxy of new features and functions. Customers cope; they tolerate the sales clerks and service engineers. They struggle with the complications and complexities that the suppliers have introduced as a result of the surveys.

Yet despite the enthusiasm there is also evidence of much confusion. For example, a survey of over 100 executives conducted by the author confirmed that customer satisfaction was considered to be critical by more managers than any other measure, yet the survey also showed that customer needs are not properly understood in most companies (even though managers claim to know how to satisfy them). Less than one-quarter of the respondents said they measured and analysed customer needs, and only half felt that it was critical to understand needs.

"In a growing number of organisations there is disillusion," comments Colin Coulson-Thomas, after surveying hundreds of senior executives on their customer satisfaction programmes.[14] He encountered comments such as: "Our approach to customers is what we can get away with, not what we can do for them" and "Most of our products and services revolve round the things we can do, rather than customer requirements."

Some questions

"Why satisfied customers defect" by Professor Earl Sasser and Thomas Jones, published in the *Harvard Business Review*,[15] presented ample evidence that customers with high satisfaction scores were defecting to competitors, despite the widespread belief that satisfaction causes loyalty. A later paper by Merlin Stone, IBM professor of marketing at Surrey European Management School, entitled *"Second-Rate Customer Service"*[16] showed why first-rate customer service does not always pay. So if raising customer satisfaction scores does not result directly in more loyalty or more profits, maybe aiming more directly at loyalty itself will work better. Bring on "relationship marketing". "Have a one-to-one with your best customers" and "form life-time relationships with them" say pundits Don Peppers and Martha Rogers.[17] In practice, what does this mean: intrusive forests of junk mail and relentless telemarketing?

Care for your customers, but remember that they are not equal, is clearly the philosophy many companies have adopted. In the place of the mass market we now have gold and platinum consumers and key-account customers, who receive different grades of care from the masses. Discriminatory practices are all the rage.

Loyalty schemes have had more detractors than satisfaction schemes from the outset, and attracted many indignant articles. In a paper entitled "Do rewards really create loyalty?",[18] two vice-presidents of Bain & Co concluded that simple rewards do not create loyalty.

More radical questions were raised by Andrew Ehrenberg, professor of marketing at South Bank Business School, in another paper, "Brand Loyalty Under the Microscope".[19] He asked: Is there such as thing as loyalty? Does it differ from brand to brand? Is loyalty predictable? Are highly loyal buyers worth having? Many managers found his answers surprising.

First, however, such questions need to be answered with careful regard to language. Satisfaction and loyalty are often assumed not only to be linked, but also to be simple, one-dimensional factors. Loyalty can mean three quite different things:

- Feeling more positively disposed towards the brand: brand endorsement.
- Buying the brand more than other brands in the category: share of category or share of wallet.
- Continuing to buy the brand over long periods of time: allegiance.

Although it is easy to assume that these three meanings correlate with each other, the evidence tells a different story. Satisfaction also has many psychological dimensions, of which some may be important correlates of loyalty and others not.

Satisfaction on the psychologist's couch

"A public opinion poll is no substitute for thought," Warren Buffet once said, but opinion polls still predominate in the measurement of satisfaction. The common format is as follows. The customer is asked to rate the product or service on an overall basis: very satisfied; fairly satisfied; neutral; fairly dissatisfied; very dissatisfied. Then a list of key features is also rated: easy to park; great for freeway driving; ideal for town; comfortable for passengers (some attributes used by the automobile industry). Based on these ratings, boards of companies approve vast expenditure budgets on projects aimed at improving the opinion poll ratings.

Yet the popular psychology behind these polls has serious flaws, which explain its inability to influence loyalty or profitability. First, the overall satisfaction rating often does not relate closely to repurchase intention. There are many reasons for this, not least the fact that general feelings of contentment may not enter the customer's mind at the time of repurchase. Second, the list of key features may not relate well to overall satisfaction rating, or to repurchase intention, or to both. The method of generating the list fails to make this connection. The list is incomplete. It is often not highly relevant.

One problem is that ranking requests are typically made without qualification, as in: "Please rate the following in order of importance." A reasonable question is: "Important for what?" Research in 1977 by Fishbein and Azjen,[20] and much subsequent research, makes clear that to link safely researched attitudes with actual behaviour, people must be allowed to explain the context of those attitudes. For example, in trying to research how the styling of a car might affect someone's attitude to purchasing that type of car, it might not generate useful data simply to ask: "Do you think Ford Fiestas are stylish?". Instead, the questions could probe deeper, and ask about style more specifically in the context of:

- Buying a Ford Fiesta.
- Buying a Ford Fiesta from the *Exchange and Mart*.
- Buying a Ford Fiesta from the *Exchange and Mart* this month.
- Buying a Ford Fiesta for your daughter from the *Exchange and Mart* this month.

According to Fishbein and Azjen, the last of these is most likely to help predict buying intentions and behaviour. Another consumer expert, Richard Oliver, comments: "If the research goal is an understanding of consumer satisfaction, then importance in product choice is an inappropriate context."[21] This leads us to question the relevance of an overall satisfaction score in the context of product purchasing.

Another even more flawed but commonplace approach is that which relies on employee feedback. An employee talking to hundreds of customers a day, five days a week, for over 40 weeks a year, and listening to them moaning about prices being too high and quality being too low, will start to believe them. But customers' moans and groans are not always relevant. If responding to customers' dreams and fantasies was really important, every market leader in every market would be the minimum-priced, maximum-quality product. This is patently not the case. Customers have lots of dreams and fantasies, and they are also prone to moan about price and quality. But it is always a trade-off; there are many markets where the more expensive products are the leaders.

Companies which act only on the basis of what employees believe about customers' thoughts and feelings, based on what they hear from them, are on a fast road to bankruptcy. This is not to say that all customers' thoughts and feelings are unimportant, but care must be taken in determining how thoughts and feelings correlate with actual customer behaviour. The proper use of satisfaction as a measurement tool is explained at more length in Part 3.

Knowing when customers really care

There is a fascination with describing and measuring exceptional performance. "The most accurate watch in the world", "Keeps babies drier", "Cuts grease quicker", "Locks in freshness", "Softens your hands while you do the dishes", "Kills bad breath but doesn't taste mediciney", "Gives you sex appeal", "Kills bugs dead". These are just some of the performance measures that managers popularly associate with satisfaction. Yet do consumers really care?

Extensive research[22] now suggests that people care much less about products and services than they do about issues such as fair trading, fraud, racial equality or crime. Many, perhaps even most, purchasing decisions do not involve consumers in a great deal of thought. Often, neither the buying situation is involving (situational involvement) nor is there long-term involvement with the product or service after the purchase (enduring involvement). Involvement is defined by Richard Oliver as: "A focused orientation towards specific products and services of a more intense nature, consisting of greater pre-purchase behaviour (for example, search), greater attention to consumption, and greater processing of consumption outcomes."[23] There is more about using involvement as a measurement tool in Part 3.

Many companies spend huge amounts responding to minor consumer discontent, as identified by satisfaction surveys and employee feedback, and yet neglect much bigger issues. By identifying the issues that involve customers, it is possible to explain why different customers react differently over matters of satisfaction and loyalty, which can help target investment more profitably.

Many managers and management commentators assume that consumer involvement in purchasing is universally high.[24] Because managers are themselves so involved with their products and services, they assume that everybody else is too. This rational view of consumers dignifies them and the products they consume.[25]

Consumers often have not only a low involvement in purchasing, but also a zone of indifference, within which they are passively contented or discontented, and where they are simply not aroused to action. As the gap between expectation and experience grows, surprise occurs, and the consumer becomes much more likely to be aroused into action. For example, if a promised pizza delivery time is 30 minutes, most consumers would not be terribly upset if it arrived as late as 45 minutes, or as early as 20 minutes. Surprise might occur if the pizza arrived in 10 minutes, and they might take action if it had not arrived after an hour. When consumers do think about performance, they compare perceived performance with their expectations: ideal, excellent, desired, predicted,

Tolerance zone and indifference zone   3.1

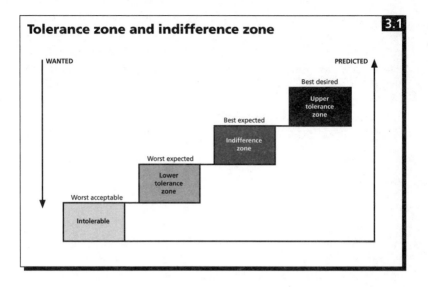

adequate, minimum tolerable, intolerable. They then react according to their tolerance zone. Figure 3.1 illustrates the concept.

The tolerance zone is bounded by "the best I would desire" and "the worst I will accept as barely fulfilling my needs". It is used as the basis of the disconfirmation approach to satisfaction. Disconfirmation is how consumers perceive performance that lies outside the zone of indifference. It has been associated with frustration, shock and dissonance, in which experience causes a spike of arousal. This spike of arousal is thought to be the motivating factor behind satisfaction.

Surprise is the most arousing factor. It causes more behavioural response than passive contentment or discontent, and therefore has greater commercial impact. Hence it is important to monitor two things: expectations by customers of what they will receive; and surprise with the difference between expectations and experience. The important role of surprise and expectations in satisfaction is implicitly recognised by the actions of some firms. "Unexpected pleasure", "customer delight" and "exceeds your expectations" are now becoming increasingly common as promotional claims. Conversely, the provision of delay information is now standard among transport operators, such as airlines and railways, as customers who expect the delay are less likely to be aroused. Hotels and restaurants also promise that there will be "no surprises" and no "hidden charges" in final bills.

What is more powerful: surprise or expectation?

Yet even though surprise is known to be more likely to spur customers into more action than mild feelings of discontent, in many circumstances it is customers' expectations which have a more powerful effect on behaviour than their past experiences. It is especially important to understand this when trying to influence future purchasing. Many managers assume that negative surprises cause brand switching and positive surprises cause repeat purchasing, but such generalisations are dangerous (see Figure 3.2).

Dissatisfaction is often not acted upon by consumers. Habits play an important part in behaviour, irrespective of thoughts and feelings, and many dissatisfied customers continue to purchase the same goods. Switching is often not the effect of dissatisfaction. Dissatisfied customers are strongly influenced in their behaviour by what they believe other people, such as family, think they should do, and by control factors such as time, skill and knowledge. Switching also arises from positive satisfaction. When consumers receive a surprisingly good experience, their curiosity is often aroused and they begin exploring and trying out alternatives. Research on positive surprises reveals that, contrary to what many gurus claim, delighted customers often become restless and are more likely to explore competitor offerings.

It is also true that repeat purchasing is sometimes a cause rather than an effect of satisfaction, and that switching likewise seems to be a cause of dissatisfaction. Customers who have switched in response to a competitor's price offer often rationalise the switch after the event by attributing dissatisfaction to the original brand. Likewise, customers who repeatedly purchase a given brand often justify their behaviour by talking about satisfaction, even when they have no experience of alternatives.

Low involvement may make past experiences less relevant, and in these situations habit often dominates. Take a long-life light-bulb, whose manufacturer claims it will last for 1,500 hours. Almost all consumers will be guided by expectations, not by direct experience. There are also internal consumer factors at work. Vividness of recall matters, and sensory imagery can be important when remembering past experience. Critical incidents, especially emotional ones such as those involving anger, may be more relevant and result in switching.

Inexperienced buyers with no previous experience are common in many markets, including the automobile market where expectations dominate. Consumer expectations can be influenced by many factors apart from experience, such as promotional claims, word-of-mouth informa-

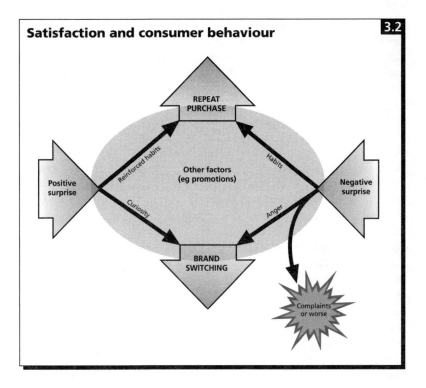

Satisfaction and consumer behaviour 3.2

REPEAT PURCHASE

Positive surprise

Reinforced habits

Habits

Other factors (eg promotions)

Negative surprise

Curiosity

Anger

BRAND SWITCHING

Complaints or worse

tion, third-party information such as consumer reports, and product cues (for example, high price often raises expectations about performance).

Measurement difficulties are common in many markets, and in many situations customers simply cannot measure product or service performance. It takes time to tell whether a baldness cure is actually promoting growth of your hair. For some categories of products, such as pensions, it is virtually impossible to tell, and the management of expectations is critical.

Control factors such as time, skill and other resources which may make it difficult to switch supplier are likely to contribute to the effects of perceived performance. Research by Earl Sasser, a professor at Harvard Business School, shows that industries vary greatly in their switching costs and associated consumer behaviour.

Studies of brand loyalty indicate that switching is rarest for low-income customers, who may want something different but cannot afford to switch, or perceive the risk of switching as high. Many products cannot be substituted, such as petrol and detergents, and the fact that buyers have a choice between many alternative brands is a matter of near indifference. People do a great number of things they would prefer to avoid, such as travelling to work on congested public transport and waiting in line in banks and at supermarket checkouts. The freedom to withdraw custom or complain effectively in areas such as education, medicine and legal advice is limited in many countries.

Sasser recognises that low satisfaction and loyalty often coexist. He describes such customers as hostages, and comments: "Hostages are stuck. These individuals experience the worst the company has to offer and must accept it. Many companies operating in a monopolistic environment see little reason to respond to the plight of hostages. After all, these customers can't go anywhere. So why bother to correct the problems?"[26] Companies should bother for two important reasons: "First, if the competitive environment suddenly shifts, these companies will then pay the price ... Second, hostages are very difficult and expensive to serve." Yet Sasser's conclusions about the need for high service and quality rest on the assumptions that a big competitor will mysteriously arrive, or that hostages are free to make an expensive nuisance of themselves. Anyone watching customers waiting in quiet frustration in a bank, post office or doctor's waiting room will consider such assumptions tenuous.

Mercenaries, however, are customers who may switch service suppliers to obtain better prices or deals, even though they are highly satisfied with their previous supplier (this is common in the automobile industry). Even when switching costs are low, consumers are generally only aroused to action when they have a strong perception that the supplier is to blame; plausible excuses from suppliers are often successful in pacifying customers.

Many factors other than dissatisfaction can lead to brand switching. These alternatives may be easily overlooked. Price promotions and running out of stock are common causes of brand switching. The cost of raising satisfaction by a few percentage points may be far more expensive than the cost of undertaking simpler, but more effective marketing actions.

Lastly, confirmation bias pervades many decisions that involve the ego, where disconfirmation may reflect badly on an individual's decision-making ability. The story of the emperor's new clothes is an example of such confirmation bias. Many fashion goods are dominated more by expectations than by performance measurement. Owners of fashionable clothes or motor cars are likely to experience disappointment, but still experience overall satisfaction.

Loyalty in the auto market

If a new Rolls-Royce is delivered with a small chip in the paint then satisfaction will be low, even though perceived quality of the Rolls-Royce is still likely to be high. A buyer of an old Lada has much lower expectations, and is likely to be happy that it runs at all. However, the emotional appeal of the Rolls-Royce may cause the customer to overlook the disappointment of the chipped paint when considering a future purchase.

The automobile market is one where many loyalty pundits wax lyrical about customers for life. Yet is loyalty really that important for success, and are car buyers loyal to manufacturers who deliver superior products? Fred Reichheld comments: "The US auto industry is an excellent example of a value proposition in desperate need of revitalisation. Customer repurchase rates of 30–40% show clear dissatisfaction with the value provided by most of the major makes ... Lexus, the luxury division of Toyota, is poised to establish itself among the royalty of loyalty ... repurchase rates hover around 60%."[27] Reichheld sets out a story of how the good guys at Lexus have beaten the bad guys at Cadillac simply by being better.

Yet this explanation of high Lexus repurchase rates omits a vital piece of evidence. In most of the automobile market, customers face a wide variety of choices, and the sheer number of alternatives reduces the probability of repurchase. For Lexus, however, the luxury price is so high that the choice of alternatives is severely limited. For Lexus in the UK, the Jaguar xj6 is its only true rival, according to *What Car* magazine.[28] Jaguar repurchase rates are also around 60%.

Managing needs and expectations

Expectations have a more important role, especially as regards repeat purchasing, than most satisfaction pundits would readily admit. Branding, advertising, PR, packaging and other traditional elements of the marketing mix potentially have an important effect on customer expectations.

Corporate marketing support is critical for sustaining customer expectations. For customer expectations to be sustained year-in, year-out, it is helpful for the brand to enter the cultural mythology. As Tim Ambler, a research fellow at London Business School, comments: "Building brands includes the business of building myths co-operatively with consumers."[29] Such long-term ambitions require sustained support. Having some yardsticks against which to measure corporate marketing support is enormously helpful (see Part 3).

Managing the traditional marketing mix needed to create such expectations involves the careful addition and subtraction of mix elements: TV, direct mail, PR, telephone calls, sales visits. Marketing mix productivity indicators, as described in Part 3, are needed to target and control the levels of marketing inputs.

The brand identity aims to provide something that customers can recognise when they are purchasing. In low-involvement situations, such as shopping, this facet of brands can be extremely important. Observational studies indicate that, on average, buyers take only 9.4 seconds from first sighting of the brand to deciding they need the product and putting it in their supermarket trolley and moving on.

Habitual customers do not have totally empty minds, but their thoughts are far from the logic machines that loyalty gurus present. Table 3.1 indicates that an amazingly high 47% of all supermarket brand choices are made when the product is actually seen. Research shows that customers must recognise the brand first, then decide if they want to buy the category. For example, snack foods are recognised first, then the decision is made to purchase; 78% of snacks are bought in this way. In the great majority of cases recognition is a visual process, requiring only memory traces associating the image with the category.

Recognition of the category for the brand through visual associations is important for most supermarket products. It is also important in direct response marketing, and pictures and other visual representations are often significant cues to enable the customer to recognise the category offered.

Recall of a brand name is important when the category is pre-planned. Many industrial products and consumer services are chosen in this way. The buyer experiences the category need first, then must mentally recall a list of possible suppliers or brands that potentially can meet that need. Brand recall is often a verbal process, requiring recall of the brand in response to a verbal cue (occurring mentally or subvocally) of the category need. Advertising can have an important role in linking brand need to category need. Recall and recognition are two key aspects of awareness, which are discussed in more detail in Part 3.

Some readers may protest about habits, pointing out that there are many unfamiliar buying situations. Yet habit is always important, especially when a person is on the point of buying something for the first time. Most people buying something for the first time are in the habit of asking questions such as "Which is the best?", to which the answer is usually the top-selling brand. Most first-time purchasers are familiar with similar products; they have often talked to friends who have used them, and they have read the popular press and magazines. Thus their pur-

Table 3.1 **Incidence of point-of-purchase brand choices for supermarket products**

Type of choice	Incidence (%)
Impulse (neither category nor brand pre-planned)	47
Brand pre-planned	35
Category pre-planned but not brand	15
Other (eg switch of pre-planned brand)	3

Products: point-of-sale choice	Incidence (%)
Snack foods	78
Cosmetics	69
Soft drinks	67
Non-prescription drugs and medicines	49
Cigarettes	33
Alcoholic beverages	20
Prescription drugs	0

Source: POPA/Du Pont Studies, see J.R. Rossiter and L. Percy, *Advertising and Communications Management*, McGraw Hill, 1997, Chapter 5, note 19.

chasing behaviour owes much to habits established in related contexts. From this standpoint the basic form of all behaviour is habitual and in unusual situations customers generally follow habits in their repertoire at least as much as in familiar situations.

Brands also need to stand out as good examples of their category. It is often said that brands need to be differentiated in order to be bought. Differentiation can take many forms, from the distinguishing but irrelevant (blue packaging, stripes on dentifrice), to minor differences (two kinds of tomato soup), to clear physical differences (combined fax, answerphone and printer). However, successful differentiation asks to be copied and generally it is (PCs with Pentium chips; shampoo for oily hair).

Comparison shoppers often complain that there are only minor differences between brands. The big differences are in the products within a category (Pentium 75 compared with Pentium 200), the detailed features, service and packaging, and the price. Yet for busy customers, who have limited time for comparison shopping, the brand provides a reassurance, or a promise of value. Measurement of this brand image endorsement is described in Part 3.

Brand loyalty under the microscope

Having measured customers' minds, measuring their behaviour is the last task. The behaviour of customers reveals habitual patterns. They will return to the same products over time through sheer force of habit. Cognitive data provide explanations of what motivates these habits. The commonest motivators are negative, such as normal depletion of the refrigerator or larder, which dominates grocery purchasing, and replacement of goods which are broken, worn out, or causing high levels of dissatisfaction. Positive motivators such as sensory gratification, intellectual stimulation or social approval are much less common.

Yet it is these positive motivators which many loyalty gurus focus on. They interpret regularities in buying behaviour in terms of a rational process, suggesting that customers rationally choose the "best" suppliers with whom they will form relationships, motivated by the "right" care, or the "right" rewards, or other "right" rational factors. The evidence is far more prosaic. Consumers are creatures of habit simply because they are creatures of habit, who believe that their habits are convenient. Purchasers of products, whether for home consumption or business use, do not, on the whole, have time to go into great detail before making a decision on what may be a trivial item of expenditure.

Choosing the product that you have bought before, or the first, second or third that you are offered, or simply the market-leading product, can be a sensible way of reducing risk without wasting time. There is evidence to suggest that this is often how purchasing decisions are made, even substantial ones such as TVs and motor cars.

Professor Andrew Ehrenberg has been looking at the behavioural data since the 1950s. At first, facts and figures were extremely scarce and hard to assemble, so his findings were not readily confirmed by other researchers. During the last five or so years much more evidence has started to emerge in France, Germany, Japan, the UK and the United States as computer data on customer purchasing behaviour have become much more widely available. Evidence of loyalty has been studied in over 50 product categories, as diverse as biscuits, beer, cars, cosmetics, cleaning materials, over-the-counter medicines and pharmaceutical prescriptions, supermarkets and TV programmes.

Four questions about loyalty, as raised by Ehrenberg,[30] are answered by the behavioural studies:

- Is there such a thing as loyalty?
- Is loyalty predictable?

■ Does the degree of brand loyalty differ much between brands?
■ Are highly loyal buyers worth having?

First, loyal behaviour does exist. People generally buy the same brands again and again, but their loyalty is polygamous; that is, they habitually buy a repertoire of several brands, one of which is dominant.

Second, different measures of loyalty generally correlate with each other. Table 3.2 shows this pattern in the powdered detergent market. Loyalty measures such as quarterly repeat purchase, first brand loyalty, share of category requirements (see glossary for definitions) all correlate. The pattern of variation in loyalty is predictable from market share alone. The bigger the brand, the more loyal are the customers. This is the normal pattern in brand analyses. Loyalty can therefore be defined from behavioural data, without assuming any deeper consumer commitment.

Third, loyalty depends on market share, but differs little between brands with similar market share. This rather contradicts the wisdom of some gurus. For example, Rapp and Collins say: "No matter how small or how large your business is, a key to making it work is 'customer development' ... customers are identified, located, persuaded, motivated, converted and cultivated in a way that maximises sales and profits."[31] Fred Reichheld proclaims: "Revenue and market share grow as the best customers are swept into the company's business, building repeat sales and ... customer spending tends to accelerate over time."[32]

Table 3.2 **Loyalty measures and market share in UK detergents (%)**

Brand	Loyalty measures			Market share
	Share of category requirements	Quarterly repeat purchase	First brand loyalty by brand	
Persil	47	75	78	30
Ariel	35	66	75	18
Bold	32	64	72	13
Daz	26	57	68	10
Surf	26	56	58	10
Average	**33**	**64**	**70**	**16**

Source: AGB data for the UK market, 52 weeks, 1986. Data analysis by Hammond (1996).

Yet the evidence from categories as diverse as cars and cosmetics paints a different picture. Differences in purchase frequency are small between brands. This can be seen in the analysis of American instant coffee purchases in Table 3.3. Even 100% brand-loyal customers differ little in purchase frequency. No brands enjoy abnormally high purchase rates, whether in coffee, cars or cosmetics.

Fourth, regular buyers of brands are always few in number, and they do not buy as much as average buyers. They are not heavy buyers of the brand and are light buyers of the category. For example, in Table 3.3 only 15% of Nescafé customers are 100% loyal. They buy coffee 4.3 times per year, compared with the average coffee buyer who buys 9 times per year (across a portfolio of brands). There are more loyal customers for large brands than for small ones.

This would be a typical pattern of brand loyalty. About 20% of people who bought Maxwell House in a year are 100% loyal (that is, they bought Maxwell House exclusively). Loyal customers bought a little more than the average brand customer, 4.2 Maxwell House purchases per year compared with 3.6 Maxwell House purchases per year. Loyal buyers are also lighter coffee buyers than average, 4.2 coffee purchases compared with 9 coffee

Table 3.3 **Purchase frequency and brand loyalty in the American instant coffee market**

| | Purchase frequency (times per year) | | | | |
	Of any coffee	Of brand	Of 100% loyal buyers	100% loyal buyers (%)	Market share of brand (%)
Maxwell House	9	3.6	20	4.2	19
Sanka	9	3.3	20	3.2	15
Tasters Choice	9	2.8	24	4.2	14
High Point	8	2.6	18	1.8	13
Folgers	9	2.7	13	3.3	11
Nescafé	11	2.9	15	4.3	8
Brim	9	2.0	17	2.4	4
Maxim	11	2.6	11	3.9	3
Average brand	**9**	**2.8**	**15**	**3.4**	**11**

Source: MRCA data over 48 weeks. Data analysis by Ehrenberg.

purchases per year. Average buyers of Maxwell House made 9 purchases of any instant coffee in the year, but bought Maxwell House only 3.6 times (a share of category requirements of 40%). Which other brands Maxwell House buyers also bought are in line with these brands' market shares and market penetrations, and this is not partitioned or segmented. In other words, Maxwell House is not particularly like or unlike any other coffee. It is just bigger.

Loyalty: five guidelines for profitable success

1 Understand people's habits. In the case of existing customers, the objective is often defensive, to exploit repetitive habits that will result in repeat purchase or renewal. For non-customers the habit to focus upon is trial. Which new things do people habitually try?

2 Understand the negative motivators of habit. Commonly, motivators are negative, such as the need to replace everyday household goods or groceries that you have run out of, or the desire to replace goods which are broken, worn out, obsolete, or causing high levels of dissatisfaction (this is the main reason behind purchasing of durables, including automobiles, refrigerators, office products, industrial plant and equipment). Such purchases are sometimes called relief purchases.

3 Understand the switching costs and benefits. Many buyers repeat their purchases because the perceived costs of switching to a different purchase are high. The emphasis on service and quality as sources of retention, according to most loyalty literature, exaggerates the amount of choice that people actually have. For example, "He or she is not an unthinking pawn to be manipulated at will by the commercial persuader ... Consumer behaviour as a rule is purposeful and goal oriented. Products and services are accepted or rejected on the basis of the extent to which they are perceived as relevant to needs and lifestyle. The individual is fully capable of ignoring everything that the marketer has to say," according to Engel, Blackwell and Miniard.[33]

4 Understand the positive reinforcers of habit. Positive reinforcers such as sensory gratification, intellectual stimulation or social approval are much less common than negative ones. Such purchases are sometimes called reward purchases.

5 Do not try to buy loyalty. Many businesses are attempting to use loyalty programmes (incentive-based promotion activities such as supermarket loyalty cards or frequent flyer programmes) to increase long-term repeat purchase behaviour. The fact that they are so easy to copy seems to undermine their effectiveness. Surveys of cardholders

show that most of them hold cards for more than one rival scheme. It is thus the "loyal" customers who have benefited for their normal habits, and the end-suppliers who have lost, by having to reduce their costs enough to pay for the loyalty schemes. So any claims that loyalty programmes create a competitive barrier seem rather weak.

Nor do price promotions have any long-term effect on loyalty. Research into their effectiveness shows that sales gains are temporary and last only for the period of the promotion. There appears to be little carry-over of sales effect into the post-promotion period. Most discount purchasers have already bought the brand at some time before (that is, it is in their repertoire), so that promotions rarely introduce a brand to a new purchaser. Purchasers seldom increase their total consumption in the category in response to a sales promotion, although they may stockpile to get a better discount. The costs of the promotion are not generally recouped, even as short-term sales gains. The customer seems to be the only person who gains, and the end-suppliers lose out through having to deliver at reduced net prices.[34]

Conclusion

In general, loyalty occurs simply because habits are convenient to the busy customer. It is therefore easy to spend a lot on misguided loyalty schemes.

Traditional marketing techniques, in particular advertising and brand management, have a powerful role in reinforcing habits and hence supporting loyalty. The combination of these techniques with good measurement tools and systems can sustain loyalty for decades. It is no coincidence that some of the longest-lived products and services in the world are heavily advertised, branded goods such as Persil and Maxwell House. Their success is ample testimony to the power of the tools, and not to a blind faith in the loyalty effect.

Tools for measuring customer satisfaction and loyalty

Ten key tools are described in Part 3:

- Satisfaction
- Customer involvement
- Brand image endorsement
- Repeat purchase
- Complaints

- Market leadership
- Distribution leadership
- Category health map
- Competitive threat map
- Marketing waste

4 Innovation

ANOTHER business obsession is the perceived need to innovate. Consumers are deluged with new miracles which they do not want, which do not work and which rapidly pass away, and still managers yearn for more innovation.

In his 1997 book, *The Innovation War*, Christoph-Friedrich von Braun compared business innovation with the arms race, and suggested that R&D was spiralling out of control. He cited the $630m per day spent on R&D in France, Germany, Japan, the UK and the United States. The book caused a storm of newspaper headlines in Germany and widespread discussion. Charles LaMantia, CEO of innovation consultants Arthur D. Little, commented: "This book is a warning to all those innovation warriors whose business actions are increasingly founded on time-based management. Any escalation spiral that is driven by competitors' actions only is as misguided as was the arms race during the Cold War."

Business history is full of failed attempts at selling the new, the improved and the different to consumers. But, as discussed in Chapters 2 and 3, consumers are creatures of habit who spurn the new, the improved and the different. They remain loyal to familiar brands over long periods, even when there are better brands, and they rate the familiar brands badly in blind tests. They are constrained by the views of others about what they consume and their limited knowledge of products. They rarely use relevant information from consumer associations, newspapers and so on about products or services. They watch advertising that seldom contains useful information about the product. Is it any wonder, then, that around nine out of ten new products that are launched this year are likely to be withdrawn before the end of next year?[1]

The fashion for innovation

Innovation has moved in and out of fashion for over 100 years. In the 1880s Thomas Edison in the United States publicly battled with Joseph Swan in the UK over the rights to the electric light bulb. Inventors caught the imagination of the public and business alike, particularly because of their combination of technical and business prowess.

In the early 1950s, with overproduction threatening on many fronts, a fundamental shift occurred in the preoccupation of people in executive suites. Innovation in product and processes had become a secondary concern. Consumers were not buying what was being produced. Most already possessed perfectly usable cookers, cars, radios, clothes, and so on. Waiting for these to wear out was intolerable. The search began for a new type of innovation which worked through "psychological obsolescence". There was talk at management conventions of "the marketing revolution" and considerable pondering on how best to stimulate consumer buying by creating wants in people that they still did not realise existed. The myth of the all powerful, innovative marketer was born.

In the years that followed the marketing industry added a new type of agency responsible for innovation. Describing themselves as design agencies, these firms helped create the psychological obsolescence that should enable technical innovators to land a good catch of consumers. Changes in consumer demand patterns translate into theories of innovation. Youth demand and fashion becomes lifestyle marketing. Increasing health and longevity translates into demographic marketing. Concern with the environment becomes green marketing. Most of these approaches required simple, low-cost changes to the product assembly process and produced more and more goods for the steadily evolving consumer demand.

By the 1980s many firms in the West had embraced these ideas of marketing-led innovation, and the associated production processes were flexible enough to accommodate the marketing-led changes, over 90% of which were line extensions, requiring a minimum of costly process change.[2] Two events, however, shook this marketing approach to its roots. The first was the arrival of Japanese competitors in the West with big differences in technical superiority. Western firms found their own processing capacity unable to match the Japanese innovations, and for a while they struggled to catch up through a concerted effort in process re-engineering. The second was the amazing growth of the personal computer industry. Small and oddly managed firms such as Apple, Intel and Microsoft beat marketing giants such as IBM and DEC with amazing, innovative products.

The mood of the time was eloquently summed up by Bennett and Cooper: "The marketing concept has diverted our attention from the product and its manufacture; instead we have focused our strategy on responses to market wants and have become preoccupied with advertising, selling and promotion ... The impact of a market-responsive strategy has been most strongly felt in the field of product innovation ... So we spend billions more convincing the customer that the product is 'new and improved' rather than spending the money in the lab to develop a significantly superior product ... A market-driven strategy provides little encouragement for technological discoveries, inventions or significant breakthroughs ... We have become a society of tinkerers and cosmeticians."[3]

Consultants thrived on these challenges to traditional marketing-led innovation. Michael Hammer and James Champy built a major consulting business on the basis of being customer-led. They wrote about process innovation in *Re-engineering the Corporation*: "Deprived of material goods, first by the Depression, then by the war, customers were more than happy to buy whatever companies offered them ... In reality a mass market never existed. Customers demand products and services designed to their unique and particular needs."[4]

Gary Hamel and C.K. Prahalad thought this was not enough. In *Competing for the Future* they wrote: "A company must be much more than customer-led. Companies claim to be re-engineering their processes from the customer backwards. Customers are notoriously lacking in foresight. Companies that create the future do more than satisfy customers, they constantly amaze them."[5]

A belief that unites most consultants, however, is the need for real differentiation as opposed to purely psychological differentiation. According to Tom Peters: "Any product or service, no matter how mundane, can become a 'high-value added' product or service; that is, there is no such thing as a non-differentiable commodity. Indeed, the more the world perceives a product/service to be a mature commodity, the greater the opportunity to differentiate it through the unending accumulation of small advantages – which eventually transforms the product, often creating wholly new markets in the process."[6]

The marketing industry realised that the trouble was not a sudden insurgence of Japanese products. Although some marketers played the real differentiation game, and a new breed of design agency appeared with names like The Value Engineers and The Added Value Company, many were sceptical of jettisoning their experience in favour of the ideas floated by consultants. The reality is that almost all Western consumer markets are mature and fully penetrated at current price levels. Differentiation is not so much in product performance as in consumer brand perception. Distribution is becoming increasingly competitive; and price competition is intense. The only real growth comes from population increases, which never exceed 1–2% per year. To thrive as an innovator, a company must wrest market share away from established brands, entice new users into a category, find process innovations to reduce costs, or be a pioneer in newly emerging categories.

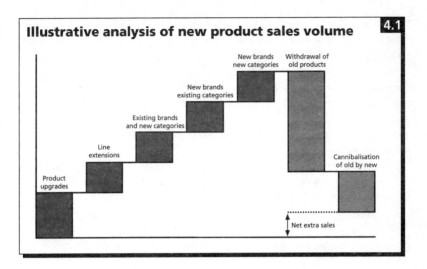

Illustrative analysis of new product sales volume 4.1

How new is new?

Talk of such radical innovation can enliven a business's annual general meeting, but the action seldom lives up to the talk. A statement in an annual report that "25% of our sales volume this year has come from new products developed in the past five years" may disguise a breakdown of "new" product innovation that looks like Figure 4.1.

New brands and products, line extensions and even product improvements are often confused by companies wishing to appear radically innovative. The reality is that real growth in GDP is only about 2% in most western economies, and corporate growth is seldom much higher. The conjuring trick for those wanting to appear radically innovative is to hide the withdrawal of old products and cannibalisation of old volume by line extensions, flanker brands and new brand names. The key to a useful definition of innovation is consumer perception, rather than the degree of technical change.

Why innovate?

The case for making an unchanged product until it stops selling is a powerful one. Bestsellers such as aspirin, Coca-Cola, Kellogg's Corn Flakes, Mars Bars, Nivea and Vaseline have continued to dominate important markets virtually unchanged for decades. As technical concepts they are close to the original product. However, if the originals are looked at in a museum or in photos, or the ingredients are studied, then small changes may be noticed. Packaging and advertising are the most visible changes, but size also changes, and ingredients such as cocaine in Coca-Cola come and go. So phrases like "new product" need careful analysis before abandoning the need for innovation altogether.

Lessons can be learned by examining the performance of firms during periods of no innovation. Innovation comes and goes in cycles as management changes. During the 1960s the British Motor Corporation chose to run its products until they and their market dropped. It argued that customers' needs were not satisfied any better by newer products from competitors such as Ford. They did not get from A to B any faster, the same number of passengers were accommodated, and they were just as comfortable. Yet the competitors became more profitable and more popular over time. The extra profit came from two sources: cost reduction, because the new model Fords were less expensive to produce than the old ones; and the added popularity of variations on the basic theme.

The radically different option

One approach to innovation is to pursue radical innovations that really differentiate a company's products and services from those of the competition. Radical differentiation has become fashionable, but what does the marketing evidence say about it? Liquid detergents provide a revealing example of evidence of consumer behaviour towards innovation. They were developed by scientists as an alternative to the traditional powdered detergents, such as Persil and Surf (from Unilever) and Ariel, Bold, Fairy and Daz (from Procter & Gamble). Most of the brands were mature, and consumers were creatures of habit. Technically, the new products were revolutionary. It took seven years of R&D to develop a fatty acid with water-softening capabilities equivalent to a phosphate and new "builders" to prevent redisposition of dirt in the wash. The organisation of the R&D was so ambitious that it is considered an important case study in global organisation theory.[7] But the key question is how did consumers perceive the innovation?

The first to market was Unilever, which faced the question of differentiation: given the technically different basis of liquid detergents, how different should consumers perceive it to be? Tom Peters, Gary Hamel and Michael Porter all seem to favour differentiation. They think it avoids consumer confusion and cannibalisation. They also favour being visionary and first to market. So Unilever was first to market with a radically different identity.

The new Unilever brand was named Wisk. Its growth from launch in the fourth quarter of 1985 was slower than is typical for line extensions, but after a year it had achieved a share of 10% (for line extensions it often takes only 3–6 months to reach peak share). Growth was achieved by stealing share from existing products, including Persil and Surf. It cannibalised 4% from Persil's 33% share, but also stole share from Ariel (3% from 19% share), and all brands lost share to the new entrant in direct proportion to their size before the launch. At first this seemed to vindicate the decision to differentiate under a new identity.

Procter & Gamble responded in the first quarter of 1987, but quite differently from Unilever. The differentiation was minimised and the product was launched as Ariel Liquid, a line extension. Within one quarter Ariel Liquid climbed to share levels that had taken Wisk a year to achieve, and, contrary to the theories of the consultants, it did not cannibalise the parent brand more than other brands. It cannibalised 2% from Ariel Powder's 16% share, but also stole 5% from Persil and 2% from Wisk. Again the losses in share were in direct proportion to brand sizes before the launch.

Unilever responded to the success of Ariel Liquid rather belatedly in the third quarter of 1988, by which time the share of Persil had deteriorated from 33% (just before the launch of Wisk) to 24%. It launched Persil Liquid. By mid-1989 Persil Liquid's share was 6% and Persil Powder's was 23%, Wisk's share had decayed to 5%, and Ariel Liquid and Powder's shares were 9% and 11% respectively. The more strongly differentiated product, Wisk, ended up in the weakest position.

This case suggests that strong differentiation can be less effective than hiding behind an existing identity, even when the new product is technically quite different, in contrast to the widespread view that stronger concepts favour a new brand name and strong differentiation. It is particularly valuable to note the differing fortunes of Wisk and Persil Liquid in the UK, since they are actually the same product.[8] The key determinant is whether consumers see the differentiation. Despite all the technical innovation, most consumers saw the liquid as an example of the detergent category, not as a new category, and there were no barriers to consumers switching from powder to liquid or back again. The key to success was for enough consumers to see the liquid detergent as relevant to them as a detergent.

This is not an isolated case. Hundreds of studies suggest that radical innovations are only occasionally adopted by creatures of habit, even when the innovations have real benefits.[9] Internal problems, such as lack of organisational commitment, can exacerbate the market issues. But the real challenges are to get the ugly duckling into the water; to see whether real customers will part with real money; to have the measurement systems needed to monitor results early; and to evaluate fast whether you have a winner or a loser.[10, 11]

The continuous improvement option

Another approach to innovation is to make many small innovative steps and the occasional big one. It is like a game of snakes and ladders. Occasionally, a player is lucky enough to land at the bottom of a ladder, which allows him to climb up to a higher level of the game's twisting path. An unlucky player can land on a snake, which whisks him to a lower level, as in the case of a firm that chooses to coast in the face of rapidly changing competition. Most of the game involves succeeding with small incremental moves.

This may not seem heroic, but it is how Agincourt was won. These incremental improvements have resulted in jet engines with double the thrust per unit weight of two decades ago; plastics that can be used at temperatures twice as high as a decade ago; and incandescent light bulbs 15 times as efficient as Edison's. Marketing's job is to make sure that the constant streams of innovation meet customers' perceived needs, and also that they are widely and rapidly adopted. A systematic marketing process can dramatically increase the chances of successful customer adoption.[12]

Launching a new product

Whether it is a radical or an incremental innovation, it is vital to research the thoughts and feelings of buyers and potential buyers before and during the launch. Care must be taken to track factors that drive product adoption behaviour.

As discussed in Chapter 3, it is possible to anticipate when attitudes predict action and when they will not.[13, 14, 15] It has been shown, for example, that people's attitudes towards a behaviour, such as attitudes to buying detergent, are consistent with that behaviour. Whereas people's attitudes towards the object, such as attitudes towards detergent, are less good as a guide to their behaviour. People who dislike cheese may still buy it as an ingredient in cooking, and people who like it may not buy it because it is not part of their diet plan. In both cases the right question is to discover their attitudes towards buying or using the object, not the object itself.

Practices in market research have been slow in responding to this dis-

Brand image map of the British detergent market 4.2

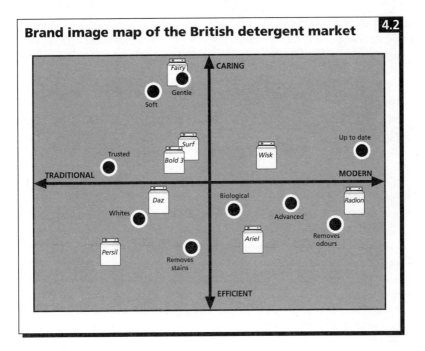

covery. Much brand research still tracks people's perceptions of the brand, not their attitudes towards buying it. Figure 4.2 shows a recent example of such a brand image map of the British detergent market.

According to brand image theory, buyers of brands that are far apart on the map should behave very differently. Thus Wisk buyers should be less likely to stop buying Persil and more likely to steal share from Ariel. However, in practice Wisk took 4% of Persil's share and only 3% from Ariel. In reality, the large distance between Wisk's brand image position and Persil's brand image position was not reflected by buying behaviour.

The Microsoft approach

Microsoft, like Proctor & Gamble, is an opportunist company. Its approach to innovation is described by Jeff Lill, technical manager of the project that became Microsoft Network: "A competitor comes in and does something interesting, then we come in and basically clone it; do it marginally better and throw some marketing clout behind it, then relentlessly make it better over the years. That's our strategy. And it has worked damn well."[16]

When the computer industry was dominated by giants such as IBM, Microsoft broke the habits of the IT industry's customers with innovations such as Windows and Word. Few markets could be more different from the household detergent market, with its habitual purchasers. Yet much of Bill Gates's success lay in his deep understanding that even in novel situations people trade on already acquired habits. The lack of success of his largest competitors, including IBM, lay in their willingness to overlook people's habitual behaviour because of their overwhelming desire to be seen to be different and better than Microsoft.

Fitting in is the root of culture. Paying closer attention to what everyone else is buying than whether it is any good is what allows societies to function, but it is not a source of progress. To engineers in firms such as IBM, and to American consulting gurus such as Gary Hamel, the best of all possible worlds would be one in which technologies competed continuously and only the best survived. But Bill Gates knew that in the real world the most successful products become standards against which other products are measured, not for their performance or cleverness, but for the extent to which they are like that standard.

Consider the habits of a person who is on the point of buying a personal computer for the first time. Most people buying something for the first time ask questions such as "Which is the best?", to which the answer is usually the bestselling brand. Most first-time PC purchasers are familiar with other electronic products, they have talked to friends who have used PCs, they have read the popular press and magazines, and they are likely to be knowledgeable about the need for standards in technical products such as video recorders (VHS and Betamax). Thus their PC purchasing behaviour owes much to habits established in related contexts. From this standpoint the basic form of all behaviour is habitual, and in unusual situations such as buying a PC customers generally follow habits in their repertoire.

Gates exploited his understanding of buyer habits while almost everyone else in the early PC industry strove to be different. Companies like IBM, Victor and Zenith wanted to set the standard with their hardware and software. Zenith's Z-100 had two processors so it could run 8-bit and 16-bit software, and it was a little cheaper than the IBM PC. The Victor 9000 had more power, more storage capacity and more memory than the IBM PC, and cost less money. IBM, Victor, Zenith and many other clone makers commissioned a custom version of Microsoft's DOS operating system for their machines, along with custom spreadsheets and word processors, all from Microsoft. Consumers became more and more dissatisfied with the differences and the resulting compatibility problems. So when Microsoft offered them a standard set of products – the MS-DOS operating system, MS-Multiplan spreadsheet (later called Excel), MS-Multiword (later called Word) – they abandoned the differentiated products like IBM-DOS, Zenith-DOS and Victor-DOS in their millions.

Successful innovation

Winning at the innovation game is a matter of understanding the habits and behaviour that will encourage or discourage willingness to try out something new and continue using it. Here are five guidelines for success.

1 Provide effective marketing support for the innovation. The concept of the innovation must, of course, be appropriate, but it will fail unless it is properly supported. The job of marketing support is to generate awareness, trial and reinforcement (ATR). Reinforcement is essential if consumers are to keep using the innovation. Even for purchases such as refrigerators and motor cars, consumers often search more for reassuring information after the purchase than before it. However, a percentage of habitual buyers and users will at any time be dissatisfied (about 15% per year in many consumer categories) and willing to try something new.

Microsoft has a massive support resource and infrastructure dedicated to the beginning of the product cycle. Awareness of Microsoft is extremely high. It integrates the marketing messages through all media. Its press office is fast, nimble and in touch, rather like a good political press office. With the press, keeping Bill out there is key. Gates is presented as a soothsayer (supported by his book, *On The Road*), and has even been portrayed in Spielberg's Saturday morning kids cartoon "Pinky and the Brain" as capable of ruling the world. When Gates says something is the future, people are often willing to give it a try. Having tried it, all the messages reinforce their choice.

2 Do not try to use persuasion, it seldom works. Most writing on innovation says or implies that innovative products obtain significant market share because consumers are persuaded to use them and keep using them. But there is little evidence that a campaign of 30-second commercials about an innovative product is likely to persuade people to do something they have so far not wanted or felt able to do, or at least been indifferent to. Similarly, word-of-mouth advice and recommendations are common from parents, teachers, the clergy, politicians and friends, but usually change nothing.

Microsoft does not try to persuade people to do something different, and its communications avoid explicitly saying that Microsoft is better or different. Instead, its trademarked slogan, *Where do you want to go today?*™, says no more than *Coke is It*, or other "here I am" slogans. By contrast, IBM has made strenuous claims that OS/2 and other PC products are different and better. The trouble is that consumers are seldom persuaded to believe suppliers who claim to be different, better, or the best.

The classic persuasion model is AIDA. It says that for each consumer there first has to be Awareness, then Interest, then Desire and lastly Action. But this persuasion view has increasingly been criticised. For example, there is seldom evidence that potential customers feel strong desire when they buy an innovative new product. Where research is used to measure desire, it finds that buyers of competitive brands often regard their own brand as highly desirable (often scores will be bunched together at, say, 8.8 out of 10), whereas they rank other brands as less desirable (often with scores for other brands bunched together at, say, 6.6).

There is no hint in AIDA that consumers already have some kind of loyalty to an existing product, nor any suggestion of what will happen after action. AIDA treats each purchase as a seduction exercise of first chatting up a cold prospect, then foreplay, and lastly closing the sale. Although AIDA may help inexperienced salespeople to fill out order forms, it seldom represents the process that customers go through in purchasing a product.

3 Be relevant. Consumers choose relevant products which to them are a good example of the category. This may seem surprisingly neutral, as many consultants recommend being the best. Yet if ten million people regard brand A good-enough and only one million regard brand B good-enough, then about ten times more people will buy brand A. Even if one million people regard brand B as amazing but ten million regard brand A good-enough, then A will still generate more volume and profit, unless B can command a much higher price.

Microsoft has been extremely good at presenting itself as an example of the personal category. *Where do you want to go today?*™ focuses on the individual and the easy possibilities. IBM, however, has great difficulty in appearing a credible, or even relevant, supplier of personal computing, because of its strong association with corporate IT. Personal computing is a category that individuals (not corporations) buy, and they choose suppliers that make it easy for them to do more with their personal computers.

Market research provides tools for tracking consumers' beliefs about the category and consumers' ratings of brands as good examples of it. Descriptions such as "personal computing" and "application software readily available" are typical category descriptions for PC operating systems (such as Windows or OS/2). For breakfast cereals "stays crispy in milk" is a category description. Over time consumers' category descriptions drift, causing dissatisfaction with existing brands and potential opportunities for innovators. Tracking the changes in consumer descriptions of a category is essential for opportunistic innovators.

John Leftwich, Microsoft's marketing vice-president, explains it like this: "My philosophy is that research should be like a video camera. Bad research is like a still camera, where someone says 'that's the situation at the moment', but they've no idea what happened before. The kind of research we do here in Microsoft is over a long period of time, and it is much more like this concept of using a video camera, showing where you've come from. You learn an ability to know what data to be confident about, and where you should have doubts about the data you're seeing. You begin to see very definitive trends as opposed to a momentary attitude."

Category description errors are surprisingly common, and can have devastating effects. In the IT industry established players like IBM have often misunderstood the changes occurring in the category with disastrous consequences. Categories should be defined by consumers' terms, and yet IBM and other IT and telecoms suppliers often describe categories in ways that few customers would understand. "Solutions", "Systems Integration Services" and "Availability Services" are terms that IBM uses in telling customers about the categories of services it offers, and telcos such as BT or Bell South use terms like "Frame Relay", "Fast Pad FRAD", and "Smart Trunk".

Yet how many customers talk like this? No customer ever asks a supplier: "Does your company sell Solutions?" or "I'm looking for a Smart Trunk" or "Can you sell me some Systems Integration". Service buyers talk about "advice" or "help" or "running things" as the services they need. It is therefore hardly surprising that if suppliers and customers use different language to describe the category there will be a disconnection. Even in more familiar areas, such as food, suppliers are often more remote from consumers than the retailers who guide consumers to the shelf holding the category. For the consumers to connect with the suppliers, they must talk the same language.

Evaluative beliefs, such as good value for money, are the second part of relevance. Values are associated with the brand, not the category. The key factor to measure is the number of people who hold the belief, not the strength of their belief. Defining the action clearly is important, for example "using product X" or "buying vitamins". Researchers then ask consumers about the advantages and disadvantages of buying the brand, or using it.

4 Research the negative actions. Negative actions, such as not buying the old product, may be seen as actions with their own rationale. It is often useful to explore these negative actions. The lack of research on negative actions became acutely embarrassing for Coca-Cola. When it planned the launch of its ill-fated new flavour, over $2m was spent researching consumers' attitudes to the new flavour, using over 200,000 taste tests. Although these showed that consumers liked the new flavour more than the old one, a small amount of research into people's attitudes to withdrawing the old product showed that consumers expected to buy the new flavour as an addition to their habitual purchases of the old Coca-Cola, and not as a replacement for it. Coca-Cola ignored the few negative questions and withdrew the old flavour. Consumers exploded angrily, and in the days that followed Coca-Cola was forced into a U-turn. It reintroduced the old cola which habitual customers liked to buy, even though they did not like its taste as much as the taste of the new cola.

5 Research "influencers", that is, people or groups that think the respondent should do the defined action. Husbands, wives, children, friends and business colleagues all have the potential to shape behaviour. This is especially true where innovation is involved. Researchers should ask if there are other people who come to mind when respondents think of buying or using the innovation.

Microsoft found that inexperienced computer users were very much influenced by referents. Most vocal among these during the late 1980s were the desktop publishing specialists. Today, Microsoft's current research on the Web platform has uncovered an influential group of web site designers. Microsoft has also been highly successful in gaining support from independent software vendors (isvs). These factors were particularly important in the battle between Windows and IBM's rival os/2 operating system in the late 1980s. At that time IBM had higher brand awareness than Microsoft. Yet the enthusiastic support of the desktop publishers, and the backing from isvs, provided Microsoft with more powerful references than IBM got from the reputation of its more established brand.

Putting your trust in marketing tools and techniques

Four concerns are commonly raised about the marketing tools and techniques that can help with determining whether innovations are likely to be profitable. Yet each may be eliminated, or at least significantly limited, by good research design and clear thinking.

1 Customer needs appear to change too fast. Research is often criticised as providing a rearview-mirror perspective, leading innovators to products that are obsolete before they are launched. Yet the speed and degree of change is greatly exaggerated, as illustrated in Figure 4.1. Even in novel situations, people trade on already acquired habits. Most first-time car purchasers are familiar with cars; they may have visited car showrooms; they will often have bargained for goods before; they have read the popular press and magazines; and they are likely to be knowledgeable about the ways of sales staff and credit arrangements. Thus their purchasing behaviour owes much to habits established in related contexts. From this standpoint the basic form of all behaviour is habitual, and in unusual situations customers follow habits in their repertoire.

2 Few customers ever know their future needs. Yet there is a difference between predicting a future need and creating a future solution. Many good innovations create their own future by offering new solutions to satisfy existing habits. Orville Redenbacher's Gourmet Popping Corn combined what the company knew about people's popcorn habits, and what it knew about people's habits as gourmet food buyers. The result was a popcorn selling at twice the price of existing brands.

Great innovators are often like great detectives. Just as Sherlock Holmes could attribute much of his success to his study of everyday habits, so too can Microsoft. The company has established a group that studies the habits of office workers with the aim of finding software solutions to support their habits. Some customers may influence the future more than others. Early adopters of innovations often define the future for the mass market. Thus for Microsoft Windows the key customers to influence were the desktop publishers, and for Microsoft on the Internet the key customers are the web site designers.

3 Attitudes do not predict behaviour. This is a common criticism of consumer testing. Yet, as noted earlier, there have been major advances in research design that make prediction of behaviour from attitudes much more certain. The likelihood of failures such as that of New Coke can be

significantly eliminated by better research design.

4 Research is hopeless at predicting future demand levels. Although this is true, many early failures have been resuscitated by continuous tracking and remedial action. Few innovations are outright successes from the start. Most need multiple adjustments during the launch period. Many studies have shown that it is not the innovation itself that fails. In the majority of cases failure is the result of a poor launch process. Often success is a matter of fixing some problems with the marketing plan, adjusting the positioning strategy, focusing the customer targeting, increasing the distribution and enhancing the product design. This is good news, as it means that a seemingly dead patient can be revived and go on to live a healthy life.

Facing facts and measuring up

Innovation at Microsoft depends on objectivity. As John Leftwich points out: "One of Microsoft's strengths is our brutal honesty with ourselves about what's happening. We are paranoid. Absolutely paranoid. We have to be thoroughly open, frank and honest about what the market tells us. Anyone who isn't will not be in business in the 21st millennium. A phenomenon that I detest, which is fairly common, is using research to prove an opinion that you already hold, or decrying research because it doesn't support an opinion that you already hold. I have seen that in my past on a number of occasions. You have to listen to what the market is telling you."

As Microsoft has grown, it has needed to embrace the best marketing tools that are available. These tools have arrived quite recently. Leftwich said: "One of the first things I did when I joined Microsoft six years ago was to build a market research function. Market research at that time was a few binders in a dusty old cupboard. Today I'd say we have one of the most sophisticated market research functions anywhere in the computer industry, a mixture of commissioned research and a number of other smart ways of collecting data. It's a mixture of what we call air cover and ground cover. Air cover is formal regular research and ground cover is day-in day-out competitive and customer tracking with a mixture of formal and semi-formal ways of collating it."

Marketing tools are tightly integrated into the whole company and not an add-on or a functional specialism. Their influence goes straight to the heart of Microsoft.

"Bill Gates and people at Redmond corporate campus are frequently in customer meetings. Bill is particularly involved in product development and he likes to have direct customer feedback through meeting customers, and feedback from customer support calls, as well as the twice-yearly formal reviews, looking at trends on market share and attitudes, competitive activity, and so on.

"Marketing tools have direct links into our developers. We feed information to the vice-presidents of development. This consists of customer feedback from meetings, support-call feedback and research analysis, as well as from usability laboratories. In addition there are the formal presentations to Bill and the developers twice a year."

Tools for measuring innovation

Eight key tools are described in Part 3:

- Trial purchase
- Awareness
- Customer involvement
- Brand image endorsement
- Innovation benchmark
- Competitive threat map
- Category potential map
- Marketing waste

5 Value

Business performance measurement, customer profitability and brand valuation have become central strategic issues for many organisations. They are of organisation-wide importance, and yet the development of management tools to address the issues is primarily driven by the finance function. More worryingly, given the central role of customers in these new "value" frameworks, marketing is often uninvolved in setting the strategic agenda.

David Norton, who with Robert Kaplan invented the balanced scorecard, has advised over 100 firms on customer and brand measurements to go on to the scorecard. Yet, when interviewed for a *Financial Times* report,[1] Norton commented that "in maybe 70% or so of companies you will find the executive teams have an inadequate understanding of the customer".

Norton did not recall having had much involvement with marketing people in setting the customer objectives on the scorecard, and commented that finance and quality were the commonest drivers of the process, whereas marketing was often "isolated and not integrated into the rest of the strategy". Kaplan commented at a recent conference that marketing became involved after the strategists had set the objectives, by providing market research tools to measure achievement of objectives.

Other evidence that, in many companies, marketing is isolated from the setting of strategic objectives was noted in previous chapters. Given the importance of these issues, there is a need for marketers to be well informed about the impact of the current accounting debate, and for them to apply their tools for measuring soft customer issues to influence companies' decisions and objectives concerning customer profitability and brand valuation. It is not good enough for marketing to be brought into the debate after the strategic agenda is decided.

The new developments in customer profitability and brand value measurement are probably a good thing. The question is, how should they be applied? Which financial elements are important, and what soft customer data also needs to be applied?

Customer profitability

As outlined in previous chapters, all customers are not created equal. Some customers buy heavily; others are light buyers. Some mainly choose a company's brand; some only occasionally choose it; and others never choose it. Some customers are expensive time wasters and make extravagant demands upon an organisation; others are quick and easy to serve. Treating all these customers equally may be a waste of both resources and money.

The profit margin obtained from different customers deviates far more than the margin from alternative products or services. This seems to be true across a broad variety of industry sectors and companies. When all the costs of serving a customer are properly allocated, a supplier may find that 50–80% of customers are unprofitable. Yet although suppliers are dependent on a smaller group of customers for the majority of profits, the big customers generally demand better service and lower prices; and the little customers who never produce a profit divert the suppliers' resources. Herein lies the marketing problem for the accountants.

It is high time accountants and marketers started working together on this issue. Yet it is generally accountants, and not marketers, who do something. Accountants have begun to encroach on marketing's territory, armed with statistics from their new accounting systems. Here are some examples of recommended actions for marketing from two American accounting professors, Robert Kaplan and Robin Cooper:

- protect existing highly profitable customers
- concede permanent loss customers to competitors
- attempt to capture high-profit customers from competitors
- discount to gain business with low cost-to-serve customers
- negotiate win-win relationships that lower cost-to-serve
- reprice expensive services based on cost-to-serve.

Coming from such distinguished accountants this advice sounds eminently sensible, and it seems pretty simple to follow. Yet it makes sense to look at how customers behave before getting rid of half of them, or offering half of them discounts and other half so-called win-win terms. At first sight the differences are quite compelling. A European specialist retailer discovered that 52% of its sales and virtually all its profits were obtained from 10% of customers. An American bank realised that 17% of customers produced all the profits. A British specialty chemicals firm produced 50% of profits from just 2% of customers. Constructing a watertight case for divesting a supplier of unprofitable customers may seem straightforward, but it is important to look at the broader picture, and at five factors in particular.

The heavy-light buyers split

Research in numerous product categories indicates that over long periods of time some customers are heavy buyers and others are light buyers. This stable pattern of heavy-light makes it tempting to target the heavy buyers. Yet there is a problem. Most suppliers never know a customer's total expenditure in the category. They merely know how much the customer spends with them, and not how much customers spend with the competitors.

Share-of-purse

The amount customers spend with a supplier equals their total spend multiplied by the supplier's proportional share-of-purse. Customers who have a low spend with a supplier may do so for various reasons. They may be low spenders in the category, but they may also be medium spenders who currently buy more from competitors. This situation is illustrated in Figure 5.1, which shows that to follow the accountants' advice to concede low-spending customers to the competition carries significant risks. Many apparently low-spending customers may actually be medium or even high spenders, who currently spend more with competitors.

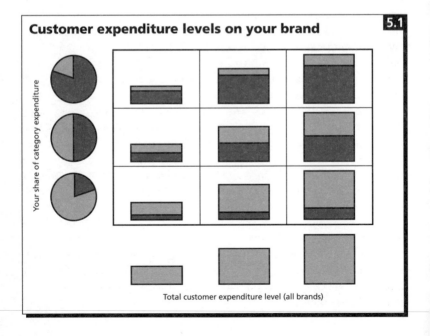

Customer expenditure levels on your brand 5.1

Your share of category expenditure

Total customer expenditure level (all brands)

Churn
This is the rate at which customers switch their share-of-purse between brands. Over time, low-share customers will churn to become high-share and vice versa. The churn process in many markets appears to be mainly random. Disturbing this stochastic process carries significant risks. Consequently, firing the low-share customers is dangerous and is likely to accelerate the erosion of the customer base. What is more, high share-of-purse customers that the supplier wants to retain will churn over time to low share-of-purse, and be fired. Meanwhile, the low-share customers who would have churned to high-share will have been lost.

Cost-to-serve
There is little doubt that different customers carry different costs-to-serve. Some customers are costly to serve and others have low costs. Yet frequently a high cost-to-serve is not a factor within the customer's control. Complaints caused by faults are costly to correct. The accountants' advice to penalise customers with high costs-to-serve will not only aggravate the complaints process, but is also likely to do irreparable damage to the supplier's reputation.

This cost-to-serve mentality seems to have gripped the imagination of many financial institutions, as well as the computer industry. Both industries are implementing so-called telephone help-lines on a grand scale, with the cost-to-serve mentality uppermost in executives' minds. Listen to any consumer programme or read the consumer press, where complaints against these practices are growing at an alarming rate. They are lampooned in many cartoons, including the popular Dilbert cartoons, where they are called "no-help-at-all lines".

The real tragedy of the cost-to-serve mentality is the opportunity missed. As long ago as the 1970s, in a series of consumer studies carried out by a US-based consultancy, Technical Assistance Research Programmes (TARP), it was established that complainants who were served well later became more loyal than the average customer and bought more. The correct factor to measure should be profit-to-serve, otherwise the extra revenue opportunities from good service will be overlooked.

Discounts or price promotions
A policy of giving discounts and price promotions to deserving customers not only further penalises customers who have complained, or have had service problems, but also seems to offer rewards to those who do not require them.

There have been extensive studies of customer behaviour towards discounts and price promotions. As discussed in Chapter 2, discounts and price promotions do not cause significant changes in buyer behaviour, and mostly they reduce profits. Furthermore, they are costly to administer. Procter & Gamble has calculated that promotions take 25% of a salesperson's time, 30% of brand management time, and that in the food industry trade promotion alone adds 2.5% to retail prices. These findings have led the company to review its discounting policy and to use more everyday low pricing.

Measuring customer profitability at Bass

Bass Brewers has developed measures to track its trade customers' profitability using sophisticated new accounting tools. Bass boasts the largest integrated sales and marketing system in Europe, involving over 500 field-based sales personnel and several hundred head-office and regionally based sales, marketing and customer services staff. Financial data are crucial to the system's success. Mike Lees, sales operation director, says: "Because there is no hiding place for costs, we are finding out lots of things, which are changing the way the sales people deal with customers."

Bass tracks a range of cost-driving activities to achieve better allocation of selling and marketing costs and gain insights into customer profitability. Customers can now be understood in terms of their true value to Bass, rather than having to be assessed by, for instance, their size, which can be misleading.

Central to the Bass approach is putting a value on what it calls "net net account profitability". According to Lees: "We see this as being a cornerstone in the whole process of how we measure the business. It really does make people think about the decisions they are taking, because they will start targeting promotions more effectively, they will be able to look at how they can raise account profitability, or see if they're putting too many resources into a particular account. This information will also be built into incentives for the sales people. This better awareness of account profitability has made our salesforce aware of the importance of looking after all the accounts, not just the biggest. Our sales teams are 'bonused' on the total profitability of their patch, among other factors."

Lees comments: "We've surprised some of our sales teams, because they have large-volume accounts which they assumed were giving good profit. But when you analyse the associated costs, these large accounts can turn out to be less attractive than some of the smaller ones. Some of these unprofitable accounts are also the ones which make the most demands on service, emergency delivery, promotional support. They shout the loudest."

Bringing a financial focus into marketing is not just a tactical move. "We are witnessing a major change in culture," says Lees. "We are much more commercially focused, which is crucial when we are in such a competitive business." As well as highlighting unprofitable accounts, profitability analysis helps the salesforce understand how they can make accounts more profitable. "It highlights the customers who are not making money – the ones who are underperforming. It also gives an indication of what the salesforce can do about it: put more activity in, or change the way they address that account."

Bass is now using its improved information to re-examine the way it services various accounts. This feeds back into the process of deciding how to approach customers, leading to review of the frequency of sales activity and the introduction of alternatives such as telephone-based account management.

Lees emphasises the importance of looking at the total value proposition, and in particular at examining profitability rather than just costs. "If you get hung up on costs, you're only seeing part of the picture. We're driven by profitability in the long term. Where we look at costs, it's a question of making sure that we are getting the best out of the costs that we're incurring." This applies to the marketing function as well as the salesforce. A better understanding of how profitability correlates with promotional activity allows marketing to make better, more commercial, decisions about how to spend its budget.

The need for a fuller understanding of the profitability implications of marketing has led to a rapprochement of the marketing and finance functions within Bass. "A lot of our deals are financially driven. Sales negotiations could include a loan or discounts on the product. Over the past year to 18 months we've aligned commercial managers in the field alongside our salespeople. Part of these commercial people's job is to develop the salesforce's financial acumen, and the other part is to improve the quality of the sales we're doing."

The commercial managers working in the field also give assistance to customers. "We have quite complex models through which we can put customers' details to help them with business planning and profit and loss analysis. We can help them determine which brands, and what approach to retail pricing, are right for them." The intention is that the commercial managers will be needed in the field for only a limited period. "Our vision is that in another 12–18 months we will have fully financially literate account managers, who don't need the financial support, or rather don't need it to the same extent – it will always be there."

Measuring intangibles

Short-term profits are not the only factors that have attracted increased attention. Assets have also been the subject of intense examination. Sir Bryan Carlsberg, secretary-general of the International Standards Committee, puts it this way: "As time goes by, more and more of the growing difference between the full value of the business and the balance sheet is explained by intangibles. We do not account for intangibles very well and perhaps cannot do so under traditional accounting."[2]

The need for measuring intangible assets has never been greater. Brand value is an important asset to measure, even if current methods still provide only an approximate answer. To take a simple example, suppose company X with net worth of $500m has raised $800m cash to buy company Y (and therefore also has $300m in liabilities). Y is worth $1,000m in future earnings potential, but its book value is only $200m. If future earnings potential is not shown on the balance sheet, after the exchange the books would show the firm as being insolvent ($200m in book assets, $300m in liabilities, no cash) as a result of paying $800m for $1,000m earnings potential.

Marketers are lining up to obtain new measurement tools to support their brands. On the whole this seems to be a good thing. More marketers are looking more carefully than ever before at what is happening to their brands. These tools, although still rather blunt instruments, enable them to make better diagnoses of the health of their brands, and to take remedial action when brands are unhealthy. Here are three tools for measuring intangibles.

Brand health

Brand health is measured by many large grocery manufacturers and retailers, and by some large firms in other sectors. They keep a diagnostic scorecard containing a matching set of brand health indicators, and monitor whether the scores go up or down. If there is a change, they usually take remedial action. Most measure at least five factors, and it is common to measure as many as 12. A few monitor 20 or more. Young & Rubicam favour four primary measures. Tim Ambler, a veteran of Grand Metropolitan, former joint managing director of International Distillers and Vintners and now a research fellow at London Business School, favours "about a dozen". David Aaker, an American brands expert, thinks "about 40" are necessary.

Popular brand health measures include output measures such as brand awareness (unprompted and total), penetration, loyalty and retention, market share and leadership. They can also include input measures such as budget support, share of voice, number of product lines and geographic distribution.

How brand health is assessed is far less important than the fact that it is measured, and that it is done consistently over time. John Leftwich, marketing vice-president at Microsoft, who has been tracking a matching set of brand health indicators since 1990, stresses the importance of taking a long-term view of trends and changes on a consistent basis.

Brand health scorecards have become common. Young & Rubicam has one standard, Millward Brown has another, and AGB Taylor Nelson offers yet another. After studying several of these brand value standards, it is apparent that none provides a panacea. The brand measurements need to be adapted to fit the business context.

Extensive research on brands suggests that the standard factors relevant to the health of one brand will be irrelevant for others. In particular, advertising-related factors are commonly included on brand scorecards, even though they may be totally irrelevant outside the consumer products world. For many brands there is a gaping hole in the off-the-shelf brand measures, in such areas as customer satisfaction, perceived quality or relative price.

Two Australian academics, John Rossiter and Larry Percy, have shown that even in heavily advertised products the relevant factors to track can vary widely. They have done extensive work on how brands work. They find two types of awareness factors. As mentioned in Chapter 2, in 65% of grocery brands **recognition** is needed at the point of purchase, as their buyers generally see the brand first and then recognise that they need it. Studies of supermarket purchasing show that buyers take less than 10 seconds from seeing the brand on display to recognising they need the category, putting it in the supermarket trolley and moving on. For the remaining 35% of grocery brands, **recall** of the brand name is needed, since the category purchase is planned in advance. So two different awareness measures are needed.

Rossiter and Percy also find that attitude can be more important than awareness, especially for non-grocery brands. They find attitude factors differ between **relief** purchases, to remove a problem, and **reward** purchases, to provide gratification or stimulation. For relief purchases, such as many household detergents or weight-control foods, customers should have knowledge of the tangible benefits that the brand promises and believe what it promises. For reward purchases, such as Haagen-Dazs or the Renault Clio, it is more important to track whether audiences like the adverts and like the brand on an emotional level. Many different measures such as brand knowledge, esteem, relevance, or perceived quality may need to be monitored, depending on the brand.

David Aaker thinks that brand health measures must be tailored to fit the brand. He is dismissive of claims that one standard framework fits all brands across all categories.[3]

Measuring brand health at British Bakeries

British Bakeries is part of Tomkins plc. With sales of about $400m, its business is split between branded goods with names such as Hovis (the UK's leading bread brand), Mother's Pride, Nimble and Granary, and own-label products for retailers, which account for just under half of the company's business.

What might on the surface seem a straightforward operation is actually quite complex, since the company has to juggle the short-term demands of daily deliveries of bread products with a long-term strategy for the brands. The brand managers work across product groups: bread, rolls, tea cakes and muffins, and speciality breads.

The emphasis on branding has grown over the last few years, with advertising playing a key role in boosting the brand, although there is a lot of promotional activity with retailers across product areas. Hovis is now first in the market in both bread and rolls, and the strategy is to continue to stretch the brand as far as possible. A few years ago, when revamping its corporate identity, the company considered changing its name to Hovis. However, it was decided that as the company was a large supplier of own-label this would give the wrong impression.

Andrew Brown, former marketing and planning director, firmly believed that marketing should be seen to be as accountable as any other part of the company: "I have wanted to show the business the value we get from our brands. It is not so much that I have been asked to do it, but that I have been keen to do so. The point has to be made and understood that marketing is an investment, not a cost."

The effectiveness of the marketing spend is gauged on an annual basis, with Brown agreeing an overall marketing budget and its broad allocation with the Tomkins board. This includes proving that advertising works: "I will have a financial justification for the amount we are spending on the brand, showing how the brand delivers this amount of money to the company and how it is growing."

A comprehensive brand health toolkit, the Stochastic Reaction Brand Monitor, from research company BJM, provides regular feedback on the effectiveness of marketing activity on the brands. It was first developed in the early 1980s in Australia and was introduced to the UK in 1987 by BJM. The measures provided by the monitor, which usually involves face-to-face interviews, are grouped into five headings: communications awareness; brand awareness; disposition, which measures consumers' overall attitudes towards or disposition to buy different brands, ranging from those who "insist on" or "prefer" to buy a brand to those who "reject" a brand; behaviour; and consumers' perceptions of brand positioning.

The demands of a day-to-day business are not allowed to prevent strategic thinking about the brands. Monitoring the brands' health to ensure that the strategy is working is critical to success.

Brand strength
Brand strength is a concept related to brand health, but it is closer to the financial aims of brand valuation. The idea of a strong brand is that it can be stretched more effectively than a weak brand. For example, the Mars brand was stretched from confectionery into ice-cream, but no ice-cream brands have yet stretched into confectionery, and so in theory ice-cream brands are not as strong as Mars. The Virgin brand has been stretched from record production to retail, airlines, cola, vodka and financial services. Both Mars and Virgin have been described as strong brands.

Financially, the idea of a strong brand is highly attractive. Simply acquire a strong small brand and, for little investment, stretch it into a strong big brand. Most firms that acquire a brand seem to fall prey to the desire to stretch their brands. When Cavenham Foods bought Bovril in the 1960s it quickly stretched it to Chicken Bovril. Pierre Cardin was extended over a decade, but its premium price was forced down. Nescafé succeeded in stretching its price and image to Nescafé Gold Blend.

So what is the secret of a strong brand? Brand gurus who claim to know the secret of brand strength often rely on a small number of selected success stories. Al Ries and Jack Trout recommend narrow brands, citing dozens of failed attempts at broad brands. David Aaker is in favour of wide brands, and believes that there is a science to widening the brand by finding extensions that fit.

Not surprisingly, the situation is rather more complex. As outlined in Chapter 4, when Wisk was launched in 1985 it initially gained 10%

category share, but by 1988 this had dropped to 5%. Ariel split into powder and liquid, moving from 19% in 1985 to 11% (powder) and 9% (liquid) in 1988, a net brand gain of 1%. Persil split into powder and liquid, moving from 33% in 1985 to 23% (powder) and 6% (liquid) in 1988, a net loss of 4%. Just who won or lost is harder to assess. If profits are important then everyone lost, owing to the higher costs of all the fragmented brands.

The high cost of brand extensions is an important issue. Many companies are now adopting some form of activity-based costing to discover their true costs, because their traditional accounting methods understated the costs of extensions. This cost information remains highly confidential, and so the true story about brand strength is unlikely to emerge until the true profitability data can be objectively studied.

Robert East, professor of consumer behaviour at Kingston University, has made extensive studies of brand extensions, and he concludes: "At present we lack a clear procedure for identifying the most important aspects of fit that will help us to plan and evaluate extensions." However, once the extension has been introduced, then brand health tracking can help determine the best remedial action, from increasing the budget, to relaunching to withdrawal. Tim Ambler similarly comments that "research is an unreliable guide to marketplace performance" for brand extensions and concludes that brand health tracking can help to "keep the failures small".

Brand valuation

Brand valuation is the third aspect of brand measurement. The concept is beguilingly simple. Brand value is the storehouse of future profits from the brand. It is what the brand has earned but has not yet paid out in profits. The task of brand valuation is to check out the storehouse today.

Although accountants and investors have always felt much more comfortable when dealing with assets they can touch, there is now widespread acceptance that brands and other intangibles are the major assets of an increasing number of companies. However, most investors still prefer to be given raw data and to do their own assessment. In the words of one investment banker, quoted by David Haigh of Brand Finance: "You can make up any values you like and put them on the balance sheet, but no one in the City is going to take the resulting balance sheet seriously. We simply add back the values we have no faith in and draw our own conclusions."

Data that City investors would like to see disclosed have been researched by the IPA, which supports the findings of Richmond Events, presented on the *Oriana* (see Chapter 1). The IPA survey found strong and growing demand from the City for more comprehensive disclosure of raw marketing data to help make investment decisions. For example, 85% of respondents want to know market share; 83% want market volume and value estimates; 74% want positioning data; and 60% want demographic profiling data. However, with regard to brand valuation, City analysts prefer to draw their own conclusions from the raw data, although 53% said that a company's own estimates of its brand value might be useful for reviewing performance.

Interbrand was the first of several firms to emerge to feed this demand for brand valuation calculations. Its approach errs towards conservatism, and its much publicised Top Brands list did not contain many rising stars or question marks: Coca-Cola, Kellogg's, McDonald's, Kodak, Marlboro, IBM, American Express, Sony, Mercedes-Benz and Nescafé. Also the subjectivity of the criteria and their assessment has resulted in much criticism.

David Aaker comments on the biases inherent in the Interbrand method: "The Interbrand system does not consider the potential of the brand to support extensions into other product classes. Spending money on advertising does not necessarily indicate effective brand building. Trademark protection, although necessary, does not of itself create brand value ... Small niche brands, for instance, may be more profitable than so-called leadership brands. Older brands may lose their brand strength. The ability of a market to create or protect margins is difficult to project. A local brand can have the advantages of connecting with customers, and thus it may be more profitable than an international brand that must deal with substantial co-ordination problems. Growth in brand sales, especially if obtained by sacrificing margins, is not necessarily healthy."

The weakness of current measures of brand strength causes the biggest problems when quantifying brand value. As noted earlier, prediction of future growth potential in terms of future brand extensions is something of a lottery. Apart from the question of the brand's strength to extend into other categories (for example, would Mars succeed in biscuits?), there is also the problem of forecasting future management support for future extensions (for example, would management support Mars moving into biscuits in 2001?).

Patrick Barwise, professor of management and marketing at London Business School, has studied the financial valuation of brands and has the following perceptive insight: "Brand equity – clever new numbers to stop management from being short-sighted – seems to me yet another example of an attempt to use the latest analytic technique to address what is in fact primarily a managerial issue. Long-term managerial problems need long-term managerial solutions. That the Japanese and the Germans are more long-termist than the Americans and British is definitely not because they use more sophisticated or adventurous accounting systems: they do not ... the short-termism of the United States and the UK is debatable, and in any case seems unlikely to be reduced by generating inherently subjective brand equity numbers."

Conclusion

Value problems are here to stay. Customer value calculations offer real opportunities to increase profitability and shareholder value. Brand asset valuation is needed to prevent dumb investment decisions being taken. There is a real need for new ways of assessing value.

Marketing knowledge about customers and brands needs to be grafted on to the traditional and not-so traditional financial data. Educated guesses from accountants about how customers and brands will behave are not the answer. Financial experts such as Kaplan and Norton accept their limitations in this area. Appropriate tools must be used to assess how customers will behave, and likewise brands.

Marketing managers must begin to work with their accountant colleagues on these problems. Their current approaches, either isolationist or patriarchal (for example, hiring marketing finance experts, such as Interbrand, to contradict and outsmart their colleagues in accounts), are not good enough. Marketing managers must get involved in solving the issue, not side-step it. Marketing myths such as "market share drives profitability",[4] "perceived quality drives value", "the key to shareholder value is in being 'different', 'creative', 'exciting', 'sexy' or all four", need to be either proved or discarded.

Tools for measuring value

Four key tools are described in Part 3:

- Brand valuation
- Marketing mix productivity
- Corporate marketing support
- Marketing waste

6 Information technology

ONE development more than any other has altered the worlds of customers and competition. It involves the relentless and expensive march of information technology (IT). As we approach the year 2000 marketers are realising that they ought to be more in control of the IT agenda. Organisations are making massive IT investments on the basis of competitive and customer issues, and marketers' opinions are not the deciding factor when such investments are being made.

Kit Grindley, professor of systems automation at the London School of Economics and a long-time observer of information technology, wryly commented: "I went to a talk shortly after the war given by the chief executive of Hotpoint. He said that marketing was now the central function. He said, 'We got here by making a good iron, which gets us into the white goods business. Now it doesn't matter what we produce, or even if we produce it, as our skill is marketing.' [Marketing] was not the fashion in the 1930s. Then everything was focused on the product, making it cheaply and well. Today there is no reason why someone should not redraw his circle and, where he put marketing at the centre of the organisation, put IT in there. It used to be the airlines and the banks where all the programmers wanted to work, because they got some kudos there. Today, it is key to get the IT strategy right in all sectors. There is nowhere that IT does not dominate your business strategy. Now, is that too confrontational for marketing people?"[1]

This chapter looks at the encounters between technology and marketing. Is technology really able to deliver some of the competitive advantages that the IT industry claims? Will it really enhance customer relationships? And can it do so, or not, without proper marketing input?

Hooked on IT

Technology is no longer just good to have; it has become an addiction. The first book on marketing and the computer appeared in 1967.[2] The following year Philip Kotler began writing about technology as providing "marketing's nerve centre".[3] However, most companies ignored such predictions, and it was the accountants who adopted the computer with most enthusiasm. CFOs and finance directors control IT in the majority of corporations; even where there are chief information officers (CIOs) and IT directors, they generally report to finance.[4]

When the mini-computer arrived in the 1970s most of the new machines went into manufacturing and distribution, but there was still speculation about IT and marketing. For instance, in 1973 accountants at Arthur Andersen commented: "Perhaps no major management area has been neglected as much as marketing in the rush to develop and implement management information systems. The movement to such systems, which has been accelerating over the past 5–10 years, has engulfed the financial areas of the business with refinements of accounting and reporting systems and new developments, such as corporate modelling ... This neglected condition may have its roots in the mistaken notion that marketing people operate by hunch and intuition."[5]

Although the mini-computer was adopted on a large scale by the manufacturing and distribution functions, consumption of computer power by the marketing function remained erratic. By 1979 the pundits were still seeking that elusive surge of progress: "There is no doubt that the 1980s will see a profound transformation in the working environment of marketing and sales management, and it seems safe to predict that among the most successful companies will be those which have decided to make efficient use of information systems as a control tool."[6]

When the personal computer started to take over in the 1980s, the long-awaited surge of so-called marketing applications finally began. "Information for competitive advantage" became the high-tech battle cry, heralding a new era of growing IT expenditure, and consolidation of power for IT managers. "Customer-facing applications" became the rage.

These new applications were warmly welcomed by the IT industry. Suppliers such as IBM and DEC were reeling from the body blows struck in the early 1980s by new PC suppliers such as Compaq and Dell. They needed new markets as the sales of accounting and operational applications had peaked. When technology was named as the key factor for competitive advantage, IT suppliers were delighted. "One of the great things about this industry is that every decade or so you get a chance to redefine the playing field", said Lou Gerstner, IBM's boss.[7]

Oddly, the idea of using IT to transform the competitive playing field came not from a marketer but from an industrial economist, Michael Porter. Since the publication of his book *Competitive Advantage* in 1985, the urgency of the IT message to senior executives, worried about foreign competition and anxious about customer dissatisfaction, has fuelled a spending binge on technology of unprecedented proportions. Every executive now faces a barrage of facts and figures on the IT investments of competitors, and feels compelled to match them.

Power and influence

However, even before Porter's book was published, the IT function (CIOS and IT directors) had become an established, costly and powerful reality in organisations. Its power meant that marketers would have trouble influencing the agenda, even though the IT agenda was being paid for by the consumer.

The driving forces that motivate IT people are size and speed. Size means gigabytes and terrabytes, unimaginably huge volumes of raw data, churned and turned by supercharged database engines. Speed means processing power, MIPS (millions of instructions per second). Big is beautiful is the name of the game, and big databases are the favourite toy. The biggest database is the customer database, so this has become the new technological dream-machine. The IT industry has not been slow in fuelling the hype. A quote from Lars Nyberg, CEO of NCR, is typical: "At NCR we develop business solutions based around innovative data warehousing technology, which helps companies focus on individual customers. By delivering increased customer satisfaction, these solutions provide a potent source of competitive advantage." Like a mantra, the words "solution", "competitive advantage" and "customer satisfaction" are intoned over and over again in such speeches, in the hope that they will lull troubled executives into buying these techno-toys.

The main reason for databases being so large is to enable the data users to send out mega-mailshots, or "one-to-one marketing" to use the popular jargon. The amount of information held on customers today is truly startling. John Cummings, an American database expert, estimates that Procter & Gamble has 44m customer records on its marketing database, Kraft Foods 40m, R.J. Reynolds 35m, Philip Morris 26m, Quaker Oats 20m, Ralston Purina 20m, Walt Disney 19m, Kellogg's 14m, and many others exist at or below this size.[8] Similarly, in the UK there are records of 20m customers held for marketing uses by organisations such as Barclaycard, British Telecom and British Gas, and many others with over 1m customer records. One consequence of there being so many organisations with so much data is that the average British household receives over 100 items of direct mail annually, and the average business manager receives over 750 items of direct mail annually. Half of these items are discarded unread, and fewer than one in 20 receives a response.

Call centres, using sophisticated computer and telecommunications technology, are another annoying application of technology. Consumers are becoming increasingly intolerant of unwanted telephone calls, selling anything from insurance to double glazing. Smooth-talking operators, claims of dramatic benefits, "last chance to buy" limitations and ease of purchase conspire to persuade casual buyers when their resistance is low.

Organisations need to proceed with more caution where technology is concerned. "The data warehouse has fallen victim to the plague of over-inflated expectations", says Kevin Strange, research director at IT analysts Gartner Group.[9] At OTR researchers commented: "It's a stark conclusion and a real surprise. The majority of data warehouses are not successful."[10] Meanwhile, consultants at Cap Gemini Sogeti conclude that "few retailers take the Web seriously", and at Ovum, David Bradshaw, a consultant studying call centre technology, has concluded: "There are eight different groups of vendors chasing this market, but none of them has a complete solution."

IT solutions

These criticisms of IT highlight real problems, even though many CIOs and IT directors wish their critics would shut up and go away. Survey after survey about IT staff draws the same conclusions: they are out of tune with their non-technical colleagues and widely distrusted by them; they are not trusted to set their own budgets or to prioritise expenditure; they do not understand customers.

The solution is to change the approach to technology. The question is what to change and how. Technology people like to emphasise processes, tasks and functions, which computers can speed up and automate. They get excited by complex flow charts, data models and systems architectures. They have favourite technologies, such as object-oriented processing (OOP) and online analytical processing (OLAP). They want to use slow, methodical project management methods to ensure their results meet "user requirements". They want to get things right first time and are annoyed and upset by frequent changes. They see the computer as being all-powerful, capable of doing anything and everything.

Marketing people, however, perceive the world as something that is rapidly changing, and they expect computer systems to keep pace with these changes. They are unimpressed by the formalism of process flows, data models and systems architectures, and see their artistic endeavours as being beyond the rational logic of the systems analyst. They are willing to experiment and get things right after a few trials. They see the computer as one of many tools, not the ultimate weapon.

IT managers often underestimate the problems with their systems. Many claim to know what is important to customers, basing their claims mostly on their own experiences as customers. When it comes to analysing what is important, most IT managers do not see the need for measurement, or else they do not have the skills to undertake measurements. Marketers are often not much better, preferring to focus on the creative campaigns that they want to run rather than listening to customers' needs and wants.

Tools to guide IT investment decisions

Marketing tools and techniques can help to improve the relationships between customers and the technologies used by businesses. They involve researching and observing the relationship between customers and technology. Each of the different levels of involvement that exist between customers and technology has its own set of requirements. These include:

- Consumer-owned technology, of which the Internet is the most widely cited example. Customers use the Internet to browse for things they want, place orders and track delivery. Levels of consumer sophistication vary greatly, as does the consumer's willingness to spend time sitting at the computer or learning how to use new applications.
- Web site designers, creating interfaces between the customer and the company. These firms are generally small, with neither the time nor the budget to do research into consumer needs and behaviour. Large firms which can afford it, such as Microsoft, see this level of interaction as extremely important, and are spending considerable amounts of time and money getting it right.
- Consumer-operated technologies, such as bank ATMs and retail kiosks, where the consumer operates the technology to place orders and track information. Concerns which apply here are similar to those involving consumer-owned technology, except that skill and training are even bigger issues. Such consumer-operated devices will probably remain few in number, at least over the next five years, as home computing seems likely dominate the field.
- Consumer indirect involvement, which includes a large number of customer-service and point-of-sale systems, where the customer interacts with an employee who operates a computer. These indirect systems include point-of-sale systems at high street locations and shopping centres. They come in a variety of formats, in particular with or without card readers. They also include home telephone systems, where the customer speaks to a sales or service representative in a computerised call centre.

Research into consumer reaction to such systems is still in the early stages, but a number of important concerns are emerging. There seem to be several trade-offs between the benefits and the costs to the consumer. Convenience can be a benefit, but the effort of providing data for a computer system may be inconvenient or annoying. On the one hand, the system may provide access to more information about products and services than a human could provide; on the other hand, the consumer may distrust the accuracy or reliability of the computer's answers.

Consumer concerns

Many consumers find the inflexibility of computers irritating, especially when accompanied by hard selling. They dislike a computer operator who is too rigid or insistent. Such concerns intensify when there are inaccuracies in their personal information, a problem that is itself likely to be compounded as computers handle ever greater volumes of data. Accuracy is crucial to building customer relationships. Other important aspects to consumers are as follows:

- Control, particularly as it affects consumers perceptions of direct mail and telemarketing. It also colours their views of the disclosure of personal information. Call centre staff who want to control the telephone conversation with a consumer may get a brief hearing before the consumer puts down the handset. Monitoring calls and researching consumer attitudes and opinions can yield helpful insights.
- Fairness. Many consumers feel overwhelmed, for example, by the smoothly scripted operator, the claims for the product and the ease of purchase. It is useful to investigate consumer opinions about fairness after sales conversations.
- Regret can be widespread after tele-purchase, and returned goods are common. It is important to monitor consumer perceptions after the contact to look for signs of regret. Privacy is an important related issue. Consumers may wish to have some control over the nature and extent of information about them being disclosed to others. Such concerns are, to some extent, controlled by privacy legislation. For example, in the American video rental industry, businesses are prevented from trading in lists showing the types of videos their customers rent (this law was brought in when a Supreme Court nominee became concerned that the press had got hold of such data about himself).

◪ Sensitivity. This depends on how much importance consumers attach to the different types of information that the computer operator asks for. Concern about sensitivity may cause them to avoid situations where they are asked for confidential information, to refuse to give information, or to give false information.

◪ Relevance may also colour consumers' perceptions of the conversation they are having with a computer operator. Consumers may question efforts by companies to collect information about them if that information is not relevant to the transaction in hand.

◪ Trust of the organisation can have a significant effect on the conversation. If the consumer trusts the organisation, then fears may be alleviated. Trust usually results when the consumer believes that the firm will perform actions that will result in a positive (and not a negative) outcome for him.

◪ Knowledge and familiarity have an important effect on consumers' perceptions and reactions to computerised systems. Many consumers have little knowledge of computers and harbour a variety of strange beliefs and myths about them. For example, a recent study by Martin Evans, professor of marketing at Bristol Business School, found that consumers generally were confused about what companies could do with their personal data, and a significant number thought that a gigantic Big Brother computer existed somewhere in the UK, collecting and consolidating all their personal data from every source and constantly compiling such data for dubious and harmful purposes.[11]

With IT many companies take a predictable series of steps. Initially, they focus on the technical mechanics of database accumulation and ignore the customer concerns. Then they find themselves at the heart of a storm of customer discontent, with letters of complaint going to the CEO or the data protection authorities. Well-intentioned but puzzled, executives find themselves asking what happened. IT soon becomes more of a damage limitation issue than a source of competitive advantage, with the focus on avoiding mega-mistakes rather than missing giga-opportunities. Thus in the United States, when the video rental records of Supreme Court nominee Robert Bork were printed in a Washington newspaper, Blockbuster Video had to act swiftly to protect its position, especially as legislators moved fast to pass the Video Privacy Protection

Act 1988, which placed constraints on all uses of video rental records.

Trust has always been an important element of good marketing. Effective marketers are taking steps to ensure that customers trust the uses being made of IT as well as enjoying the convenience it affords. A good example from the United States is W.M. Green, a mail order firm that includes with every catalogue a "Help Us Mail Smarter" statement. Green codes its mailing labels so that customers can easily deduce the source of the customer's name and address; for example: "If the first number of your source code is 1 or 2, your name is on our mailing list because you have recently purchased from us." Green also asks customers to indicate on a simple checklist whether they wish to be removed from the mailing list, have their name made available to other companies, or have their name used for other marketing purposes. As well as increasing customer trust, Green keeps its database up-to-date, separates hot from cold prospects and optimises its marketing budget.

Another example of good practice comes from telemarketing. In this sector it has become all too common for organisations to use computers to time telephone conversations, and so hassle and hurry consumers that they often become irritable or annoyed, and even hang up. Rudi Oetting, a telemarketing expert, takes up the story:

"By tracking yields, using the computer, we've found that telemarketing agents who are intuitively good communicators, even though they may not have been trained particularly effectively, may have a revenue performance as much as 100% higher than their colleagues. The interesting thing is that their companies don't know this. The reason the companies don't know this is that they are unduly preoccupied with cost per hour, which is also measured by the computer, and with trying to increase the number of sales per hour. But that actually reduces the amount of yield from their single biggest asset: their customer database.

"It is realistic to expect that someone dialling automatically might be able to talk to 50% more customers per hour, say 12 instead of eight. But a cost-driven organisation will try to get them to talk to 25. If you do that, all you're doing is pitching; there's no dialogue and no sensitivity. We've continuously found on in-bound operations in particular that catalogue companies and others are leaving millions on the table because of being cost-driven."

Rudi Oetting and Geri Gantman believe that a computer-induced fixation on costs can lead companies to offer their salesforce the wrong incentives. They cite the example of a $650m multicatalogue operation which was paying almost $5 an hour incentive at 17 calls per hour, because at 17 calls per hour a representative gets $850 worth of orders. However, Oetting and Gantman found that at ten calls an hour, when representatives got no incentive payment, they were taking nine more orders per 100 calls and $6 more per order.

Keeping IT in perspective

Enthusiasts from the IT industry claim that companies already have more data than they need, and the biggest challenge is in harnessing existing data. Don Peppers and Martha Rogers comment in *The One-to-One Future*: "Almost anything that is in the public record has already been collected and compiled into a database by some enterprising mailing list company somewhere ... Births, deaths, marriages. Property sales, building certificates and mortgages. Bankruptcies. Divorces. The number of children you have and their birthdates, any crimes you've ever been convicted of, and whether any bad payment judgments have ever been levied against you, among other things. All from public records."[12]

There is undoubtedly a vast array of information out there on public computers. But much of it is more relevant to blackmailing than to marketing. Much of the information that is needed for marketing is simply not held on computers. Table 6.1 shows the areas that are usefully computerised, and also the areas where traditional research is more important. It follows the input-output format. Moving from left to right, computers are well suited to measuring the marketing inputs that a firm makes. They can measure all activities, including marketing ones, and assign them with associated costs.

Customers' thoughts and feelings are, however, almost impossible to measure using in-house computer systems. Such systems generally have sales or service as their primary purpose, and the research tools they contain are therefore rudimentary, having been added only as an afterthought. This has not stopped companies asking their sales reps and service staff to survey customer opinions using computerised questionnaires. These exercises are often unsuccessful and can be downright misleading. Sampling is likely to be unrepresentative, since the customers are chosen by members of staff, and the information is likely to be biased. Staff have little or no training in research methods. Customers do not expect to be treated in such a way by staff, and they are likely to say what they think their contact ought to hear, rather than what they really think or feel.

Customer thoughts and feelings can in practice be measured only using small research samples rather than mega-databases. Market

Table 6.1 **What technology can and cannot measure**

	Marketing inputs	Customer thoughts and feelings	Customer actions and behaviour	Business value output
Own company performance	YES	NO	TO SOME EXTENT	TO SOME EXTENT
	Computers give good measures of input activities and costs	Computerised collection of such customer data is incomplete	Computers cannot yet track lifetime behaviour and loyalty	Computers track profitability but not long-term value
Competitive comparisons	NO	NO	NO	NO
	Computers alone cannot provide competitive comparisons	Computerised collection of such customer data is incomplete	Computerised collection of such customer data is incomplete	Computers alone cannot provide competitive comparisons

research still has a vital role to play in measuring customer needs, attitudes, opinions and satisfaction.

Customer actions and behaviour can be measured to some extent by computers, which can track product enquiries and sales in terms of both money and unit volume. However, computers generally do not provide an adequate view of customers' lifetime behaviour or their loyalty. They can track each individual sales transaction, but they are unable to link any one transaction with earlier transactions by the same customer. This means that most computer systems do not reveal whether a customer is a heavy or light, frequent or infrequent, increasing or decreasing buyer.

Tracking customer behaviour over time is one of the key goals for computer enthusiasts. Customer identifiers, such as account numbers, loyalty card numbers or credit card numbers, can provide the missing link which enables customer loyalty and lifetime behaviour to be tracked. However, because most customers carry and use multiple cards and identifiers, the links that computers can establish are often incomplete.

Panel and survey research is still the major source for accurate data on customer lifetime behaviour patterns, purchase frequency, loyalty and switching. Such research is widespread in the branded food and drinks market, but much less common in other markets.

Lastly, looking at the bottom row of Table 6.1, competitive comparisons cannot be made using computers. More conventional research methods have to be employed. Research is needed to assess relative inputs (such as share of voice in advertising); to assess relative thoughts and feelings (such as relative satisfaction of a firm's customers and its competitors' customers); to track customer activity regarding competitors (such as market share, share of category requirements and relative loyalty of customers); and to track the relative profitability of a firm's activities.

Marrying IT and marketing

In 1988 Warren McFarlan, dean of studies at Harvard Business School, predicted that "in five years there will be two types of company, those who use the computer as a marketing tool, and those who face bankruptcy". Because of a blitz of statements like this, it is perhaps not surprising that at the touch of a button whole forests of trees are felled in order to dispatch marketing shots to consumers, who instantly bin them.

Marketing tools and techniques can help the database user to target more effectively. Giving consumers an opportunity to opt out of mailshots and other forms of contact can reduce annoyance and improve profitability. Categorising consumers on the basis of actual behaviour, rather than the more traditional criteria of demographics and geodemographics, can increase relevance to consumers and profitability to marketers. Tracking campaigns over many years can help identify those groups of consumers with high response rates and those who never respond.

Market research can help identify how consumers feel and think about the mailshots and offers they receive. It can help improve the way products and services are categorised and described, by overturning traditional categories which no longer address consumers' real needs and wants. It can help uncover why certain items are relevant to consumers. It can reveal how consumers prefer to go about selecting and deciding on purchases. It can show what satisfies them and what causes dissatisfaction. All these factors should have an influence on the computerised approaches that businesses make to customers.

IT can be a powerful aid to market research, but it also has the power to damage customer relations. "Most managers have given little systematic thought to the social issues inevitably implicated in database marketing programs," concluded Frank Cespedes, a professor at Harvard Business School, and Jeff Smith, an assistant professor at Georgetown University.[13]

"Consumers view companies as enemies, not allies. They don't welcome our advances. They arm themselves to fight back." This grim conclusion emerged from a recent *Harvard Business Review* article on the realities behind the myth of one-to-one marketing and databases.[14]

William Rees-Mogg, a veteran British journalist and board director, comments: "Most senior managers now at board level have only a superficial understanding of information technology; boards are bad at deciding what they need; consultants are expensive, hard to monitor and of variable quality; their recommendations are often inappropriate to the real needs of the business; the technology and software seldom deliver what the consultants have promised, and always cost more than the board have budgeted for; the IT systems need to be updated continuously; the once-for-all capital expenditure turns out to be an annual commitment, tending to rise year after year; the improvement in efficiency is less than has been forecast, and staff savings are much less – indeed sometimes staff numbers actually rise; profit gains are much smaller and the IT investment is much bigger than the board had hoped for; instead of being a profitable investment, IT turns out to be a running cost."[15]

Tools for measuring IT

Six key tools are described in Part 3:

- Repeat purchase
- Satisfaction
- Customer involvement
- Innovation benchmark
- Competitive threat map
- Marketing waste

PART 2

A NEW APPROACH TO MARKETING

7 Marketing measurement frameworks

MEASUREMENT has long been accepted as a necessity for controlling financial performance, and the management accounting discipline has created a coherent framework for collecting and analysing financial data. No comparable discipline yet exists in marketing; there is a theoretical framework, but practice lags behind.

The details of a common approach to marketing measurement may not be completely agreed, but the basic principles are widely accepted. At its most basic the aim of marketing measurement is to establish the relationships between marketing inputs and outputs, including financial outputs (see Figure 7.1). This simple input-output framework dates from the 1950s, and has its origins in studies done at Harvard Business School by Neil Borden, which were published in 1964 in an article entitled *The Concept of the Marketing Mix*.[1]

Measures of the inputs and the outputs have been constantly developed throughout the 30-year period following Borden's work. Output measures are primarily financial, but input measures include financial measures and activity measures, such as advertising activity. Competitive benchmarks of inputs and outputs are increasingly common.

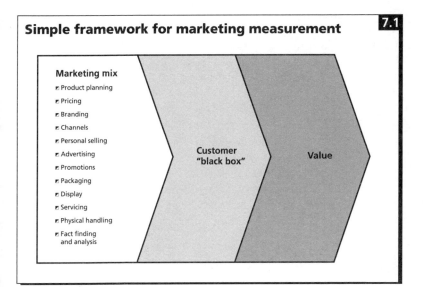

Simple framework for marketing measurement 7.1

Marketing mix
- Product planning
- Pricing
- Branding
- Channels
- Personal selling
- Advertising
- Promotions
- Packaging
- Display
- Servicing
- Physical handling
- Fact finding and analysis

Customer "black box"

Value

However, this simplistic framework has some obvious drawbacks, as noted by Mike Wilson, visiting professor of marketing at Cranfield School of Management and chairman of Europe's biggest marketing consultancy, Marketing Improvements: "Most of us in marketing know what we want to achieve, which is hopefully profit in relation to assets, however you care to measure it. And we know that we have a certain number of inputs, such as PR, advertising, new product development, salesforce, channel strategy, and so on. The problem is that all of this goes into a great black box with the results coming out the other end. The difficulty is that the black box is being influenced all the time by other things than your own marketing, such as continuous market change, continuous competitive change, continuous legislative change in many industries. Nevertheless, companies are increasingly looking for insights into the black box, to find what has worked and so should be repeated."

Looking into the black box

There have been a number of different attempts to discover how and why customers respond to marketing inputs to generate revenue. Probably the best known are the research findings originating from the Profit Impact of Market Strategy (PIMS) database.

General Electric (GE) has been searching for general principles linking marketing inputs to outputs since the 1960s. In 1974 Sidney Schoeffler, professor of economics at the University of Massachusetts, demonstrated a strong correlation between market share and profitability by using a database of GE businesses, and disproved the claimed correlation between profitability and a host of other factors at the same time. Later Bradley Gale, Sidney Schoeffler, and Harvard's Bob Buzzell and Ralph Sultan expanded Schoeffler's GE database into the PIMS database by adding data from hundreds of other companies and refining the research methodology. Now the PIMS database contains an extensive body of empirical evidence from over 7,000 business units. Two empirical findings stand out from analyses run on the PIMS data: the association between market share and profitability; and the association between perceived quality and return on investment (see Figure 7.2).

The criteria for winning the American Malcolm Baldridge National Quality Award have been heavily influenced by findings from the PIMS database. Consequently, the award structure represents a sophisticated version of the marketing measurement framework shown in Figure 7.1. Although some past winners have not been consistently successful, the award provides one of the most complete descriptions of what an organ-

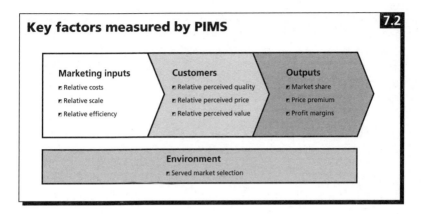

Key factors measured by PIMS — 7.2

Marketing inputs	Customers	Outputs
▪ Relative costs	▪ Relative perceived quality	▪ Market share
▪ Relative scale	▪ Relative perceived price	▪ Price premium
▪ Relative efficiency	▪ Relative perceived value	▪ Profit margins

Environment
▪ Served market selection

isation capable of consistently delivering superior value to customers looks like. It stresses the importance of actions based on facts, data and analysis measures; the need for customer-perceived quality; the search for underlying causes of customer satisfaction; and the need to benchmark strategic processes in the light of customer perceptions and the competitive environment.

Bradley Gale notes that: "You can't expect the Baldridge award to do what it was not designed to do. It is an award for quality, not an award for customer value management or strategic management."[2] In his book *Managing Customer Value* he notes some of the important areas not covered in Baldridge, in particular measures of: financial control; strategic management (what category of business should a firm be in?); market segmentation (Baldridge averages across market segments); and innovation and creation of new categories of product or service.

A market research framework

At the same time as the quality and satisfaction frameworks were being developed, the market research industry was beginning to find some insights into the black box (see Figure 7.3).

Although interesting, the inputs measured by the market research industry are somewhat biased by the agenda of the marketing departments, which pay for the majority of its studies. The success or failure of advertising, brands and new product launches are still the main focus of the market research industry's work. Customer satisfaction research represents only about 6% of market research activity, is not usually commissioned by marketing departments, and is often hived off into specialist

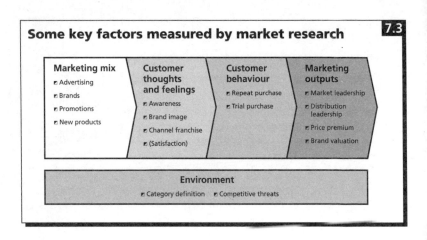

Some key factors measured by market research `7.3`

Marketing mix	Customer thoughts and feelings	Customer behaviour	Marketing outputs
▪ Advertising	▪ Awareness	▪ Repeat purchase	▪ Market leadership
▪ Brands	▪ Brand image	▪ Trial purchase	▪ Distribution leadership
▪ Promotions	▪ Channel franchise		▪ Price premium
▪ New products	▪ (Satisfaction)		▪ Brand valuation

Environment
▪ Category definition   ▪ Competitive threats

subdivisions of the big research agencies. Hence it is not generally taken into account in frameworks such as that in Figure 7.3.

Apart from its inherent bias towards investigating issues of importance to the marketing department, another shortcoming of frameworks generated by the market research industry is their willingness to ignore outputs like sales revenue. David Wethey, managing director of Agency Assessments, a firm that advises clients on choosing advertising agencies, comments: "You can go to Millward Brown or Taylor Nelson AGB and they will provide you with measurements that prove you are doing your advertising right. But there has to be something wrong with this, for everyone can't be a winner."

Linking long-term and short-term marketing measures

Tim Ambler, a research fellow at London Business School, describes the current thinking using this simple equation:

$$\text{Marketing performance} = \text{short-term results (results - costs)} + \text{change in brand equity}$$

To track both short-term and long-term effects, he advocates the use of a scorecard containing several measures. On the question of how many measures and which ones, he comments: "My own preference is for 10–15. How brand equity is assessed is far less important than the fact that it is, and consistently. The numbers do not matter, but the trends do. So does consistency between measures. If perceived quality and relative price are both up, book your holiday, but if relative price is up and perceived quality is down, start taking the Zantac."

Ambler's keen perception about the importance of effective marketing measurements has been strongly endorsed by the UK Marketing Council. In April 1997 it launched the Marketing Metrics project under Ambler's guidance. Other sponsors include The Marketing Society, The Institute of Practitioners in Advertising, London Business School and, more recently, the Marketing Science Institute (US), the SPCA and Cranfield School of Management. The project will study current and best practices in marketing measurement, particularly for senior management, with the aim of providing guidelines that will enable marketing measurement to "command sufficient credibility to be accepted as key indicators of business success alongside accounting measures".

The Marketing Science Institute in the United States has also been active in the promotion of good marketing measurement. Most recently it established the MAX (Managing Advertising Expenditures) programme, launched in December 1996. Paul Root, president of MSI, comments: "The primary goal of the MAX program is to understand and improve the advertising budgeting process."

Putting the measures together at BT

As noted, measurements in isolation reveal far less than measurements seen together. Single figures do not matter but trends do. Also developing models that link inputs to outputs can tell us more than visually scanning trend data. British Telecom (BT) is one of the few companies to track several measures in parallel and also to develop models. It provided a rare glimpse of some of its sophisticated tracking machinery when presenting a winning paper in the IPA Advertising Effectiveness awards.[3]

BT has been using advertising aimed at stimulating consumer use of the telephone for a decade, spending at least £40m annually in the process. During this period it has developed a formidable array of measurement and tracking tools that enable it to fine tune its marketing and get the maximum value from its advertising spend. Using a sophisticated statistical technique called multiple regression analysis, BT developed models of consumer demand with tracking data from 111 monthly periods between April 1986 and June 1995. From this the revenue impact of the campaigns was estimated at £294m, compared with a cost of £56m for media and production. So even extremely subtle effects may have an enormous financial pay-off. In BT's case there were significant quality differences between the three campaigns studied (see Table 7.1).

Table 7.1 **Campaign quality impact at BT**

Campaign	Revenue (% return from 100 TVRs)	Index
"It's good to talk"	1.75	398
"Beattie"	1.05	236
"Get through to someone"	0.44	100

Quality of marketing is reflected in changes in people's attitudes, interests and opinions. These changes can be dramatic compared with economic behaviour; swings of 5–50% or more often result from marketing inputs. However, these indicators are little more than crude indicators of quality. Even so, in the absence of significant economic shifts, social science measures can be useful indicators.

The BT case also shows that extreme attitude shifts in the short term are common. For example, the company's "It's good to talk" campaign was associated with opinion changes of over 200% in some cases. After the campaign there was a 217% increase among women who said "the advertising reminded me to call someone and I rang them". BT found that these extreme attitude changes are rarely sustained in the long term. For example, it tracks the number of people who think call charges are high over many years, not just one campaign. This long-term perspective is vital when judging marketing effectiveness.

MSAT: a new tool for auditing measurement

Most traditional measurement systems fit into one or the other of the frameworks in Figures 7.2 and 7.3. Looking at them together provides a broader picture, combining the interests and thinking of the board with that of the marketing department.

The Measurement Systems Assessment Tool (MSAT) Framework, developed by the author in 1997, is used to audit this broader view of what companies measure, and to explore how they assess their own performance in choosing and using measurement systems. To date 130 organisations have completed MSAT questionnaires, a sample that makes it possible to draw preliminary conclusions about how organisations are using tools. MSAT assesses 30 of the most widely used tools (see list and definitions in Appendix 2). The aim of the survey is to offer an objective assessment of how managers choose tools, what they use, and how satisfied they are with them.[4]

The survey responses so far show that organisations used an average of 12 tools in 1997. Many techniques are new and experimental. In 1997 about half of the tools in use were still being tested as pilots. Managers expected to convert about half their pilots into full implementations within 18 months, and they expected their organisations to take on 1.6 new tools in the next year. They also expected to stop using at least one tool because of poor performance, although the 70% of failures are reported to be internal, caused by poor training or misuse of the tool.

Despite the lip-service that is paid to best practice, most managers seem to want new toys. As many as 60% disagreed with the statement "Using tried and trusted methods is more important than choosing the latest new methods". Expertise and authority were also undervalued, with 57% of managers disagreeing with the statement "It is better to gain experience of using the same tools and techniques for many years". In contrast, 95% of managers said "Creative vision and foresight are very important when choosing new tools" and 96% said "I like to keep delivering innovative improvements to the tools and techniques I use".

About half the tools in use are described as being critical to running the organisation. However, satisfaction with the tools is not great; less than one-quarter of the managers describe themselves as completely satisfied. There is also a strong correlation between what managers report as critical and what they see as easy to implement. This is somewhat reminiscent of the comment by Robert McNamara, former president of Ford, adviser to presidents Kennedy and Johnson, and former head of the World Bank: "The first step is to measure whatever can be easily measured. That is okay as far as it goes. The second step is to disregard that which can't easily be measured or to give it an arbitrary quantitative value. This is artificial and misleading. The third step is to presume that what can't be measured easily isn't important. This is blindness. The fourth step is to say that what can't easily be measured really doesn't exist. This is suicide".

A broader framework for measurement: five perspectives

Based on the 1997 MSAT studies, and also the picture that is emerging from the Metrics project, the author has constructed a broader framework to show the combined measurement framework that is emerging (see Figure 7.4). It is called the five perspectives because it covers:

- Inputs
- Customer motivation

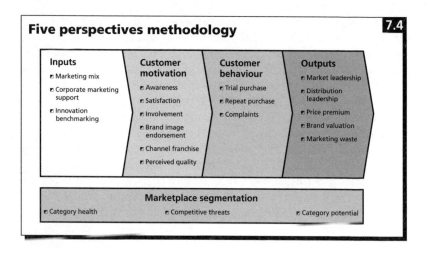

Five perspectives methodology · 7.4

Inputs	Customer motivation	Customer behaviour	Outputs
Marketing mix	Awareness	Trial purchase	Market leadership
Corporate marketing support	Satisfaction	Repeat purchase	Distribution leadership
Innovation benchmarking	Involvement	Complaints	Price premium
	Brand image endorsement		Brand valuation
	Channel franchise		Marketing waste
	Perceived quality		

Marketplace segmentation

Category health · Competitive threats · Category potential

- Customer behaviour
- Outputs
- Marketplace segmentation

This framework synthesises Figures 7.2 and 7.3. The 20 measures in Figure 7.4 are described in more detail in Part 3.

Input measures

The input measures shown in Figure 7.4 – marketing mix productivity, corporate marketing support and innovation benchmarking – all depend on effective tracking of marketing activities and allocation of financial numbers to those activities.

Activity-based costing (ABC) is the perhaps the most influential new financial tool underlying these input measurements. Although it is fairly new, the piloting of ABC is widespread and has been found in over half the MSAT benchmark group. As noted in Chapter 5, ABC differs from traditional costing systems in the treatment of resources that are not directly volume related; for example, advertising, promotions, special batch set-up for private-label products and new product development. Traditional costing commonly distorts the allocation of costs. For example, low-volume products are often undercosted, and so many product extensions that are traditionally reported to be profitable are actually unprofitable.

About one-third of users express some dissatisfaction with ABC and over 10% have found it so unsatisfactory that they do not plan to continue with it. The main source of dissatisfaction appears to be the time and effort involved in implementing ABC. Yet its benefits can be tremendous.

Strategic benchmarking of key processes is perhaps the most influential of the non-financial strategic tools. Also comparatively new, it has become surprisingly widespread, again mainly as pilots. Less dissatisfaction is expressed with strategic process benchmarking than with ABC, but even so benchmarking is seen as less critical than rather more mundane input measures.

Customer motivation: thoughts and feelings

Measurements of customers' thoughts and feelings in the form of customer satisfaction measures were used by about two-thirds of the MSAT survey respondents. They have come to be regarded as an established technique rather than experimental or a pilot. Even companies with a strong financial focus still consider customer satisfaction to be critical.

All other measures of customers thoughts and feelings are far less common than satisfaction. Thus perceived quality was measured by only one-third of the MSAT respondents. There are a few exceptions in a few industries, such as branded food and drinks, where these measures are much more common and more mature.

Customer behaviour

Measurements of customers' actions and behaviour are commonly confused with measures of thoughts and feelings. As noted earlier, behaviour should be measured independently of cognitive issues. Only about one-quarter of the MSAT benchmark companies use behaviour measures, compared with three-quarters which measure customer satisfaction.

Repeat purchasing ought to be a pattern that most firms study in depth. After all, according to studies by management consultants Bain & Co, small increases in repeat purchasing rates (say 5%) can result in disproportionately large increases in profits (often there are increases in profits of over 50%). Yet only about one-quarter of the MSAT benchmark companies measure this important factor.

Trial purchases are analysed by a similarly small number of firms. Yet such analysis can yield valuable insights. Rentokil Initial not only monitors customer attitudes to service, but also tracks all cancelled contracts to ascertain the reason for the cancellation. It finds that such analysis gives indications about competitive trends and activities, any possible decline in its service and pricing issues. It also gives information about the type of customer. For example, there is a much higher rate of termination in small restaurants compared with large restaurants, because ownership of small ones changes more often.

Complaints is an area where simple tracking procedures are common. About three-quarters of the MSAT benchmark companies have procedures for handling customer complaints. However, given the lack of data on repeat purchasing and customer needs, it is unlikely that many companies learn much from the complaining behaviour of their customers.

Output measures

All companies measure revenue and profit in aggregate, but few can track these figures to the associated marketing inputs. Nor can many organisations relate the profits to the customers who generate them, even though all customers generate different profits.

Customer profitability measurement has become a critical goal for many organisations. In the MSAT survey it is being tracked in over one-third of the benchmark group, but in about two-thirds of cases the measurements are pilots, not full implementations. So about 90% of firms have little or no sound knowledge of the different levels of profit that different customers produce. Yet many studies suggest that the majority of customers are unprofitable, sometimes as many as 90%.

A few organisations have taken the customer profitability concept one stage further by linking profitability with customer retention and loyalty. Some have quantified the links between customer selection ("experienced salespeople are much better at finding and recruiting the best customers"), customer referral and customer retention ("long-term employees create higher customer loyalty"). Customer profitability appears to grow over time in many cases. As customers get to know a business they generally interact more efficiently with it. Spending by most customers increases over time, following the initial purchase. This is sometimes referred to as cross-selling. Over time a customer is also more likely to generate referral business. Customers who are repeat buyers are more likely to buy at a premium price. The majority of managers tracking customer profitability are satisfied with the tools they are using, but about half are unsure whether the information is really business-critical for managing relationships with consumers.

Market leadership is widely discussed in business literature and at conferences, so it is somewhat surprising to discover that only half the MSAT respondents routinely track market share. The shortfall seems to be mostly among industrial and business-to-business marketers, where the major market research agencies offer ad hoc research rather than regular measurements.

Price premium is another measure that ought to figure highly. It is, after all, one of the primary results of quality programmes and branding. So it is again surprising to discover that relative price tracking is used by only one-third of the MSAT respondents.

Distribution leadership is also important in many sectors where retail or trade channels are important. Yet only 11% of the MSAT sample tracked distribution. In part, this low figure is explained by the fact that not all industries use trade channels, but its use was also far lower than trade channel profitability, which is measured by 27% of the sample.

Marketplace segmentation

Marketplace segmentation provides the broader context for the first four perspectives. All customers are not created equal, and this perspective reflects the differences.

The market segmentation measures shown in Figure 7.4 (category health, category potential, competitive threats) depend on effective segmentation of the marketplace. They reflect the attractiveness of the segments and the competitive threats by segment. A company's strategy can then be defined by those segments which it chooses to target. The five perspectives framework should then identify the target segments, and for each segment set objectives for inputs, motivation, behaviour and outputs.

KMAT™: a framework for assessing knowledge

For an organisation to progress it needs more than just an accumulation of the latest tools; it needs a coherent framework for integrating the data gained from the tools into a consistent understanding of its customers and markets. The Arthur Andersen KMAT™ (Knowledge Management Assessment Tool) framework identifies five factors affecting an organisation's ability to do this: measurement; process; technology; culture; and leadership. Of these five, measurement is often the weak point. The problem is nearly always the collection of data rather than the analysis. Companies usually collect data that are easy to gather, not data that are useful or accurate. They then apply rocket-science analysis to comparatively worthless data.

KMAT™ shows that process problems frequently underlie measurement problems. Speed is often given higher priority than accuracy or relevance. Information must be collected quickly, even if it is bad. Personal interviews are downgraded to telephone interviews, which are then changed to postal questionnaires, all in pursuit of quick, cheap data. Too often information technology is recommended as the solution, even before the problem is known. The problem is that IT attracts enthusiasts, and enthusiasts try to control the measurement agenda. The prevailing attitude is that if it is on the computer it must be true.

Cultural issues go hand in hand with process problems. The marketing industry pays researchers extremely badly, and in-house researchers have no career path. Training in measurement is rare, and skills shortages are a widely cited reason for problems with measurement. Employees are expected to interview customers, obtain honest answers and record them accurately. This sounds pretty basic, but good interviewing is a highly skilled activity. Problems are compounded when research is global. Good researchers have questionnaires translated into the local language, then back into English.

Lastly, leadership, or the lack of it, lies at the heart of many issues. Senior executives allow inexperienced junior staff to select the tools because they do not perceive the need for world-class measurements. Political infighting is often symptomatic of weak leadership. Most marketing managers would agree that measurement is a topic charged with political implications and corporate infighting.

Four steps towards understanding customers and markets

In most organisations progress passes through recognisable stages, and improving knowledge about customers and markets is no different. In marketing there are four steps. These steps are not jumps. Each covers a broad spectrum of approaches. They evolve into each other, but their philosophy is different. They are:

1 Cost and product driven
2 Customer tool proliferation
3 Co-ordinated customer data
4 Integrated customer knowledge

This stepped development process has been noted by several observers. The author and his colleague, Merlin Stone, described it in 1987 in *Database Marketing*. David Norton wrote about it at the same time, in the context of computerised knowledge. In 1993, Bradley Gale found a similar sequence, when he wrote *Managing Customer Value*. And in 1998 Robert Kaplan and Robin Cooper described a similar series of steps in the development of activity-based costing in *Cost and Effect*.

Table 7.2 shows what happens at each of these four stages in the five areas identified as critical by the KMAT™ framework.

Table 7.2 **Four steps in development of marketing knowledge**

Knowledge factor (KMAT)	Step 1 Cost and product driven	Step 2 Customer tool proliferation	Step 3 Co-ordinated customer metrics	Step 4 Integrated customer knowledge
Measurement	Mostly cost and management accounting; hard to analyse for marketing purposes	Tool proliferation; quality, needs loyalty, satisfaction all measured in different ways	Rationalisation and standardisation of marketing tools	Dissemination of measurement; used to grow organisational knowledge
Process	Processes satisfy departmental needs; finance has biggest share of measurements	Processes satisfy individual needs; local ownership of information	Processes satisfy corporate needs and cross-departmental boundaries	Processes support problem-solving teams with high degree of flexibility
Technology	Central computer operations, usually controlled by finance	Islands of automation, under control of local IT users; local databases and networks	Central computer operation, strong CIO at board level; market research still separate	Networked computer operation; market research integrated; chief knowledge officer (CKO)
Culture	Role culture dominated by strong finance function; control and authority are not to be transgressed	People culture where satisfying friends is an accepted way of life; loyalty to peers	Power culture requiring loyalty to the organisation; rewards for those who support marketing	Task culture where it is acceptable to challenge authority; reward for task performance by team
Leadership	Autocratic rule by finance on measurement; board-level support for finance leadership	Department heads encourage staff initiatives and often discourage steering committees	Autocratic rule by marketing, often a charismatic boss	Network of expert contacts, constant skill development and exhibiting skills, with status for solving problems
Example	Most small and medium-sized businesses	Recently privatised utilities; banks	Packaged food and drinks companies	Some IT companies (HP, Microsoft); pharmaceuticals companies

Step 1: Cost and product driven

At step 1 the company is driven by managing the costs of producing and delivering a standard range of products. Measurements consist of budgeting and traditional management accounting. Marketing measurements consist of sales revenue reports (monthly or quarterly) and allocated marketing costs. Data are held in the accounting systems, and may also be held in a database. They are hard to analyse for marketing purposes, for example, to identify profitable customers, or to assess campaign profitability.

Processes are hierarchical. Departmental boundaries are rigid. Customers are managed in one way by the sales department and in another by credit control and operations. Sales forecasts are often prepared by operations or finance. Different standards and policies for customer service are applied by different departments. Finance generally has the final say on the development of any new measurement process.

Technology is used primarily to support finance and operations. A customer may appear many times on more than one computer system, such as order processing and accounts receivable. Multiple records may exist for the same customer on the sales ledger, since there is often no incentive for accounting to co-ordinate its customer records. Traditionally, such computer data are not readily available for marketing purposes, and the marketing department finds it extremely difficult to obtain the data it needs.

Culturally, everyone has a job to do. Rules and controls are not to be transgressed. Marketing is regarded as a sideline. Employees see no reason for gathering marketing information. They often distrust marketing, seeing it as the department which most often enjoys expense-account lunches, with staff who are often away from their desks or even away from the office, and who seem to have fun, as well as the department which is never accountable for results.

Leadership is often autocratic, with financial issues dominating. The board does not allocate resources to efforts that increase the organisation's knowledge of its customers. It sees marketing as tactical, something added on to existing products and services. There may be no mention of marketing measurements when new investments in products or services are under consideration. Marketing is often driven by a particular sponsor on the board, so when that sponsor goes, or changes his or her priorities, the role of marketing may change.

Organisations which are still at step 1 are the norm in the small and medium-sized business sector. The Chartered Institute of Marketing and

The Marketing Council have set up initiatives to help such organisations progress. Public-sector organisations are generally also in this position. Eventually, such organisations come to recognise the need to become more responsive to customers, and usually they move on to step 2.

Step 2: Customer tool proliferation
In step 2 marketing knowledge begins to grow, but only in pockets here and there throughout the organisation. If it uses several channels of distribution, or has several product or service lines, there may be different areas of knowledge for each. A specialist salesforce, or call centre, may have its own customer data because it needs particular information that is relevant to its own department or unit. Tools for measuring various aspects of customer relationships begin to proliferate, and information begins to accumulate. However, these islands of information often contain facts and figures that are incompatible and unconnected.

Each department or unit may have some information that it needs for its own purposes. But there is often great frustration because other departments will not gather or disclose information that they need. This may be because each "owner" of an item of knowledge guards it jealously. In large organisations disputes about information ownership and sharing are common. The result is often poor service. A bank customer, for example, may receive many contradictory messages and communications, conflicting mailshots, telemarketing, and so on, because the departments concerned have lots of customer data but there is no co-ordination.

Measurement goes beyond financial data. Tools to measure customer factors begin to proliferate. There are often independent pilots of such measures as customer satisfaction, as well as customer databases and lists in various departments. New soft measures of customers start to be used as well as the traditional hard data. There is a lack of standards, calibration is poor, and many managers disbelieve the soft data.

Processes are still confined within departmental boundaries. They are often the work of one enthusiastic manager, whose individual needs they are aimed at satisfying. Local customer information gathering is developed. Many members of the organisation are involved in looking for ideas in traditional and non-traditional places. Market research is sponsored on an ad hoc basis by individual managers. Information is perceived to be owned by individuals, and ownership often becomes a contentious issue.

Technology use is mainly departmental, and personal computing is common. Finance still has a strong influence, but mainly to control expenditure on end-user computing. Users often see marketing data as a resource that they personally own. Disputes about ownership of customer data are common. There is little effort to co-ordinate technological data-gathering with market research, and often the two are incompatible.

A culture of empowerment is frequently associated with this step. Individuals are encouraged to do their own thing and to take responsibility for their own learning. Loyalty to their peers and friends is common. Although some departments and individuals actively support the gathering of customer information, other departments, such as customer service, and opinionated individuals actively resist it on the grounds that it does not meet their aims. The gathering of soft data is not considered to be important by some departments, such as finance and operations, and there is no corporate view of the need for knowledge of customers. The culture supports the hoarding and ownership of knowledge.

Leaders encourage learning to support existing core competencies and create new ones. However, the leaders are happy to see tools being acquired haphazardly, and do not see any need for co-ordination. Some leaders may even fear co-ordination, equating it with empire building.

Step 2 is necessary and a lot of companies are at this stage. Many of the building blocks needed for step 3 are contained in step 2, such as marketing databases and online marketing analysis tools, market research skills and relationships with market research agencies.

Step 3: Co-ordinated customer tools

At step 3 the measurement tools are co-ordinated so that outputs from one tool can be fed into another. Segmentation and analysis become consistent, and gaps are filled where vital tools were missing at step 2. The emphasis is not on accumulation of more and more tools, but on integration of existing tools. The aim is not to collect more and more facts about customers, but to develop a depth and breadth of understanding. Key questions are:

- Who are our customers?
- What do they need and what satisfies their needs?
- How do they behave?
- How profitable are our activities that satisfy customer needs?

The whole organisation works to answer these questions by pooling its knowledge, acquiring information from other sources where there are gaps. It rearranges its processes so that its knowledge is properly co-ordinated.

At this stage everyone in the organisation has agreed on a set of measures that they are committed to supporting in all departments. Knowledge gaps are systematically identified. Pilots of the balanced scorecard may be tried (see Chapter 8 for a description of the balanced scorecard). Rationalisation of the step 2 measurements occurs, and standards are developed to make the information more consistent and more credible. Processes are rationalised further and streamlined. The aim is often to fit a "corporate" need.

Well-defined processes are now used to close the knowledge gaps. Processes are developed that cross departmental boundaries, and resistance to change is actively discouraged, often through central power and support from senior levels.

Karen Guerra, general manager of Colgate-Palmolive in the UK and Ireland, comments: "When I joined Colgate-Palmolive in 1983 we had brand profitability according to contribution but not down to operating profit. We had some customer (retailer) profitability measures but they were pretty basic. Managing the business was a case of smelling it and guessing." Today the processes ensure that the view of the customer is seamless and integrated across functions. Having that clear vision is essential, maintains Guerra: "Giving costs or providing a service are only worthwhile if you know what the endgame looks like. This means you have a vision of which customers you want to support and why, and what shape and profile you think the business could have in three to five years' time. We do have that. We often say here that if you don't think you can measure something at least try, because if you can measure it you can see if you are doing something right or wrong. It gives you a benchmark by which you can assess what you are doing."

Technology is brought back under central control. A single customer database is developed, creating an institutional memory that is accessible to the entire enterprise. Technology is used to link all members of the enterprise to one another. There is often a powerful chief information officer (CIO) who holds sway at board level. Centralisation is necessary to create the expensive infrastructure needed, as step 2 systems rarely have sufficient budgets to create the infrastructure to cross departmental boundaries. Computerised information systems are integrated under the influence of the CIO. However, it is usual for market research to be run separately from IT, and it is often inconsistent.

A power culture demanding loyalty to the organisation and its mission is usual at this stage. Those who support marketing are rewarded (for example, by linking bonuses to customer satisfaction measures). Leadership is often strong and autocratic, with a strong marketing emphasis. The board understands the profit-generating potential of its marketing knowledge assets, and encourages their development by the whole organisation. The leadership acknowledges customer knowledge as a major objective for all departments in the organisation.

Yet this pooled knowledge can create problems. In particular, if a marketing database is available to all marketers, the result will probably be too many direct mail campaigns and too much telemarketing. In a large organisation this may be a serious problem. The number of one-to-one relationships with customers may become untenable. As a result, many marketing initiatives seem trivial and useless instead of unique and valuable. Customers maintain literally hundreds of one-to-one relationships in their personal lives, with partners, colleagues, friends and acquaintances, but only a handful of these are close and committed.

"It's overkill," said a woman interviewed for a Harvard Business School study, talking about the many direct mail and telephone contacts she receives. "One is more meaningless than the next. I must get ten mailings every day. When I go away, the accumulation is remarkable. I never look inside the mailings any more. I just throw them all away."

Step 4: Integrated customer knowledge
Many firms between steps 1 and 3 gather and co-ordinate information, but they never integrate it with the policies and controls for the whole business. They allow individual managers to use marketing media in ways that collectively annoy customers. In step 4 the organisation integrates and internalises its knowledge, and uses it to satisfy customer needs and drive profitability.

Few companies reach this stage. Some, however, such as Microsoft and Hewlett-Packard and several pharmaceuticals companies, do appear to have moved beyond step 3. They seem better at listening to their customers and responding to them (although some commentators accuse Microsoft of going back a step). The most noticeable feature of such firms is the scientific or task culture, where it is acceptable to challenge authority. As the culture shifts towards a scientific approach, managers become better at balancing their customer and financial objectives. The organisation finds ways to link marketing knowledge with financial results. Measurements such as the balanced scorecard can help. So can campaign co-ordination and category management, to minimise cluttered communications and product disorder.

Ian Ryder, worldwide director, brand management and communications at Hewlett-Packard, comments: "As a company we are addicted to profitable growth. We are very happy with a margin of 7–8%, providing that we grow every year by at least 20%. And that is injected into the whole company culture. This is what allows us to develop our citizenship and community programmes." The strong culture also encourages honesty and objectivity. As Ryder points out: "A key strength is the ability to challenge. We are not hierarchical here. Rather than tell people what to do, which probably wouldn't work, senior management would say: 'This seems like a good idea, have you thought about it? What would be the impact on your business?' It is also ingrained, probably because it is a throw-back to the engineering background, for people to be self-critical and look for ways to improve things. This is helpful because it means we can change more quickly."

Similarly, John Leftwich, marketing vice-president at Microsoft, points out: "One of Microsoft's strengths is our brutal honesty with ourselves about what's happening. We are absolutely paranoid. We have to be thoroughly open, frank and honest about what the market tells us. Anyone who isn't will not be in business in the 21st millennium."

Processes support problem-solving teams, with a high degree of flexibility. The organisation formalises the process of transferring best practices, including documentation and lessons learned. Networked computers assist in the process of information sharing. IT becomes a knowledge tool. Market research becomes integrated with information technology.

Boehringer-Ingelheim, a pharmaceuticals company, has gone further than most to integrate its knowledge. Zinta Krumins, head of business information and support, explains: "When I joined the company in the late 1980s there were sales data going to sales management and marketing data going to marketing people. Gradually, as the market research role developed, it seemed to be sensible to bring together both sets of data. As there were no analysts on the sales side, it made sense to have market research analysts looking at that information. So then we had market research plus salesforce information, and that became the Business Information and Support Department." At Boehringer-Ingelheim, Krumins's role spans strategic information technology, market research and employee feedback.

Where marketing knowledge stands today

Most organisations are entrenched in step 2. They are actively acquiring more and more tools, without giving much thought to the contention and chaos this may be causing. But some are finding they have reached the limit. As marketing professionalism increases, attempts are being made to co-ordinate and progress to step 3 or even step 4. However, for the foreseeable future, the trends encouraging the increased use of measurement tools and techniques are likely to continue.

Fragmentation of product and service categories is making it necessary for companies to develop goods more carefully, and to improve the targeting of communications. As the marketing environment becomes more cluttered, it is harder to find images and messages which will be seen and heard by consumers. As retailers and other intermediaries become more computerised, and more power is concentrated in a few hands, it becomes harder for suppliers to satisfy trade customers. More information is needed to ensure that trade customers are satisfied and will remain loyal.

The fashion for getting closer to the customer shows no sign of ending. Rather, those who follow the customer gospel are realising the complexities of their job and are demanding more and better information. Financial managers are also demanding more credible information to justify ever-escalating expenditure on customer projects. To implement the measurement framework in this chapter and move towards step 4, it is necessary to develop a more co-ordinated approach to understanding customers and markets.

8 Implementing a new marketing strategy

RETHINKING your marketing approach requires hard examination of assumptions that have been made about customers, markets and products. This chapter outlines how you can go about it.

Testing strategic assumptions

The first stage is to consider how your current marketing strategy relates to your business strategy. It is important to remember the comments of Sir Clive Thompson, Sir Colin Marshall and other senior businessmen quoted in Chapter 1: marketing strategy is business strategy. In challenging marketing assumptions, companies are also challenging the basis of their overall corporate strategy.

It is also critical that these assumptions are continually tested, to destruction if need be. John Leftwich, marketing vice-president at Microsoft, thinks it is essential that companies respond to what the market tells them. He says: "I'll give you a small and poignant example that relates to the Internet. One of our sales reps visited a South American university campus, and afterwards he sent an e-mail to Bill saying: 'Bill I have to tell you I've just visited an important South American university and nobody is using our software, they're all using Mosaic.' Now we enjoy high market share and this e-mail hammered home to Bill that something was going on in the market. In this brave new world of ours all these graduates were coming up, none of whom had seen our software. That, coupled with other things, really jolted us into action. It's that direct input from the market that speaks volumes about the way we listen and respond to the market. It is easy to ignore the market and yet we don't because we can't afford to."[1]

Some useful questions to get the process started are listed on pages 122 and 123. In theory, the factors that need to be measured to create this bigger picture should be defined by linking the strategy, or mission and vision, to specific objectives and measures. If the statements in mission or vision or strategy say little that is helpful in setting clear objectives, a useful procedure is to work backwards from the financial effects sought, looking first at the customer problems and opportunities, and second at the projects and processes needed to address them.

Some questions to ask about strategic assumptions

Management and measurement
- Do investors have access to all the key marketing indicators for assessing the company's performance?
- Does senior management take a balanced cause-and-effect view in making strategic decisions (marketing mix inputs, customer motivation and behaviour, financial outputs)?
- Is there high-level integration of marketing measurements (bringing together market research, customer satisfaction, quality, customer information systems)?
- How fully has management evaluated the health and future potential of different category sectors, customer segments, distribution channels and brands?
- What effort is expended to measure the financial impact of different marketing options?
- How well are marketing objectives and measurements at the top communicated and implemented down the line?

Customer behaviour and motivation research
- When did you last conduct research studies which fundamentally re-examined customers' categorisation of their needs and wants (descriptive categories, for example, fast, big; and evaluative categories, for example, downmarket)?
- How fully do you understand the nature of routine behaviour (for example, shopping habits)?
- Do your predictions of customer behaviour accurately reflect customer involvement and inertia (for example, low involvement, high inertia), and emotional compared with rational motivation?
- When did you last conduct research studies which fundamentally re-examined customers' experiences of buying, owning and using the products or services offered by you and your competitors?

Processes have become the focus of change for many companies. Although marketing process initiatives are often meant to cause changes in customer behaviour, the precise mechanisms that cause these changes should be explained, and they should be based on real knowledge about the customer base. There are three keys to this.

- How effectively do you link measurement of customer satisfaction to customer buying behaviour?
- How fully do you understand the role and influence of brands on buying behaviour?
- Do you combine brand, satisfaction and other motivational research to explain and predict what drives buying behaviour?

Marketing mix inputs
- What evidence do you have about the customer and financial consequences of stretching or contracting your brands or product lines?
- Can you adequately measure quality and track the effect of quality changes?
- What do you really know about the effects of price changes and promotions on customer profitability?
- Do you fully understand the impact of market coverage and quality of distribution on consumer behaviour and profitability?
- What do you know about the financial consequences of alternative distribution strategies?
- Do you have clear customer communications objectives, and are the quality and quantity of communications effective?
- What do your sales resources actually do for customers, and could they be more profitably resourced?
- Can you adequately measure service and track the effect of service changes on customers and profits?

Employee feedback and review
- How effectively do you encourage employees to feed back their insights about changing customer needs and wants and other market changes?
- How frequently do managers review their assumptions about the market forces that drive effectiveness?

The first is to focus on the right process level. Although there may be a number of high-level generic processes in most companies (for example, product development, customer acquisition, order fulfilment and manufacturing), inside each process is a series of subprocesses (see Figure 8.1). The key to process re-engineering, and the reason its benefits prove so

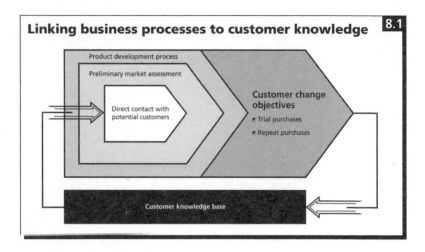

Linking business processes to customer knowledge `8.1`

Product development process

Preliminary market assessment

Direct contact with potential customers

Customer change objectives

- Trial purchases
- Repeat purchases

Customer knowledge base

elusive, is that the secrets lie in the differences in the details, not in the similarities at the generic or high level.

The second is to provide customer knowledge to guide these detailed processes. Processes transform inputs of all types into outputs according to guidance rules, and a key guiding ingredient is knowledge about customers (see Figure 8.2).

The third is to use IT creatively to enable customer knowledge to be delivered to the right process at the right time. Successful customer relationship systems provide a set of building blocks ("objects" in IT jargon), with which companies can build their own solutions. It takes a lot of time, effort and money to design the architecture for such systems, and to do the distinctive building work.

Defining a marketing measurement strategy in a telecoms firm

The Strategic Intent document of a medium-sized telecommunications company included a three-year profit growth target of £500m, and managers were struggling to find a way to achieve it. The £70m spent on measurements and associated systems during the previous year seemed to have been to no effect.

To find out what measurements were needed, a two-day workshop for senior management was arranged. On the first day the group agreed a list of ten key customer issues. They used their own best estimates of the factors that affected these issues to calculate their impact. They estimated that there was approximately £270m in financial benefits to be gained

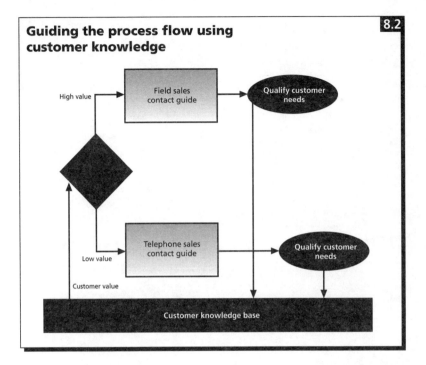

8.2

Guiding the process flow using customer knowledge

from solving problems that they had identified (see Figure 8.3 on the next page, columns A and B).

For example, consider the first problem in Figure 8.3. This was expressed as "Customer-facing staff are unable to turn every communication with customers into a retention opportunity". The group then developed a model of the benefits of solving the problem: 200,000 domestic customers lost each year at £100 each (average) = £20m revenue; £5m contribution; 5% of business customers lost each year from a total of £800m = £40m; £10m contribution; and so on. They estimated that profit opportunities totalling £22m would be lost if this problem were unsolved.

Measurement had a key role in enabling these benefits to be achieved. On the second day the group looked at the process changes needed (Figure 8.3, column C).

As they went through each problem the group became more adept at developing models to estimate the size of their business problems. By the end of the workshop their gut fears had become tangible. And although these fears were confirmed, investigating the company's problems

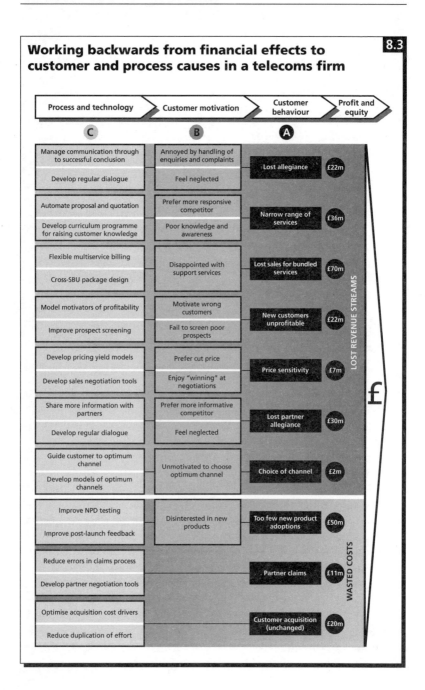

8.3

Working backwards from financial effects to customer and process causes in a telecoms firm

Process and technology > Customer motivation > Customer behaviour > Profit and equity

C — **B** — **A**

Process and technology	Customer motivation	Customer behaviour	
Manage communication through to successful conclusion / Develop regular dialogue	Annoyed by handling of enquiries and complaints / Feel neglected	Lost allegiance	£22m
Automate proposal and quotation / Develop curriculum programme for raising customer knowledge	Prefer more responsive competitor / Poor knowledge and awareness	Narrow range of services	£36m
Flexible multiservice billing / Cross-SBU package design	Disappointed with support services	Lost sales for bundled services	£70m
Model motivators of profitability / Improve prospect screening	Motivate wrong customers / Fail to screen poor prospects	New customers unprofitable	£22m
Develop pricing yield models / Develop sales negotiation tools	Prefer cut price / Enjoy "winning" at negotiations	Price sensitivity	£7m
Share more information with partners / Develop regular dialogue	Prefer more informative competitor / Feel neglected	Lost partner allegiance	£30m
Guide customer to optimum channel / Develop models of optimum channels	Unmotivated to choose optimum channel	Choice of channel	£2m
Improve NPD testing / Improve post-launch feedback	Disinterested in new products	Too few new product adoptions	£50m
Reduce errors in claims process / Develop partner negotiation tools		Partner claims	£11m
Optimise acquisition cost drivers / Reduce duplication of effort		Customer acquisition (unchanged)	£20m

LOST REVENUE STREAMS

WASTED COSTS

£

through measurement became a way of solving its strategic implementation problems.

Finding the budget

Although it invariably takes time and money to discover the answers to some customer-oriented questions, finding the money may be a problem if you want to do research that seriously questions the status quo. Andrew Ehrenberg, professor of marketing at South Bank Business School, has recently drawn attention to this issue. He points out that it is rare for marketing to receive much, if any, of an R&D budget, so he has set up a Marketing R&D Initiative[2] to obtain funding for research that will explore some of the commonest assumptions in marketing. Areas being researched include: pricing; distribution; competition and loyalty; branding and differentiation; advertising; and sales promotions. The R&D Initiative now has over 30 large US backers (including Amex, Bristol Myers Squibb, Colgate, General Motors and Kodak) and over 60 from Europe (including Barclays, BAe, Cable & Wireless, Marks & Spencer and Shell).

Identify strategic initiatives directed to radical improvements

Most companies have many initiatives under way at a time (for example, in total quality management, satisfaction and innovation), as well as endless marketing campaigns. A new marketing measurement initiative could become lost in all this activity. It is important to choose marketing measurement projects which have an immediate impact, and which create enthusiasm and support for the initiative throughout the company.

BT, for example, has now formalised its campaign objective-setting and measurement (see Figure 8.4). Adrian Hosford, the manager responsible for the professionalisation of BT's advertising and sales promotion after privatisation, has described the campaign management and co-ordination system as one of the corporation's major successes.

Hewlett-Packard (HP) is another positive example. It has developed a sophisticated management system which effectively addresses these issues (see Figure 8.5). HP is highly measurement oriented, measuring the chain of causes that effect profitable growth, and in particular linking customer objectives and measurements to performance improvement initiatives and campaigns. According to Ian Ryder, worldwide director, brand management and communications: "We start off with the business plans, and then see whether we have the processes in place to make them work. Then those improvement projects are linked directly into the business plans, and the measurements are put around them."[3]

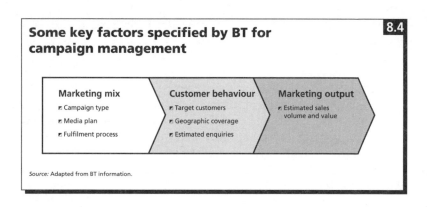

Some key factors specified by BT for campaign management　8.4

Marketing mix	Customer behaviour	Marketing output
▪ Campaign type	▪ Target customers	▪ Estimated sales volume and value
▪ Media plan	▪ Geographic coverage	
▪ Fulfilment process	▪ Estimated enquiries	

Source: Adapted from BT information.

The company aims to go even further to understand customer needs and values. "We are now looking at customers in different ways to find out different things, because if there is one standard way, you get only one viewpoint. So, customer complaints will tell you what is on their minds at the moment, but won't tell you everything. So the highest level is imagining what customers themselves haven't thought about."

Setting customer objectives for improvement initiatives and campaigns requires marketing experience. One skill that can be helpful is in setting campaign objectives. Campaigns are the natural units for marketing improvements. New campaigns need not just be about advertising or sales promotion, they can be about new products, new services, or a whole new organisation. Experienced marketing managers take this integrated marketing approach, and can mobilise a wide range of resources

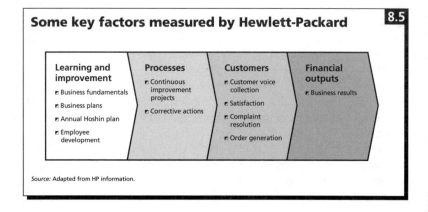

Some key factors measured by Hewlett-Packard　8.5

Learning and improvement	Processes	Customers	Financial outputs
▪ Business fundamentals	▪ Continuous improvement projects	▪ Customer voice collection	▪ Business results
▪ Business plans	▪ Corrective actions	▪ Satisfaction	
▪ Annual Hoshin plan		▪ Complaint resolution	
▪ Employee development		▪ Order generation	

Source: Adapted from HP information.

inside and outside the organisation. They also have the skill to define a precise campaign brief, including customer and financial objectives.

Campaigns is another area of improvement for HP. Much of its customer communication spending is channelled through a series of campaigns to generate sales leads, and the effectiveness of the campaign is of paramount importance. Yet judging its effectiveness is not always easy, as it involves tracking both customers and financial results. First the cost of the campaign is recorded. Then the leads it generates are tracked and the cost per lead calculated. Then the customer potential is reviewed (customers using IBM systems are known to have lower potential for HP). A win-loss analysis is conducted, taking account of customer potential and any process problems (such as late delivery of leads). Lastly, the cost wasted is calculated, and the lessons learned are fed back for future campaigns.

Many marketing managers can tell horror stories about the difficulties they have had in trying to obtain hard evidence from company systems to support their campaign or project decisions. Tracking campaigns, new products and strategic initiatives is generally fraught with difficulties. The problem is exacerbated by the constraints imposed by the periodic reporting systems used for budgetary control. Yet these managers' practical experience of the measurement problems can provide valuable awareness of which areas would be the most effective candidates for new marketing measurement projects.

Choosing a balanced team

It is important to get the right balance between specialists and generalists on the team responsible for auditing and reviewing marketing performance. This will help secure commitment from a cross-section of functions and from people at a sufficiently senior level.

Studies of power struggles in businesses[4] show that the most common focus for friction is those departments of a company which are most involved with customers, such as marketing and sales. According to extensive research on management politics, these departments are twice as likely to be involved in political infighting as manufacturing, human resources or accounting. Sometimes interdepartmental strife is so extreme that it is hard to believe they are part of the same company.

Conflicting departmental objectives, as illustrated in Table 8.1, are often unrecognised in large organisations and waste huge amounts of management time, with hours spent in endless rounds of interdepartmental committees and the like.

In the case of the telecoms company discussed above, the cross-func-

Table 8.1 **Conflict in the objectives in a typical organisation**

Department	Wants	Which causes	To be less good at
Marketing	Customers to receive personalised service	Operations	Containing costs by spending less time with customer
Finance	Pricing to cover short-term costs	Sales	Negotiating to secure long-term customer loyalty
Credit control	Credit limits to reflect financial risk criteria	Sales	Winning business from long-term prospects
Computing	Databases to be shared across departments	All other departments	Reducing their overheads
Manufacturing	Standard product features	Product development	Creating a competitive product range
Purchasing	Lowest cost bids	Manufacturing	Quality control, failure and defect reduction
Sales	Enquiries to be qualified by whoever takes the message	Operations	Reducing cost of telephone time and effort
Advertising	Long-term budgets to support brand	All other departments	Obtaining funding for other valid investments
Operations	Standardised service to meet BS5750	Marketing	Offering differentiated service levels to various market segments

Source: Robert Shaw, *Journal of Marketing Practice*, Vol. 2, No. 3, 1996.

- Marketing often wants low pricing to develop loyalty, easy credit terms, easy collection procedures and confidentiality. Finance typically wants pricing to cover costs, tough credit terms, tough collection procedures and full credit disclosure.
- Manufacturing often wants standard orders, ease of fabrication and long production lead time. Marketing wants bespoke orders, aesthetic appearance and short lead time.
- Logistics often wants standard distribution route, bulk delivery, full trucks, cheap labour. Marketing wants convenient delivery time, split delivery, fast delivery and good service.

tional debate ended with the recognition that measurements based on shared resources were needed. Customer database development, and satisfaction and branding research received support from the whole organisation. This support was based on common agreed customer objectives.

However, there was a major power struggle between the sales and marketing department and the operations department. The latter had 600 staff who answered 3m customer calls per year. They operated on behalf of four strategic business units, covering large, medium and small businesses and domestic customers. Their costs were considered to be high when compared with other benchmarked utilities. After the operations director in charge of the department had agreed to the £500m Strategic Intent profit growth target, a series of excuses were made for avoiding co-operative ventures with marketing.

Better performance management at the telecoms company had the potential to cause major disruption to the status quo. It required many changes to existing practices and processes: adding codes to the existing ledgers and operational systems to identify customers and products (as well as accounts and stock-keeping units); summarising the customer transactions in multiple directions; extracting the customer and product data; storing them on a database; adding extra codes to facilitate segmentation analysis; obtaining software tools to analyse and report on databases. In the past there had been no attempt to bring together marketing and operations. The CEO had let both groups work to their own departmental agendas. Getting these groups together at the workshops and defining the customer problems, the process causes and financial effects (see Figure 8.3) were crucial to breaking this deadlock.

Framing the discussions around the topic of "customer problems" was helpful. It allowed the two groups to discover a great deal of common ground. Previously, discussions had focused on processes and degenerated into an unproductive tug-of-war between marketing and operations.

Ordering the discussions, first of customers, then processes and lastly finance, helped overcome the many barriers to change. These included the expectations of: sales management (who "own" call reports and account plans); marketing managers (who "own" market research and analysis); operational management (who "own" order-processing, service, warranty and other records); financial management (who "own" the sales ledger records); and computer staff (who "own" the hardware, software and networks). The logic of what needed to be done helped overcome their reticence to co-operate.

Risk management

Implementing a new marketing measurement system is clearly a risky business. HP has a detailed system for containing such risk which is worth reviewing (see Figure 8.6). For new products the project is screened through a series of "gates". At each gate it is assessed for viability before it is allowed through to the next. Measures involving organisation, customers and financial factors are assessed at each stage. HP's original approach was based on the NewProd methodology developed by Robert

Cooper and described in his book *Winning at New Products*.[5] More recently, HP has streamlined this procedure to speed it up, without making the process more risk prone. For example, new inkjet printers were developed in 22 months, compared with four years previously.[6]

The balanced scorecard as a strategic management system

In many organisations there is growing recognition of the need for greater balance between different financial and non-financial objectives. Kaplan and Norton's balanced scorecard[7] is a strategic tool which aims to revolutionise the measurement of corporate performance. So far it has been adopted by over 50% of major corporations, according to the author's MSAT research.

The balanced scorecard is a positive approach for the future of marketing, since it helps both companies and financial markets to look beyond past financial results towards measuring future potential, in particular customer issues. Figure 8.7 (page 134) shows the balanced scorecard in a cause-and-effect layout, rather than in the more common diamond shape. Organisations use scorecards as a management system, not just a measurement method. The scorecard framework provides not only rearview and sideview mirrors, but also headlights to illuminate future strategy.

HP's philosophy, The HP Way, stresses the importance of many stakeholders in a business, so it may seem unsurprising that HP uses the balanced scorecard. It has been doing so for almost a decade, far in advance of most organisations, and so can probably be credited with partly inventing the idea. HP uses scorecards at both the business and the individual level. For example, a sales manager would probably be measured on sales, and a marketing manager on the conversion rate of opportunities into orders. "While in practice these measures are not handed down from on high, if they weren't on the scorecards questions would probably be asked," says Ian Ryder. The emphasis is on individual generation of ideas, however, with people putting on their scorecards the measures they feel are important to their performance, although a manager might make suggestions.

Ryder comments: "We learned quickly that measurements like that generally don't cascade through the business but end up just replacing financial accountability measures. They are then not a self-assessment tool which shows how well someone is doing in their job. We even invested in an IT system to try and do the cascading, but we quickly learned the hard way that measurement is all about what people believe

New product risk management stages in NewProd   8.6

STAGE	PROCESS	CUSTOMER	FINANCIAL
1. Predevelopment financial analysis	Process plans and activity estimates	Market share estimates	Formal economic criteria
2. Preliminary market assessment		Direct contact with potential customers	
3. Preliminary technical assessment	Engineering and process concepts		
4. Detailed market study		Customer needs, competition, prices, market size	
5. Predevelopment financial analysis			Revised financial analysis
6. Product development	Process layouts		
7. In-house product testing	Product prototypes		
8. Customer tests of product		Blind tests, focus groups, trials	
9. Trial sell		Market test data	
10. Trial production	Revised prototypes		
11. Pre-launch analysis	Revised process layouts	Revised market figures	Revised financial analysis
12. Production start-up	Full production		
13. Market launch		Customer data	Campaign tracking data

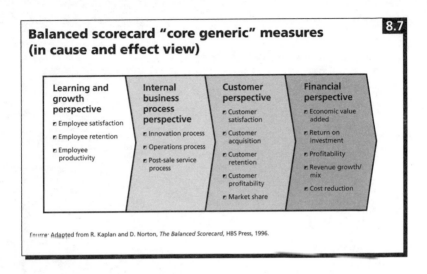

Balanced scorecard "core generic" measures (in cause and effect view) `8.7`

Learning and growth perspective	Internal business process perspective	Customer perspective	Financial perspective
◪ Employee satisfaction	◪ Innovation process	◪ Customer satisfaction	◪ Economic value added
◪ Employee retention	◪ Operations process	◪ Customer acquisition	◪ Return on investment
◪ Employee productivity	◪ Post-sale service process	◪ Customer retention	◪ Profitability
		◪ Customer profitability	◪ Revenue growth/ mix
		◪ Market share	◪ Cost reduction

Source: Adapted from R. Kaplan and D. Norton, *The Balanced Scorecard*, HBS Press, 1996.

they are measuring in themselves. Measurement is owned by the people." So every scorecard in the organisation will be different.

HP's experience highlights the benefits of scorecards as well as the dangers of inexperienced managers choosing generic measures, such as customer satisfaction. A director of one of the world's largest logistics organisations told the author that she and other directors debated for hours what should be the chosen customer measures to put on their balanced scorecard. After several fruitless hours one of the directors suggested that they look at what standard measures were suggested in Kaplan and Norton's book, and so they reached agreement.

Kaplan and Norton defend their use of generic measures as follows:

- ◪ "The core measurement group of customer outcomes is generic across all kinds of organisations.[8]
- ◪ Customer retention and customer acquisition are driven by meeting customers' needs. Customer satisfaction provides feedback on how well the company is doing.[9]
- ◪ Only when customers rate their buying experience as completely or extremely satisfied can a company count on their repeat purchasing behaviour.[10]
- ◪ Market share is straightforward once the targeted customer group or market segment has been specified. Industry groups, trade associations, government statistics, and other public data sources

can often provide estimates of total market size."[11]

One of the key messages of this book is that measures must be tailored carefully to fit the business context, and it is therefore wise to look beyond the generic Kaplan and Norton measures. Part 3 makes some suggestions about where to look.

Feedback and strategic learning

Successful marketing requires a strong commitment to feedback and strategic learning. Marketing knowledge is really no better than a set of plausible hypotheses about cause and effect. Improvement requires a strong commitment to hypothesis testing. Do not underestimate the need for diagnostic measurement and detective work in the quest for learning. Skills in these areas are scarce resources, and it can pay to centralise and integrate market research and information systems under the control of one experienced knowledge manager.

Boehringer-Ingelheim is a pharmaceuticals company manufacturing, distributing and marketing a range of medicines. It specialises in respiratory products, but it is diversifying into new areas (such as antirheumatic) as well as bringing out new respiratory products. Boehringer considers feedback and strategic learning to be critical. The company successfully combined market research, customer-process feedback and performance management information under one team.

Zinta Krumins, head of business information and support, says: "If you look at the quality of representatives employed by the pharmaceuticals industry, the majority are perfectly able to understand the information, provided they receive appropriate training. Of course, training is essential; the representative needs to become, in effect, the business manager of their own little area, and they need strategies and analysis techniques. You do need to provide analysis facilities centrally, because the representatives are there to talk to people about the products, rather than to be analysts. But most representatives are intellectually quite capable of doing the analysis for themselves."

HP, too, provides support for learning. It has hired a team of roving consultants to help managers diagnose the more difficult problems. The consultants work wherever necessary, some focusing on strategic planning, some on customers and others on the underlying processes. The objective is to try and make the consultants act more as *agents provocateurs*, standing slightly apart from the business where they are working and challenging existing practices in the push for more improvements.

Summary: translating strategy into action

Managers in a variety of industries that the author has studied have attempted to improve their marketing performance management. Not all the experiences have been successful, and several commented that the "customer performance stuff" is not as easy as they had expected.

Success requires a deep understanding of how to satisfy customer needs profitably, at both the strategic and the tactical level. This is where marketing managers' skills urgently need to be applied. Yet it is also a big challenge which some marketers seem unwilling to accept.

Some marketing managers prefer the firefighting and excitement of the latest campaigns instead of the hard, sometimes boring, strategic teamwork. A few are genuinely puzzled by some of the figures and mathematics. As David Norton, who developed the balanced scorecard, commented: "I have worked in over 100 organisations and I would say in maybe 70% or so you will find they have an inadequate understanding of the customer ... Interestingly, my phone doesn't ring much from marketing people."

PART 3

MARKETING TOOLS

9 Tools and ground rules

THE previous chapters have explained how useful, even crucial, marketing tools are in understanding what is really happening in the marketplace. Part 3 of this book lists 20 of the more important techniques and briefly explains their application, as well as a few pitfalls in using them. The choice of techniques was driven by the five key issues in Chapters 2–6: quality; customer satisfaction and loyalty; innovation; value; and information technology (see Figure 9.1). But before you look at the measures, here are some useful ground rules.

Establish the business need

Using the wrong measures for the business will result in unnecessary labour, wasted money and missed opportunities. The business need for some organisations is growth, whereas for others it is to defend their existing market dominance. Different business needs will result in the use of different measures. In order to make intelligent decisions about which measurement tools to use, managers must first develop a full understanding of their company's problems and its priorities.

Ensure the tools are relevant

Existing tools may once have supported important decisions, but the business context may have changed while the measurements continue to be used. For example, environmental scanning may have been important when regulatory changes were imminent, but maintaining such expensive research on a permanent basis may be wasting budgets which should be applied to more pressing issues.

Choose the best tools for the job

Managers must remain impartial and unbiased when selecting, implementing and integrating measures. Tools must produce results and should be used only if:

- they genuinely support the decisions that managers take;
- the information they may generate is not already freely available;
- their use does not take so much time and effort as to be counterproductive;
- the information they generate will be accepted by everyone;

Marketing tools for measuring key boardroom issues

9.1

STRATEGIC BOARDROOM ISSUES

VALUE
- Brand valuation
- Marketing mix productivity
- Corporate marketing support
- Marketing waste

QUALITY
- Price premium
- Quality (perceived and actual)
- Brand image endorsement
- Marketing waste

INNOVATION
- Trial purchase
- Awareness
- Involvement
- Brand image endorsement
- Innovation benchmark
- Competitive threat map
- Category potential map
- Marketing waste

CUSTOMER SATISFACTION AND LOYALTY
- Repeat purchase
- Complaints
- Satisfaction
- Involvement
- Brand image endorsement
- Market leadership
- Distribution leadership
- Competitive threat map
- Category health map
- Marketing waste

INFORMATION TECHNOLOGY
- Repeat purchase
- Satisfaction
- Involvement
- Innovation benchmark
- Competitive threat map
- Marketing waste

◪ there are not cheaper and easier ways of measuring the same
thing.

Commit the resources needed

Lukewarm effort is likely to produce half-baked results. More significantly, lack of commitment carries the danger of producing results that
may hinder success or even cause harm, which will undermine the case
for measurements. Organisations must demonstrate their commitment
and, if using new measures, will need to be resilient. There will often be
obstacles and it is common for measures to need to go through a debug-
ging period.

Look long term

Measurement tools are not a quick fix. A long-term perspective is necessary to deliver continuity and consistency. It also helps to gauge how
much further there is to go. The KMAT™ assessment tool and the four-step
plan (see Chapter 7) can help with getting the perspective right, as can
experience of implementing other measurements.

Link cause and effect

Each tool is part of a bigger toolkit. It is important to avoid a narrow perspective when working out the causes and effects of customer behaviour.
The five perspectives framework in Chapter 7 can help in ensuring a balanced choice of measures.

CATEGORY HEALTH

Focus on: Marketing environment
Measures: Category size (volume and revenue)
    Category surplus (profitability after channels have taken their share)
    Consumer needs and wants for category
    Trade customer power indicators
Presented as: Scorecard of key indicators
Yardstick: Category health for all competitors, averaged across all participants, not just your own firm
Significance: Failing category health indicates the need for a strategic review and possibly for exit
Released: Annual or periodic audit

Description and methodology

A category is the set of products or services judged to be substitutes or alternatives in satisfying certain needs and wants by the users for whom such needs and wants are relevant. This definition is customer oriented, in that customer needs and wants have primacy. It is also called a need market.

Category health is a scorecard of indicators, which collectively show whether all competing suppliers serving a category are doing well or badly. If your brand is the best brand of muffin, but the muffin category is stagnant or, worse, declining in total volume and profits, then the real value of your muffin brand is likely to be declining too.

Common uses and interpretations

Strategists often ask the question: "What category should we invest in?" They are generally looking for large categories, fast growth and high profitability. The search for attractive categories was at the heart of the portfolio approach to strategic planning, which was a dominant theme a decade ago and still has considerable influence on corporate behaviour. Marketers ask similar questions, usually: "What category position should we invest in?" They too cite size, growth and margin as primary health indicators.

Causes and theory

Category health should be mapped across all the positions within the category – upmarket, downmarket, and so on. The two commonest dimensions to map are perceived quality and perceived price. Other

dimensions such as specific product features or benefits may be important in positioning. The key dimensions of the category exist in customers' minds. Mapping customers' minds may sound futuristic and the
maths a bit advanced, but the concept is straightforward.

It is sensible to split a category into sectors, based on customer
descriptions (plain and milk chocolate) or their values (upmarket or
downmarket). You may analyse the health of a category or a sector, each
in exactly the same way. Some analysts map the category according to
descriptive or value dimensions, and plot the movement of customer
sales and revenue across the map (eg, moving upmarket) to support their
strategic decisions.

Problems and cautions

Category definition is fraught with problems, and it is essential to draw
the boundaries of the category effectively. A common problem is to
ignore the customer needs and wants and to focus on the technical features of the products and services, or on the industry boundaries. For
example, to cross the English Channel, P&O Ferries and the Eurostar train
serve the same category (of need), but they are in very different industries,
whereas a local UK operator, such as South West Trains, and Eurostar are
in the same industry, but their customers have very different needs. The
ultimate definition of a category is a management judgment, taking into
consideration research evidence on customer needs and wants, what
products and services are alternatives or substitutes, and what significant
strategic decisions are on the table.

It seems obvious that size, growth or margin should make categories
such as software or financial services more attractive than, for example,
categories such as coal or tobacco (although tobacco sectors outside the
United States and Europe remain attractive). Yet the very obviousness of
their health is a problem, for they are superficially attractive to everyone.
Perceiving the attractiveness of personal computing and financial services, many firms have entered these categories, and this reduces category
profitability as quickly as entry can occur. The biggest money losers are
often firms with no relevant competitive advantage, which see the appeal
of a growing market. Observe Exxon's losses in personal computing or
B.A.T's in insurance. Observe also how some conglomerates have built
highly successful businesses by targeting acquisitions in categories which
other firms saw as objectively unattractive.

Profit Impact of Market Strategy (PIMS analysis shows only a minimal
link between market growth and return on investment. Market profit-

ability has strong cyclical elements, and it is common for there to be good or bad years for all participants in the same market. Once these cyclical effects are removed, little of the difference in profitability is explained by what market they are in. Studies of US Federal Trade Commission (FTC) line of business data show that the main drivers of profitability are specific to the business unit, the market effect is minor, and the impact of corporate brand is minuscule.

It does not follow that a firm should enter an attractive category; the issue is how much of that attractiveness, or lack of it, is already discounted. The efficiency of markets ensures that market selection is not a basis for competitive advantage, except when it provides a means of exploiting a distinctive capability which is specific to a particular firm.

The same distinction must follow for market positioning. PIMS analysis shows that high returns are associated with high-quality positions within a category. These are not returns related to market position as such. For if one position were more profitable than another, and equally attainable, then others would adopt it and the profitability would be diluted.

The high returns from quality positions reward the underlying competitive advantage, which allows only a few firms to attain high relative quality. For these firms, the competitive advantage is best exploited in a high-quality position. It does not follow that the same position would produce the same returns for other firms. The success of Mercedes does not mean that it would be possible or sensible to recommend the same market position for Honda. Each firm should select a market position which reflects its quite different sources of competitive advantage.

The confusion between category health and competitive advantage is a particularly common management error. The Next group provides a chastening example. Next successfully identified an underdeveloped market for fashion apparel of moderate quality for women and men aged 20–35. Its sales and profits grew rapidly. Mistakenly believing that its good fortune rested not on an attractive market but on its internal processes, it diversified into mail order, interior design and financial services, with marked lack of success. At the same time, established retailers with real process strengths invaded its market and brought Next to the verge of collapse. (It has since focused on its core business and recovered.)

Category health is important, but simply choosing healthy categories is not sufficient for sustaining competitive advantage. Those who enter a market first occasionally sustain advantage in new markets, but most new markets can be entered and if profitable they will be entered by others, and profits will be diluted. For this reason tracking indicators of competitor-power, consumer-power and trade-customer-power, alongside category size, growth and margin should be used.

Related topics

Category potential is another indicator to watch, alongside category health. If category health is good, and category potential is high or rising, then the category is likely to be attractive for investment. Competitive threats are also useful indicators for strategists to watch.

Selected references

Category or product-market definition is discussed in a paper by Day, Shocker and Srivastava. Baden-Fuller and Stopford look at creative approaches to reappraising mature categories. Market attractiveness was originally studied by strategic planners, especially the portfolio planners. For an up-to-date critical assessment, Kay presents an excellent review, especially in Chapters 9 and 11. Buzzell and Gale review the PIMS evidence, and Rumelt analyses the FTC evidence. The track record of late entrants to a category is reviewed by Schnaars.

G.S. Day, A.D. Shocker and R.K. Srivastava, "Customer oriented approaches to identifying product-markets", *Journal of Marketing*, Fall 1979.

C. Baden-Fuller and J.M. Stopford, *Rejuvenating the Mature Business*, Routledge, 1992.

J. Kay, *Foundations of Corporate Success*, Oxford, 1993.

R.D. Buzzell and B.T. Gale, The PIMS Principles, Free Press, 1987.

R.P. Rumelt, "How much does industry matter?", *Strategic Management Journal*, 12/3 March 1991, pp. 167–86.

S.P. Schnaars, *Managing Imitation Strategies*, Free Press, 1994.

CATEGORY POTENTIAL

Focus on: Marketing environment

Measures: Category health forecast (size, growth, margin)

Category penetration in potential market (including geodemographic segments of global category; fragmentation, concentration)

Forecasting assumption tracking (defining assumptions that go into forecasts and tracking them)

Life cycle stage (product/process technology; standardisation, commoditisation, customisation; frequency of product changes)

Innovation record of category suppliers

Presented as: Scorecard of key forecasts

Yardstick: Category forecast for all competitors, averaged across all participants, not just your own firm

Significance: Growing category potential indicates the need for a strategic review and possibly for investment

Released: Annual or periodic audit

Description and methodology

Category potential is a scorecard of indicators of future category health, which can help forecast whether participants in a category will do well or badly in the future. If your brand is the best mainframe computer, and the mainframe category is large, profitable and steadily growing, but the future potential for mainframe computers is poor, then the future value of your mainframe brand is likely to decline.

Common uses and interpretations

Strategists are interested in the question: "What category should we invest in for the future?" Because significant investment in technology is likely to be involved, it is common for strategists to become particularly interested in technology forecasting. Marketers are also interested in future positioning, often in response to weakening of current positioning.

Causes and theory

Forecasting generally works first by extrapolating past trends in category health, and second by adjusting trends to take into account other underlying factors, usually by building forecasting models. Choosing which underlying factors to take into account is an important but difficult process. The choice of models is dictated by expert opinion, and often there will be broad consensus among a group of experts on the choice of factors driving the trends. Judgmental forecasts based on the wisdom of experience are also used extensively in some industries, where formal models are eschewed. These are common in categories where change is especially rapid.

Problems and cautions

Many categories seem to be changing at breakneck speed, and this makes many strategists nervous of using customer research as a basis for future category assessment. Instead, they often keep track of the rapid switching changes in functions and features of competing and emerging products and technologies.

When monitoring trends be sceptical about headlines such as "Nobody smokes any more" or "Nobody eats white bread any more". Such attention grabbing is aimed primarily at selling more newspapers or promoting the forecaster's business. Forecasters also generally focus too narrowly on their own category and forget environmental factors that may affect customers.

Beware too of short-term waves, which can obscure your view of long-term tidal flows. Long-term trends involve millions of people and their habits, and they happen extremely slowly. People do not all wake in the middle of the night and stop smoking or stop eating white bread. A few do change and their "new product adoption" behaviour is worth tracking, but it must be kept in perspective.

How can you tell the difference between a fad and a trend? Trends usually have to be observed for a decade or more. They should involve how consumers perceive the category, not the technologists' view of what is changing and what is constant. Often the underlying customer needs remain constant even though the technology keeps switching – in this case watch out for the early adopters. But at other times the customer needs change before the category does – in this case tracking of lifestyles and customer behaviour can provide important clues about unmet needs and wants, which will influence the category potential.

Related topics

Category potential by its very nature is not closely related to other topics, except in so far as trend extrapolation is concerned. New business growth, pre-purchase behaviour (eg, enquiries) and post-purchase behaviour (eg, complaints) will sometimes provide further clues about potential.

Selected references

The references given for category health are relevant. There is also extensive literature on forecasting. One of the best studies of forecasting was carried out by Ascher in 1978. A more up-to-date and less technical account has recently been given by Sherden.

W. Ascher, Forecasting: An appraisal for policy makers and planners, John Hopkins University Press, 1978.

W.A. Sherden, The Fortune Sellers: the big business of buying and selling predictions, Wiley, 1998.

COMPETITIVE THREATS

Focus on:	Marketing environment
Measures:	Competitive concentration (eg, joint ventures, coalitions, partnerships)
	Market share forecasts for substitute categories
	Entry barrier size (and underlying factors)
	Financial strength of new entrants
	Total market share of recent entrants
	Exit rate of competitors
Presented as:	Scorecard of key indicators
Yardstick:	Relevant case examples of threats; experience
Significance:	Competitive factors that may be overlooked when routinely monitoring existing competition
Released:	Annual audit and continuous monitoring by the press office

Description and methodology

Competitive threat is a scorecard of indicators, which can help forecast whether competitive advantage in a category is likely to change. Ideally, a scorecard is developed which allows relative competitive advantage in different categories to be compared as a basis for strategic investment allocation across the categories.

Common uses and interpretations

Competitive problems arise from two main sources. First, as an extrapolation of past trends in existing competition. These problems can largely be seen from trends in indicators such as market leadership, brand preference and other indicators, which are included elsewhere in this part of the book. Second, from competitive threats from extended rivalry, which need special attention. These threats are the subject of this section.

Causes and theory

Competitive threats have come to be much better understood as a result of the work of Michael Porter on the competitive structure of industries. One threat is industry restructuring, in particular concentration of competition and creation of power-brands by mergers, acquisitions, joint ventures, coalitions and partnerships. These co-operative developments can be overlooked by those focused on the trends in the individual competitor indicators. Monitoring of structural changes can be important to strategists, in particular mergers and joint ventures, mergers which transform technology possibilities, changes in distribution channels, and application of new technology by industry outsiders.

A number of retail firms have entered financial services through joint-venture and partnership arrangements. Such developments can remain unregistered in more traditional measurement systems until the threats have become a reality.

Competition through the creation of substitute categories may be overlooked in the analysis of competitive health or potential. Substitutes that deserve most attention are those that improve price-quality-value, or are produced by industries earning higher profits (and therefore attract more intense investment).

In the UK First Direct and Direct Line are banking and insurance examples of the creation of substitute categories. At first they were so small that they did not appear on more conventional measurement studies. However, because their growth was rapid and their visibility high, they are now widely recognised as competitive threats. Toyota entered house-building through its automobile manufacturing technology.

When monitoring new entrants a number of factors need to be assessed. New entrants' motivation may be different from that of existing entrants, and it may affect their positioning. For example, foreign competition may offer lower prices, as a result of different financial strategies from those of the existing competition. The financial strength of new entrants may also be so large that they can afford to wage war in a way that existing competitors cannot.

Problems and cautions

Competitive environment monitoring can become a complex and costly exercise. Yet much of the information needed can be collected by judicious reading of the press. There are strong arguments in favour of having a periodic audit, say annually, of these competitive threats, but otherwise leaving the job to a diligent press office. A great deal depends on the speed of change in the industry.

One reason for formalising the monitoring of competitive threats is that otherwise they may be excluded from the formal measurement system, which often concentrates on the top three or five competitors, but overlooks the smaller but deadlier competitors. It is also important to co-ordinate competitor analysis across departments, so that all important views are taken into account.

Microsoft was late in responding to Netscape because it monitored its larger competitors such as Lotus, Novell and Oracle and did not bother with Netscape at first, because its strategic importance as a competitor was not registered and its size was too small to warrant attention.

Related topics

In deciding upon the best response to competitive threats (eg, invest to grow, harvest past investment, divest or exit) management should take into account category health and potential as well as threats. There is often a tendency just to react to threats, rather than to assess them in the context of category health and potential.

Selected references

The classic work on competitive threats is still Porter. Kay also provides important insights.

J. Kay, *Foundations of Corporate Success*, Oxford, 1993.
M. Porter, *Competitive Strategy*, Free Press, 1980.

MARKET LEADERSHIP

Focus on: Outputs of marketing activity

Measures: Volume share (by category, category sector)

                Value share

                Range share (broad or narrow)

                Penetration (including customer concentration – reliance on few customers)

Presented as: Percentage of market occupied by brand or product

Yardstick: Ranking of your share or penetration against competition

Significance: High share is an indicator of competitive strength

Released: Monthly in fast-moving consumer goods markets, less regularly in other markets

Description and methodology

Market leadership is measured by using one or more indicators, such as relative market share (either unit volume or value), relative purchase penetration (purchase penetration being the percentage of potential purchasers in a population who have purchased your brand at least once in this period), or relative ownership penetration (ownership penetration being the percentage of potential owners who own your brand). From these indicators the relative ranking of your brand can be calculated.

Common uses and interpretations

Market leadership is the indicator managers use to track competitive strength, and it is a premium factor driving management's expectations about profitability and shareholder value. The idea of market leadership is familiar and widely quoted, but it is not necessarily an accurate indicator. It is used to assess customers' preference for your brand rather than competing brands. Market leadership is often achieved by having a large number of brands and brand extensions within one category. For example, Procter & Gamble and Lever Brothers have over decades played a competitive game of maximising aggregate market share of the household detergent category through adding, subtracting and repositioning new brands and brand extensions.

Causes and theory

Competitive advantage is often linked with market leadership. However, it is not linked with the aggregate market leadership. Instead, the link is with single-brand leadership. Individual brands that lead a category have a marketing advantage. The key variable seems to be their high penetration, that is, the high proportion of potential buyers who buy the brand. Leading brands are bought by more people, and those who buy them are also more loyal, that is, they buy more of the brand. This effect of this on non-leading brands is known as double jeopardy, the theory of which is as follows.

Suppose there are two brands, A and B, exactly equal in function, quality, price, and so on, but A is known to many consumers and B to only a few. If people are asked which of A or B is their favourite, nearly all of those who know brand A will say "A", because few of them (like people in general) have heard of B. In contrast, of the few who do know brand B, most also know brand A (as most people do). Since A and B are of equal merit they have to split their votes, with only some of them saying B is their favourite and others saying A, or "don't know", or "can't decide". Of the few who know B, fewer than for A can call it their favourite. So the challenge for the less popular brand is not only to equal the quality of its better known competitor, but also to make itself more widely accepted.

The other issue with aggregate market leadership is the cost of fragmentation. Where a leadership position is accumulated from several smaller, non-leading brands, there are likely to be diseconomies of scale associated with smaller brands.

Problems and cautions

Market share and leadership can fluctuate in the short term for many insignificant reasons, such as pipeline (getting goods to market) and discounts. The assumption that company performance should be judged against the average performance of all companies is not always valid. If you make a mistake in category definition and ignore brands which have an effect on yours, or include brands whose progress is irrelevant to yours, you can be led to make unfortunate errors.

A decline in market share may not be bad. Sometimes a company deliberately loses share in order to drop unprofitable product lines or bad customers. Where there are many varieties in the category, looking at range share may also be helpful. Where there are one or two dominant customers, concentrating on a few customers can also be revealing.

Selected references

Market leadership has been studied by strategic planners for almost half a century. Early studies tried to justify leadership on the basis of economies of scale. Buzzell and Gale give a good summary of this work, as well as some pragmatic analysis of the PIMS database. Double jeopardy was first described by McPhee in the 1960s, as a result of studies of TV viewing. It was later extensively researched by Ehrenberg from the 1960s to the present day. The cost of fragmented brands and product lines has recently received careful attention from management accountants, under the guise of activity-based costing. Kaplan and Cooper give a comprehensive account of this difficult subject.

R.D. Buzzell and B. T. Gale, *The PIMS Principles*, Free Press, 1987.
A. Ehrenberg, *Repeat Buying*, Griffin Oxford, 1988.
R. Kaplan and R. Cooper, *Cost and Effect*, HBS Press, 1998.

DISTRIBUTION LEADERSHIP

Focus on: Outputs of channel-marketing activity
Inputs to consumer marketing

Measures: Coverage (geographic and demographic)
Range listings (quality of distribution)
In-stock and out-of-stock maintenance
Display quality
Share of market surplus
Percentage of sales through retail own brand and private label

Presented as: Percentage of distribution outlets occupied by brand or product

Yardstick: Ranking of your share of distribution against competition; trends

Significance: Distribution leadership indicates channel preference

Released: Weekly, monthly or quarterly

Description and methodology

Distribution leadership is measured by using one or more indicators, such as distribution coverage (eg, listings by channel type, geography); range (eg, percentage of product lines listed); in-stock maintenance (eg, percentage of lines in stock at channel outlets); display quality (eg, shelf facings and location, special displays and promotions). Calculating these can require complex calculations involving weighting the data by channel type and volume. From these indicators the relative ranking of your brand can be calculated. For example, Colgate has enjoyed distribution leadership in the oral hygiene category. Brands that have such leadership are sometimes referred to as the category captain, and they can significantly influence retailers' merchandising and range management.

The methods used to gather these data usually involve a regular channel audit (weekly, monthly or quarterly) at a representative sample of channel outlets. In the case of listings, they also involve feedback from the key account managers and field salesforce.

Another important type of distribution measure is the share of market surplus. This indicates the split of gross profit between the channel and the supplier. Useful indicators are percentage of sales on promotion and distributor margin. Even consumer market leaders can have a low share of surplus because of the power of the channel.

Common uses and interpretations

Distribution leadership is a factor that managers use to assess competitive strength. In the case of commodity products, where consumer preference is weak, distribution leadership may be the leading indicator.

As the trend in retailing continues towards reducing the range of suppliers, and as efficient consumer response becomes a driving force in channel management, so the importance of distribution leadership is likely to continue. Small changes in reported distribution leadership may provide early indicators of worsening channel relationships.

Causes and theory

Channel management has recently received a great deal of attention from consultants. As a result of findings from financial reviews and activity-based costing studies, channel managers have begun to reduce the number of suppliers with whom they deal. This has been accompanied by greater financial acumen in the purchasing process.

Computerisation of the supply chain has greatly increased management information, particularly on the channel side. Suppliers sometimes benefit from this channel-generated information, but often they have to provide their own data through channel audits. Efficient consumer response is the buzz phrase used to tighten supplier-channel relationships using IT. The theoretical aim is improving consumer satisfaction, but often the technology is used more tactically for cost-cutting and increasing channel power.

Suppliers have developed their own capabilities through key account management (KAM). Greater financial and strategic acumen has been required of key account managers to deal with the increasing purchasing sophistication of channels. Measurement plays an important part in this process.

Problems and cautions

Distribution leadership often fluctuates in the short term for reasons which may, or may not, be significant. Data collection and sampling problems can introduce spurious changes in the data, but there may be significant supply chain problems. It is therefore important to be vigilant in this area, but be prepared for a significant number of false alarms.

Data problems typically result from inaccuracies and incompleteness. Systematic errors can occur, especially if the data are collected by sales staff, whose own performance is being judged using the data. It is often practical to audit only a sample of channel outlets, so the sample should be updated from time to time to reflect changes in channel composition.

It is important to compare coverage and other physical distribution measures with financial ones, such as sales on promotion. In some cases, there may be a high cost attached to good physical coverage, in terms of high discounts and promotions. It is also important to compare general listings with range and actual distribution. Channels often make agreements with key account managers and field sales representatives which need to be policed. Channels can be highly creative in the way they exploit listing agreements to their own advantage. As well as looking strategically at distribution leadership, it is also important to be constantly vigilant for tactical issues (ie, details of each individual delivery). Distribution is an area where physical supply chain problems can be extremely damaging. The distribution indicators often provide the first signs of these types of problems.

Related topics

Channel relationship indicators (such as channel satisfaction) may help in diagnosing changes in distribution leadership.

Selected references

Distribution leadership has received limited attention. The main emphasis in the literature is on physical distribution. Most of the major consultancies, including Coopers & Lybrand and McKinsey, have published reports on this subject, but few provide a detailed account of the measurements needed.

PRICE PREMIUM

Focus on: Outputs of marketing activity
Measures: Price of a basket of goods and services relative to competition
Perceived price
Presented as: Financial premium and/or percentage
Yardstick: Prices of similar items from a representative cross-section of competitors
Significance: A long-term premium price indicates a valuable brand
Released: Weekly or monthly

Description and methodology

Price premiums measure the price of a basket of goods and services purchased at a point in time relative to similar items from a representative cross-section of competitors. In a market with many competitors, the choice and weighting of which competitors and which competing items to include is important. The basket's composition and weighting should reflect the major items with which you compete. Some indices cover only flagship items; others cover a wide range of items weighted according to sales volume. Weights are updated periodically to reflect the changing position of competitors. Prices can also vary significantly by sales channel, and the measures must then be weighted according to channel volume.

Common uses and interpretations

Price premium is the indicator most managers use to track added value, and it is an important factor driving management's expectations about profitability and shareholder value. The idea of premium price is familiar and widely quoted, but it is not necessarily an accurate indicator. It is used to assess customers' willingness to pay more for your offerings than for competing offerings.

Causes and theory

Premium prices may be accepted by customers if they perceive high quality in the product or service. Conversely, price may also act as an indicator of to quality, along with other indicators.

Premium price may deter purchase more strongly when it is above a reference price. Reference prices differ between categories, channels and individual consumers.

Price should not be regarded as self-evident. Customer perceptions are important in determining their responses to prices. Method of displaying price, and comparison price display, can have a significant effect. Also a large proportion of purchasers may be unaware of the prices of the goods they buy.

Price changes are difficult to understand as upward movements may cause customer responses that are different from responses to the equivalent downward movements. Promotional offers complicate customers' perceptions of prices. Measures need to show price premiums both exclusive and inclusive of any promotions.

Customers have become more knowledgeable about a wider range of items and, as markets have moved to overcapacity, price premiums have become more difficult to sustain. Also, with low inflation, consumers have become more critical of price increases. Low-price substitutes, such as retail own brands and direct selling brands, are now regularly challenging brand leaders.

Problems and cautions
By poor selection of the competitors, items or weightings, the price premium can give a misleading view of the competitive advantage. For example, Compaq used IBM as its main frame of reference at a time when Dell and Gateway were making major inroads into the PC market at much lower prices. Hence Compaq's premium price over time became a problem which was overlooked as a result of poor measurement.

Related topics
Perceived quality and perceived value are two other indicators to watch alongside price premium. If perceived quality and value are rising at the same time as price premium, this is a cause for celebration. However, if price premium is rising but quality or value are steady or falling there may be problems. For example, in the late 1990s Compaq's perceived quality and value did not support its premium price. So the company reduced its price premium to bring it more into line with Dell and Gateway, which offered comparable quality at a lower price.

Selected references
Pricing was originally studied by economists. The principles of price discrimination were established by Pigou, and price positioning by Hotelling. More recent economics texts include Gabor, Porter, Philips and Devinney. Nagle presents an excellent summary of the various methods used to measure price sensitivity and demand. From a marketing perspective, East provides a useful summary in Chapter 4 of his book.

T.M. Devinney, *Issues in Pricing Theory and Research*, Lexington Books, 1988.

R. East, *Consumer Behaviour*, Prentice Hall, 1997.

A. Gabor, *Pricing: Principles and Practices*, Heinemann Educational Books, 1977.

H. Hotelling, "Stability in Competition", *Economic Journal*, 39, March 1929, pp. 41–52.

T. Nagle, *The Strategy and Tactics of Pricing*, McGraw Hill, 1988.

L. Philips, *The Economics of Price Discrimination*, Cambridge University Press, 1983.

A.C. Pigou, *The Economics of Welfare*, Macmillan, 1920.

M. Porter, *Competitive Advantage*, The Free Press, 1980.

BRAND VALUATION

Focus on: Marketing outputs
Measures: Financial valuation of the brand
Presented as: Asset valuation
Yardstick: Trends in valuation
Significance: Useful for mergers, acquisitions, royalties, shareholder
                  value reviews and group strategy reviews
Released: Ad hoc

Description and methodology
Brand valuation is the valuation of the brand as an intangible asset.

Common uses and interpretations
In the UK acquired brands can be capitalised on the balance sheet under the provisions of the new accounting standard FRS10, which established that only acquired brands can be capitalised on the balance sheet. The valuation has to be checked annually, and although it may need to be reduced, it cannot be increased above the original figure. Non-acquired brands cannot be included on the balance sheet.

Some companies are beginning to measure brands as assets to strengthen their balance sheets, which in some cases has increased their borrowing potential. It also has the effect of ensuring the company is fully valued on the basis of available information, that is, there are no hidden assets.

Shareholder value reviews are becoming popular as companies seek to minimise the risk of an unwelcome, underpriced predatory approach, and to demonstrate to their investors and brokers that they are building value. Internal strategy reviews may also benefit from brand valuation, when setting objectives for acceptable future rates of return, and when considering strategies for brand extensions, rebranding, franchising and divestment. In practice, these strategy reviews have become much more common than the purely financial applications.

Causes and theory
The valuation of anything is what someone is prepared to pay. The practical approach is to prepare valuations based on many scenarios: net book value; cash flow; market value. These may indicate a ballpark figure and become important in negotiating. In the case of market value, it is worth noting that a premium of, say, 30% may have to be paid to ensure a successful bid, and often more if the bid is hostile or contested.

The excess of acquisition cost over net book value (asset valuation after amortisation and depreciation) may end up on the balance sheet. Whether it is expressed as goodwill or brand valuation is largely a matter of presentation, and has no effect on the profit and loss account or net book value after acquisition.

A purchaser may be willing to pay more than the net book value, generally because the acquired assets are able to generate an abnormally high cash flow. Most valuation techniques for brand valuation choose to use this premium cash flow approach, and apply a discounted cash flow figure or multiple to capitalise it. For example, if a can of soft drink retails at 50 cents and its generic equivalent sells at 40 cents, the price premium is 10 cents. The manufacturing costs could be identical. So if the sales volume is 230m cans the brand premium is $23m, and if the brand marketing costs are $3m the net cash generation for the brand would be $20m per year. At a discount rate of 5%, a brand valuation of $400m results. (This is a grossly simplified example.)

Problems and cautions

Brand valuation has mainly been applied to long-established brands in mature industries with stable structures. It is unclear how it would apply to new brands, such as Netscape, Orange, Planet Hollywood or Versace, for which there is limited historical data and much of the value lies in future potential.

For many brands it is virtually impossible to find an equivalent generic product with which to make comparisons. For example, Walkers Crisps not only carry the Walkers brand, they also have one of the most efficient food plants in Europe, a rigorous quality programme and a superior supply chain. Comparison with other crisps, unbranded or not, is fraught with difficulties.

Future potential is often an issue. Future cash flows can be divided into those that derive from past activity and those that come from future activities. Future activities depend heavily on future brand management: will the brand be starved or overfed? The answer is inevitably little better than guesswork.

Future value may not come from consumer-led cash flow but from market value. For example, the Virgin brand has been exploited personally by Richard Branson more for Virgin's market value as a tradable entity (which accrues to Branson) than for its consumer franchise to the various companies that bear the Virgin brand.

Related topics

Brand valuation is an isolated topic. However, the capitalisation rate built into brand valuation calculations depends on category health and potential, competitive threats and indicators of brand health, such as market leadership.

Selected references

A special issue of the *Journal of Brand Management* (Vol. 5, No. 4) was devoted to the subject, and the subsequent issue (Vol. 5, No. 5) contained several more papers.

D. Haigh, *Strategic Control of Marketing Finance*, FT Pitman, 1994.
R. Perrier (ed.), *Brand Valuation*, Premier Books, 1998.

REPEAT PURCHASE

Focus on: Behaviour of repeat customers

Measures: Periodic repeat purchase frequency
Proportion of buyers who are 100% loyal
First brand loyalty
Share of category requirement
Switching matrix
Churn
Allegiance measures
Customer switching costs

Presented as: Percentage measure (one of the above)

Yardstick: Loyalty of buyers of similar items from a representative cross-section of competitors

Significance: High relative loyalty usually correlates with market leadership; if not there may be a significant underlying cause

Released: Monthly or quarterly

Description and methodology

Repeat purchase is measured as the likelihood of customers repurchasing your brand. Measuring it for competing brands as well as your own brand is essential for an understanding of loyalty. Records of periodic repurchases by individual customers provide the basic data for loyalty measurement. Internal records of periodic repurchases by individual customers, such as those from the sales ledger, can be used to calculate the periodic repeat purchase rate for your product. However, this measure takes no account of competition.

Patterns of loyalty for the whole category are more revealing. Measures include 100% loyals (ie, percentage of brand buyers who buy only that brand in a given time period), first brand loyalty (ie, proportion of purchase devoted to the household's most popular brand over the period), and share of category requirement (ie, proportion of category sales given to a brand by those who buy it at all). Data for these competitive measures have to be obtained from customer research, such as shopper panels, diary panels and telephone surveys.

An alternative competitive loyalty measure is the switching matrix. This shows the proportion of customers who buy one brand, and then buy a different brand next time. This can often be obtained by surveying lost customers.

Common uses and interpretations

Repeat purchase is the measure many managers use as tangible evidence of loyalty, brand value, quality or satisfaction. In many categories measurement of loyalty is a recent innovation, and managers are still coming to terms with its significance.

For many service suppliers, where contract renewal is important (such as electricity, gas, water, insurance), repeat purchase is the only loyalty measure commonly used, generated by internal computer systems. There is no compelling reason why the competitive indicators, such as share of category requirements, should not be measured (but this is not relevant for local monopoly suppliers such as some utilities).

For infrequently purchased products (such as automobiles) the main competitive loyalty measure used is the switching matrix. However, competitive switching effects are often overlooked when using this approach, and in particular there are no data available to assess long-term allegiance and turnover of customers.

Causes and theory

Studies of loyalty measures in a wide range of markets show that the various measures are correlated, so in theory only one measure of loyalty is needed. Andrew Ehrenberg, professor of marketing at South Bank Business School, and others have also found that loyalty measures often correlate with market leadership; that is, leaders have more loyal customers. Ehrenberg interprets loyalty as a statistical effect, rather than something caused by quality or satisfaction. Studies of quality and satisfaction generally confirm this finding; loyalty is often not correlated with quality or satisfaction.

Random patterns of switching are often called churn, and in many markets churn seems to be the main (dis)loyalty effect. However, in some markets there is a steady drift away from a brand that goes beyond churn. Studying this has given rise to an important new loyalty measure: allegiance or defection.

To measure allegiance requires repeat purchase measures over a consecutive series of periods, say six quarters. Pure churn would result in the same repeat purchase rate in the second, third and subsequent quarters. A steady decline in the repeat purchase rate indicates that some buyers have stopped buying the brand permanently, and the rate of decline can be used as an indicator of allegiance or true defection.

Problems and cautions

The commonest problems with loyalty measurement concern failure to measure competition and confusion between stochastic effects (churn) and real loyalty (allegiance). These issues have been outlined above.

Related topics

Low involvement and high inertia are likely to favour stochastic loyalty effects, so measuring inertia and involvement is essential to deciphering the loyalty effect.

Links between loyalty and quality, satisfaction or brand image are clearly of importance to management, but in many studies researchers have failed to find such links in practice.

Selected references

Ehrenberg has carried out the most extensive studies of repeat purchase data in the UK, the United States and other countries. His book is thorough, but a difficult read. East's more recent book gives a much more accessible account of the subject.

A. Ehrenberg, *Repeat Buying*, Griffin Oxford, 1988.
R. East, *Consumer Behaviour*, Prentice Hall, 1997.

TRIAL PURCHASE

Focus on: Behaviour of first-time customers

Measures: New category penetration rate in potential market

New category repeat rate post-trial

Brand penetration for early adopters of new category

New brand (or brand extension) penetration rate in existing category

New brand repeat rate post-trial

New brand cannibalisation of existing brands

Cross-sales trial rate for existing brand purchasers

Cost per trial customer

Presented as: Various penetration and purchase rate figures

Lifetime value over time is a useful presentation mode for cross-sales

Yardstick: Trends after new category launch

Trends after brand extension

Significance: New categories, or new brands, or cross-sales

Released: Monthly or quarterly

Description and methodology

Trial purchase is a measure of the behaviour of first-time purchasers. Three things may need to be measured: trials of the category; trials of the brand; trials of a product within the brand. Methods used to collect the data are similar to those for repeat purchase. Care needs to be taken over the definition of first-time buyers to ensure that light buyers are not confused with first-time buyers.

Common uses and interpretations

For new categories, category health must be measured as well as repeat purchase post-trial. The brand penetration (or share) of early adopters also needs to be monitored.

For a new brand, or a brand extension, in an existing category, it is critical to measure the penetration rate, and it is important to know whether there were sufficient repeat purchases post-trial. It is also important to measure cannibalisation of existing brands by the new brand or extension.

For brands where the range is extensive, measuring the cross-sales of other product lines to brand customers over time can reveal whether the prior purchase of the brand boosts sales of the other product lines. For brands, this is sometimes referred to as a halo effect; it is also called brand leverage. For direct sales, key account management (KAM) and relationship marketing, the expansion of cross-sales over time is critical to success. This is sometimes presented as the lifetime value of the customer, where over time the customer tries first one product, then two, and so on.

Causes and theory

New category adoption by customers has been studied extensively. The existence of a recognisable group of new-product adopters has been found in many new categories. These customers are generally less risk-averse than the average customer. Winning their preference can be important for early entrants; however, their customer values are likely to differ significantly from the bulk of the market. New brands and extensions are ripe with theory, compared with the limited amount of empirical evidence. Most studies suggest that rapid penetration of a category is essential to success; slow steady penetration rarely succeeds (perhaps owing as much to investor confidence as to consumer preference).

Cannibalisation of a firm's existing brands is a major concern. With a line extension there may be more loss of sales if the parent is perceived to be similar to the new entrant, in formulation, packaging, positioning, targeting, distribution or physical proximity, compared with other brands. However, empirical studies show this cannibalisation effect occurs less often than theoreticians suggests.

Cross-sales are discussed in most books on relationship marketing, and also in relation to direct mail, telephone selling, field sales and KAM. Yet surprisingly little is known about cross-sales, beyond the obvious fact that it is sensible for communications to include some cross-sales message. Lifetime value is starting to be studied, but as yet little is known about what is normal, excellent or abysmal growth in lifetime value.

There are a variety of marketing devices available to gain early customer trial, such as heavy initial price cuts (used widely in fast-moving consumer goods and mortgages), product sampling, demonstrations, couponing, and so on. A key issue is to select the most appropriate type of marketing mix, and cost per trier is an important measurement.

Problems and cautions

New categories need to be tracked carefully, not only for trial purchase, but also for repeat-purchase post-trial. Studies by Ehrenberg and others have noted the significance of poor post-trial repeat rates. Further investigation of psychological factors, such as satisfaction and perceived quality, may help diagnose such problems.

With new brands and extensions it is important not be swayed by creative theories about positioning and cannibalisation. It is more critical to monitor the market's response than to theorise about it. With success rates of only one in ten for launches in many categories, it is more important to detect and address quickly a poor launch than to waste time theorising about the perfect launch.

Related topics

Psychological measures of customer trust and confidence in the category and brand should be monitored alongside behavioural measures. It is also important to know marketing mix productivity.

Selected references

Moore has given an excellent account of the trial and new-product adoption process in high-tech industries. Utterbach provides insights on the adoption of new technologies generally, and especially the adoption of standards. Brand extensions have been researched widely in academic literature. Many accounts are theoretical. East gives a good empirical account of cannibalisation by extensions in mature markets. The cross-sales phenomenon, although briefly mentioned in many books and reports, lacks any substantial body of published research.

G. Moore, *Inside the Tornado*, Harper Business, 1995.
J.M. Utterbach, *Mastering the Dynamics of Innovation*, HBS Press, 1996.
R. East, *Consumer Behaviour*, Prentice Hall, 1997.

COMPLAINTS

Focus on: Behaviour of users (not always the same as purchasers)

Measures: Numbers of complaints received in the period

Backlog of complaints being processed

Sources of complaints (product, service, or departmental staff member)

Reasons for complaint

Priority

Presented as: Numbers of complaints

Ratios (complaints per thousand units)

Percentage split, by source and reason

Yardstick: Cross-brand comparisons of complaint levels

Growth trends

Competitive benchmarks, if such data can be obtained

Significance: Early warning of product or service problems

Released: Monthly or quarterly

Description and methodology

Complaints are measured in terms of the numbers arising per period, sources of complaint, reasons and priority. Measurements are most often collected by the internal department responsible for handling them. In large organisations collating complaints statistics can be difficult.

Common uses and interpretations

Complaints are used by management as indicators of quality problems in product manufacturing, sales and service, or post-sales support. Complaints are correctly recognised by management as a normal part of customer behaviour. However, there is wide variation in the ways that managers respond to complaints.

Causes and theory

As a broad generalisation, only about one in ten dissatisfied customers voice a complaint. So it is wrong to equate complaints with dissatisfaction. Action following dissatisfaction can take three forms: exit (which may be measured by repeat purchase problems); voice (ie, complaints); other antisocial behaviour (eg, vandalism, rudeness to staff). Complaining is often an alternative to exit, and there is evidence that well-handled complaints can increase repeat purchase probability.

Complaining behaviour is influenced by expected outcomes, normative influences and control factors. Positive expected outcomes such as replacement, apology and better goods may motivate complaining. Negative outcomes such as wasted time and embarrassment may discourage it. Normative influences include the influence of others on behaviour. For example, dissatisfied customers may complain to impress their friends, or because they intend to tell their spouse about the "drama" later.

Control factors include resources and skills that make complaining easier or harder. Other control factors include time, money and confidence. Vulnerable customers, such as people who are elderly, ill or disadvantaged, often complain less than others.

Problems and cautions

Notwithstanding the good reasons for monitoring complaints, managers are often reluctant to do so. Indeed, there is evidence that management reluctance to register complaints grows as the problem becomes more serious. Although some companies try to make it easy to complain by influencing expectations, norms and control factors, there are still significant barriers to complaining in most markets.

It is good practice to prioritise complaints, from those with serious commercial consequences, through temporary customer distress, to customer inconvenience, and so on. Different priorities warrant different treatments, and there should be an escalation procedure for serious problems. Although prioritisation and escalation procedures are applied in some service industries, such as elevator maintenance, their adoption is not widespread.

Related topics

Complaining is related to satisfaction and quality. Analysing the sources of and reasons for complaints can add significantly to the understanding of satisfaction and quality issues.

Selected references

Complaints have been studied extensively since the 1960s. Oliver has been one of the long-standing experts in the area of complaints and satisfaction research, and his recent book is an outstanding contribution to the subject.

R. Oliver, *Satisfaction*, McGraw Hill, 1997.

AWARENESS

Focus on:	Customers' thoughts and feelings
Measures:	Brand recall (for a category)
	Brand recognition
	Brand consideration
	Brand familiarity
Presented as:	Percentage awareness among a segment of the population
Yardstick:	Awareness of similar items from a representative cross-section of competitors
Significance:	Falling brand awareness may be one of the factors underlying reduction in trial purchase rate (new customers unaware), or poor repeat purchase rates
Released:	Monthly or quarterly

Description and methodology

Brand awareness is measured by people's ability to identify (recognise or recall) the brand in sufficient detail to influence purchase. It is potentially more relevant to non-buyers, for whom low awareness may be a barrier to purchase.

Two measures should be considered. Brand recall measures the ability of potential category buyers to recall the brands which are examples of the category. For example, in the personal computers category potential buyers may be aware of Dell and Gateway. Brand recognition measures the ability of brand cues (visual and auditory) to lead to a consideration of whether the category is needed. For example, with Coca-Cola people look at the product first and then consider whether the category is needed. There is often a delay of only a few seconds between recognition and purchase.

Common uses and interpretations

Managers often use awareness as a measure of advertising effectiveness; they frequently equate awareness with brand name recall.

Causes and theory

Buying-sequence models are important in marketing. They are also relevant to understanding how awareness works. They describe the stages of behaviour, thought and emotion preceding, accompanying and following purchase. Awareness is an important aspect of many of these models.

Generic models such as AIDA (awareness, interest, decision, action), which are applied to every product or service, are widespread. However, it is clear that different sequences apply in different contexts, and managers should construct their own models to fit their business context. Within these models, the role of awareness differs significantly.

The distinction between brand recall and brand recognition arises because there are two main buying-sequence models in which awareness is important. At the point of purchase brand recognition is more important. The purest case of brand recognition occurs with so-called impulse purchases. For many products purchased in the supermarket, there is no thought of buying the brand, or even the category, before the brand is encountered. Some high-value items, such as insurance or consultancy services, are also impulse purchases. They are bought as a result of a sales approach rather than deliberate, preconceived search. In a great many cases brand recognition is a non-verbal process, involving visual and other emotional cues, especially if the category need is not pressing.

Before the point of purchase brand recall is more important. When the customer has experienced only the category need, brand recall is most influential. Brand recall is almost always a verbal process, requiring verbal name recall of the brand in response to a verbal cue (occurring mentally or subvocally) of the category need. The key is paired association between the category need and the brand name.

Problems and cautions

The design of awareness research is complex, which may explain why its quality can be poor. It is important to be careful about prompts given to informants. For example, how is the category described to them? Do you distinguish between first mentions and others? Is a brand list shown? (this is known as prompted recall). Unprompted or spontaneous recall is also known as salience.

You also need to know whether they claim to have ever bought the brand and the category, whether they are lapsed users, whether they bought or used in the last six months, and so on. Within these groups you can create segments by claimed buying behaviour and so forth. As well as awareness, consideration of individual brands before purchase can be illuminating. Similarly, familiarity with brand attributes can be an important aspect of awareness.

Note that brand awareness and advertising awareness are different. To monitor elements of the marketing mix at a micro level, it may be important to monitor both types of brand awareness. This is because people may be aware of advertising but unaware of the brand it promotes, or they may be aware of the brand but unaware of its advertising.

Related topics

Trial purchase and repeat purchase rates may be affected by awareness.

Selected references

There is extensive literature on consumer behaviour, and most textbooks give an account of awareness. Rossiter and Percy give one of the best accounts.

J.R. Rossiter and L. Percy, *Advertising and Communications Management*, McGraw Hill, 1997.

SATISFACTION

Focus on: Customers thoughts and feelings
Measures: Meeting expectations
                  Exceeding expectations (positively or negatively)
                  Meeting and/or exceeding ideals
                  Fulfilment of needs
                  Gratification of wants and desires
                  Fairness
                  Regret and hindsight
Presented as: Score on a multipoint scale
Yardstick: Satisfaction of buyers of similar items from a representative
                  cross-section of competitors
Significance: Trends upwards or downwards in relative satisfaction may
                  indicate a significant underlying cause, such as poor quality
Released: Quarterly, or periodic audit

Description and methodology

Satisfaction is measured in terms of customers' attainment of goals through the consumption of products and use of services. It is relevant only to existing buyers, for whom satisfaction may be a reinforcing or pleasurable experience. People have many types of goals, as reflected by the variety of satisfaction measures available. The measures should be linked to the criteria for repurchase (or future purchase intention).

Common uses and interpretations

Satisfaction is the measure used by many managers as evidence that their manufacturing, distribution and service are giving what customers they want. They commonly associate low satisfaction with customer disloyalty, although the connection is not easily demonstrated, and in many categories the link between satisfaction and loyalty is weak. The most widely used measure of satisfaction is meeting expectations.

Causes and theory

Buying-sequence models should include an explanation of why customers purchase things, and satisfaction with previous purchases can figure in them. There are several different buying situations and associated models, which take different approaches to satisfaction measurement.

The basic reason people buy is simply to restock items they have used or which are needed to solve (such as medicines) or avoid (such as sun cream) a problem. Another reason is that they see the purchase as an enhancement, adding to the positive value of their lives.

The most common measure, meeting customer expectations, has been widely demonstrated to have little or no impact on purchasing. Negatively exceeding expectations can have a negative impact on repeat purchases; however, in many circumstances its impact is limited. Positively exceeding expectations can reinforce repeat purchasing; however, it can also cause more comparison shopping and, hence, switching.

Satisfaction surveys can also include lists of needs and wants, with the aim of understanding more about the fulfilment of specific needs or gratification of wants. Recent developments include studies of fairness; for example, in financial services perceived unfairness can be a significant issue. Studies of regrets, or hindsight, can also be revealing; for example, with IT outsourcing contracts it has been discovered that customer regret often sets in around two years after the contract was signed.

Problems and cautions

Satisfaction measurement should relate satisfaction to the future purchase process, or else to complaining behaviour. Questions such as "I always buy A, but I wonder if it is wise?" help establish such links.

An important limitation of satisfaction measures is that they do not apply to non-customers, and thus do not extend beyond the existing customer base. For some brands, such as Disney, satisfaction levels may be high, but for EuroDisney the low penetration (ie, few Europeans have any experience of theme parks) means that satisfaction is not as important a measure as it is in the United States (where penetration is much higher).

Another complication is that satisfaction aggregated across all types of customers can become insensitive and difficult to interpret. Thus it is often necessary to develop a range of satisfaction measures by segment.

Because of inexperience in this specialist field, in-house measurement of satisfaction often provides poorer information than surveys contracted out to a research firm. Some of the worst information comes from in-house surveys linked to bonus schemes, which are often subject to serious bias.

Related topics

Satisfaction is closely related to quality. Its effects on consumer behaviour show up in the area of repeat purchase

Selected references

Oliver is a long-standing expert in satisfaction research; *Satisfaction* (McGraw Hill, 1997) is an outstanding contribution to the subject.

CUSTOMER INVOLVEMENT

Focus on: Customers' thoughts and feelings

Measures: Average intensity of category involvement

Percentage of high-involvement purchasers

Average level of category inertia

Percentage of habitual purchasers

Presented as: Score on multipoint scale

Yardstick: Relative involvement with other brands in category

Relative involvement with other categories

Significance: High involvement in the category, or in competing brands, may cause customers to search for alternatives, causing repeat purchase rate to fall

Released: Monthly, quarterly or ad hoc

Description and methodology

Involvement is measured by using one or more indicators of the degree of arousal associated with a purchase. Most involvement scales measure intensity of arousal. For example, intense involvement in running shoes may arouse an active search for information on differences between Nike and Reebok, and a critical evaluation of them.

In some cases customers experience a long-term personal interest in one or more products and appear to have enduring involvement; for example, stereo buffs, auto enthusiasts and gourmets. In certain contexts there is temporary situational involvement; for example, students buying their first business suits. Measures should differentiate between these.

Involvement in a category may not be all-encompassing but focus on some target factor; for example, environmental safety in automobiles, health or weight in convenience foods, packaging for gifts.

Inertia, also referred to as habit, is a related factor, where the purchase context provides a stimulus which evokes previously established behaviour. Habits side-step decision-making and leave people free to concentrate on the few problems where past experience does not provide a ready response. People generally think about their actions after the habitual event rather than before. Measures of inertia, or habit, are needed to calculate the lack of arousal associated with a purchase.

Common uses and interpretations

Involvement, the formal measurement of which is fairly new, depends on the object or situation, and changes need to be monitored and addressed. In particular, involvement depends on the perceived importance of the purchase and the perceived risk. For example, between 1990 and 1995 PC operating systems became a habit purchase (dominated by Microsoft Windows), but around 1995 involvement in the Internet escalated, threatening Microsoft's habitual dominance.

Involvement also depends to some extent on individuals, on their hobbies, interests, and so on. These change over time, and tracking them can be important. For example, Adidas lost market share to Nike through not registering consumer involvement in recreational running and jogging, and not adjusting its product ranges to involve the consumer.

Causes and theory

Customer decision-making varies significantly with the type and context of the purchase decision. There are enormous differences between buying table salt, a business suit or a new house. New and important purchases elicit extended problem solving (EPS), with problem recognition, search for alternatives, purchase and post-purchase activities, such as recommending the product to others. Yet in many situations customers do not have the motivation, time or resources to conduct EPS, and engage instead in more limited problem solving (LPS).

High involvement motivates EPS and low involvement LPS, so they greatly affect the importance of awareness, brand image, satisfaction and other cognitive factors in purchasing behaviour. If only a small proportion of the market is highly involved, then some other strategies for dealing with the uninvolved majority may be required. Other factors that may increase EPS are the opportunity (which often depends on the time available) and the ability of the customer to process the information (which may be affected by personal knowledge and the complexity of the decision).

EPS has dominated customer theory for decades, especially in the United States. Yet it is hard to find examples where buyers engage in anything other than the most simple comparison shopping, search for alternatives, or value analysis. Many purchases are high inertia, low involvement.

Problems and cautions

Involvement is as important a category indicator as it is a brand indicator and it should be linked to the purchase process if it is to be a useful predictor of purchases. However, it is advertising involvement that is most often measured.

It is understandable for managers to empathise most with heavily involved customers. Yet in many markets these customers are a minority. For example, PC companies and dealers communicate much better with experienced users than with the possibly larger group who are struggling to understand. One reason the Japanese were able successfully to penetrate the US motor-cycle market was because most dealers were more interested in bike enthusiasts than in the mass market.

Related topics
Repeat purchase is likely to be influenced by changes in involvement.

Selected references
Krugman popularised the idea of involvement as a way of explaining the different levels of cognitive activity created by advertising and purchasing situations. He argued that when people had low involvement in a product, advertising could still affect their behaviour by strengthening recognition and recall (see Awareness). Since then there have been numerous attempts to describe and explain involvement. East provides a good account.

R. East, *Consumer Behaviour*, Prentice Hall, 1997.
H.E. Krugman, "The impact of television advertising: learning without involvement", *Public Opinion Quarterly*, 29, 1965, pp. 349–356.

BRAND IMAGE ENDORSEMENT

Focus on: Customers' thoughts and feelings
Measures: Relevance
                   Credibility
                   Distinctiveness
Presented as: Scorecard with several multipoint scales
Yardstick: Brand image endorsement of one or two key competitors
Significance: Advertising, packaging, PR or corporate image investments
Released: Quarterly or ad hoc

Description and methodology

A brand is a name, term, sign, symbol or design, or a combination of these, which is intended to identify the products or services of one seller or group of sellers and to differentiate them from those of competitors.

Brand image endorsement is a scorecard of measures, which collectively show whether buyers prefer the brand to its competitors (including retail own label products). This can be complex, consisting of a mental structure with a number of components. Three key measures of brand image endorsement are: relevance; credibility; and distinctiveness. Satisfaction and perceived quality (which are described elsewhere) are sometimes included on this scorecard. Attitudinal surveys are used to collect the data needed as a basis for these measures.

Common uses and interpretations

Brand image endorsement is commonly used by managers as a measure of advertising effectiveness. However, there is increasing recognition that the brand image and its endorsement by customers reflects the organisation's marketing efforts as a whole.

Causes and theory

Research into customer expectations of brands indicates that relevance, credibility and distinctiveness are particularly important. Relevance means that the brand is expected to offer products or services that are claimed to provide the expected features and functional benefits customers desire. For example, many buyers of computers would expect IBM to offer services relevant to their needs. Buyers of automobiles are unlikely to expect IBM to offer anything relevant to them.

Credibility means that the brand is expected to fit the customer's needs and wants, and to fulfil the promise of value. Many buyers will choose a branded product on trust, without checking the features in detail, on the basis of credibility. Extensions may stretch a brand's credibility, but not its relevance. For example, buyers of mainframe computers will sometimes choose IBM on trust; it has credibility. Buyers of PC software are unlikely to consider IBM, even though most are aware that IBM offers PC software. So IBM chose to keep the Lotus brand for its PC software, rather than extend the IBM brand.

Distinctiveness means that the brand can readily be recognised by buyers. For market leaders this often means heavy investment in promoting the brand. Near-substitute items, such as Perrier and Evian, rely on advertising and packaging. Coke and Pepsi rely on advertising, packaging and subtle taste differences. Differentiated brands such as shredded wheat and corn flakes differ much more, but are still directly substitutable for many customers. Brand extensions, where the brand is used in different categories, sometimes do not advertise in all the categories but rely on umbrella brand publicity. Virgin is a good example of this approach (although it may be suffering from relevance and credibility problems in some categories).

Buying-sequence models may help determine the relative importance of relevance, credibility or distinctiveness. Distinctiveness may be more important when purchase involvement is low; for example, in carbonated drinks Coke and Pepsi are similar in relevance and credibility, so distinctiveness becomes a key factor. Credibility may be more important in categories where perceived quality is important (eg, for high-quality automobiles BMW has more credibility than Ford), or perceived risk is high (eg, in management consulting a firm like McKinsey is more credible than a low-profile small firm). Relevance may be more important to new entrants in high-quality or high-risk categories; eg, in management consulting, McKinsey is more relevant than British Telecom Consulting Division; in this case BT rebranded its consulting business as Syntegra.

Problems and cautions, and related topics

It is important to measure attitudes towards purchasing the brand, not simply attitudes towards the brand.

Satisfaction and perceived quality indicate brand health, and brand image endorsement indicators explain how brand health has changed.

Selected references

There is extensive literature on consumer behaviour towards brands, and most textbooks give an account of brand image indicators. Aaker gives one of the best accounts in *Building Strong Brands*, Free Press, 1996.

CHANNEL FRANCHISE

Focus on: Trade customers' thoughts and feelings

Measures: Channel recognition as the "category leader" or "preferred supplier"

                 Channel ease of doing business

                 Channel perceived quality of product

                 Channel perceived quality of people

                 Channel perceived market leadership

                 Channel perceived added value

                 Trade customer potential

Presented as: Scores on multipoint scales, weighted towards preferred channel partners

Yardstick: Relative scores of leading competitors in the category

Significance: Strong channel franchise can dramatically affect distribution leadership

Released: Quarterly, annually or ad hoc

Description and methodology

Channel franchise measures trade or distributor attitudes to suppliers, and determines their relative bargaining power. The most privileged relationship is sometimes referred to as the channel captain, or the preferred supplier or partner.

This information is collected by surveying the attitudes and opinions of channel personnel. Most often the purchasing manager is interviewed, but the survey may also include other relevant channel people. As channel relationships move towards teamwork, there is growing recognition of the need to interview members of the team.

Common uses and interpretations

Managers use channel franchise to predict and diagnose problems with distribution leadership. Having a privileged relationship with preferred channel partners may not only ensure good coverage, but also reduce the costs of doing business with trade partners and improve such things as stock levels, display, and so on. Psychological factors in the relationship may provide helpful insights into the physical relationship between supplier and channel.

Causes and theory

In many markets channel power is strong, and so an effective channel franchise is extremely important. But the study and theory of channel franchises is not well developed.

Channel companies say the principal factors influencing their relationship with suppliers are: ease of doing business; product quality; people quality; market leadership; added value; and company culture. Channel relationships have recently been studied under the title Efficient Consumer Response (ECR). According to PricewaterhouseCoopers, ECR recognises five levels of relationships which may be used to measure the overall franchise:

1 Traditional salesman
2 Advanced salesman
3 Category sales manager
4 Trusted adviser
5 Strategic alliance partner

Problems and cautions

Measurement is still generally in the hands of the sales representative or account manager. It is therefore vulnerable to bias or distortion, especially if remuneration is tied to any of the measures. Not all channel partners are equal. Some are preferable to others, and it pays to rank partners for attractiveness. Weightings should be applied to the channel franchise data to reflect the differences in attractiveness of channel partners.

Related topics

Distribution leadership is directly affected by channel franchise.

Selected references

Channel franchise has received limited attention in the literature, the main emphasis being on physical distribution. Most of the major consultancies, including Coopers & Lybrand and McKinsey, have published reports on this subject, but few provide a detailed account of the measurements needed.

J. Corstjens and M. Corstjens, *Store Wars*, Wiley, 1995.

QUALITY

Focus on: Customers' thoughts and feelings
Marketing inputs (also)

Measures: Perceived quality (experience and reputation)
Actual (conformance) quality

Presented as: Score for multiple quality factors on a multipoint sliding scale
Number of problem-free products (no returns or complaints) per million

Yardstick: Relative quality (actual and perceived) of selected competitors

Significance: Perceived quality has a significant effect on repeat and trial purchase
Actual quality has an effect on repeat purchase

Released: Quarterly or ad hoc

Description and methodology

Quality is measured in two ways: as a marketing input measure; and as a measure of customer perceptions. Actual quality (commonly known as conformance quality) is a technical measure a supplier applies to the quality of what it produces/does. The department closest to the customer generally assesses quality, but quality measures at process steps are often included. Other methods include blind testing by consumers and mystery shopping.

Perceived quality is customers' perception of the quality of a product or service. According to this view, what the supplier thinks of its own quality does not matter; it is the customers' opinions that count. Service quality is more difficult to control and measure than product quality.

Surveys of customer opinions are used to gather data for measuring perceived quality. Customers are often asked about the perceived quality of competing products. Yardsticks used can include:

- Ideal quality versus expected quality
- Best in category versus worst in category
- Consistent quality versus inconsistent
- Finest quality versus average versus inferior

Perceived quality is sometimes included as one of the dimensions of brand image endorsement. However, since it may also be important when brand image is less so, it has been included as a separate indicator.

Common uses and interpretations

Quality, together with satisfaction, is a measure many managers now use as evidence that their manufacturing, distribution and service are giving customers what they want. Like satisfaction, low quality is commonly associated with customer disloyalty, although this connection is not easily demonstrated, and in many categories the link between quality and loyalty is weak.

Causes and theory

In the belief that quality derives from technical excellence, many suppliers have gone to great lengths to ensure that their product or service reaches certain standards, such as the number of rejects or defects being less than so many per million. More recent thinking has placed more emphasis on perceived quality than conformance quality. A series of analyses of the PIMS database by Buzzell and Gale showed strong correlation between perceived quality and profitability.

Consumers' perceptions of quality are often at odds with conformance quality. For example, in the airline industry conformance quality is typically measured in terms of on-time arrivals, problem-free baggage handling and minimal flight cancellations. Consumer quality perceptions are influenced more by aircraft congestion (percentage of seats filled), which is at odds with airline profit goals.

Quality differs from satisfaction in certain important respects. For example, low satisfaction may result from a small blemish on a luxury product, but the customer may still not doubt the high quality of the product. Quality is more about ideals and excellence; satisfaction is more about expectations and predictions. Quality is widely perceived without direct experience; satisfaction requires experience. Quality is significantly influenced by social norms, focusing on a few quality factors; satisfaction judgments can result from any factor experienced. Quality is primarily long term; satisfaction is more short term or event driven.

Problems and cautions

Confusion between quality, satisfaction and loyalty, and a mistaken tendency to equate them, has led to many poor investments in quality programmes which have not yielded the expected customer responses and associated profits.

Quality's influence on profitability is strongest in the contribution it makes to the signals about a product's value positioning, a matter in which advertising can play an important part. Conformance quality can take a long time to affect perceived quality and hence value positioning. Short-term gains can therefore be made more easily through advertising and packaging than quality programmes. For example, Daewoo success-fully used advertising to position itself as a high quality brand in terms of service, long before anyone had significant actual experience of it.

Related topics

Satisfaction and loyalty are important related factors. Prepurchase behaviour, such as enquiries, can also provide useful clues when the product or service is new.

Selected references

Quality has an extensive literature, going back to the seminal work of W.E. Deming, J.M. Juran and Philip Crosby. For a critical appraisal of this work, Howe, Gaeddert and Howe provide a valuable introduction. The relationship between conformance and perceived quality, and the profitability associated with the latter, is well described by Gale. Oliver gives a state-of-the-art description of the relationship between quality and satisfaction.

R.J. Howe, D. Gaeddert and M.A. Howe, *Quality On Trial*, West Publishing Company, 1992.

B. Gale, *Managing Customer Value*, Free Press, 1994.

R. Oliver, *Satisfaction*, McGraw Hill, 1997.

CORPORATE MARKETING SUPPORT

Focus on:	Marketing inputs
Measures:	Total marketing budget (and previous year's budget)
	Total marketing turnover/expense (gross margin) ratio
	Brand
	Brand expense allocation to marketing mix
	Quarterly budget adjustments
Presented as:	Ratios and actual monetary figures
Yardstick:	Ratios or actual expenses for representative cross-section of competitors
	Budget benchmarking models (for brands)
	Budget allocation models (across the marketing mix)
Significance:	A non-optimal budget will harm cash flow
Released:	Annually, or at quarterly intervals when budget adjustments take place

Description and methodology

Corporate marketing support indicates how much support corporate managers give to marketing, and in particular the allocation of budgets to brands and across the marketing mix. The information comes from financial systems and spreadsheet analysis of them. Competitive data is collected by a variety of intelligence-gathering techniques.

Common uses and interpretations

Corporate marketing support is of interest to investors and senior managers. Its importance is to evaluate whether management is starving marketing or overspending. Investors are taking a growing interest in disclosure of total marketing spend and the competitive ratios involved. These marketing disclosures are just one of many sources of information used to evaluate overall investment decisions.

Managers use expenditure-support yardsticks to help them determine the total budget and its allocation. The most common yardstick is last year's budget plus an increase roughly in line with inflation, but this approach has many associated problems.

Others include the percentage of turnover (or gross margin) approach, where a fixed percentage (often arbitrary) of turnover is allocated to marketing; activity-driven approaches, where the budget is actually allocated to activities and allowed to vary depending on the volume of those activities; and the quarterly (or periodic) budget review, whereby the annual budget is reviewed and usually cut, with marketing often taking a fairly heavy hit.

Causes and theory

At least three theoretical approaches are available, and it is good practice to develop scenarios based on more than one.

Budget benchmarking models are available for brands. The most well-known is based on the PIMS database of over 3,000 companies and their brands. The PIMS procedure involves taking data on the marketing budgets of a sample of competitors and modelling the impact of these budgets on their financial outputs.

Activity-based costing models are being developed by some organisations to help them link budgets to the activities which drive them. This helps overcome a common criticism of budgeting: that it fails to take account of growth and decline in marketing activities.

Budget allocation models are also available. These use historical data to evaluate the best allocation across the marketing mix.

Problems and cautions

Thorny problems concerning what should go in the marketing budget include: organisational problems of what really constitutes marketing; accounting problems of what constitutes a fixed compared with a variable cost; and the problems of the marketing mix. For historical reasons, most organisations' marketing budgets contain items which do not really belong in marketing, such as company cars (all employees, not just the salesforce), certain warehousing costs, specific distribution costs and certain manufacturing costs. Conversely, salesforce costs may not be included, nor may customer service budgets, costs of product development, and so on. Activity-based costing provides a partial answer to many of these organisational issues. By tying the budgets to specific activities, rather than to people on the organisation chart, comparisons can be made more realistic.

Another common problem is determining what the variable cost of the brand actually is. Many traditional management accounting systems do not bother to distinguish adequately between fixed and variable costs, throwing brand profit and losses into confusion. Where activity-based costing has been implemented successfully, the variable cost issue will normally have been addressed. Then there is the important matter of how to measure the quality as well as the quantity of marketing support; that is, strong versus weak advertising and effective versus ineffective R&D. Last but not least, judgments about the mix of spend are critical. Big investment in short-term tactical activities such as price promotions and discounts carry little prospect of building real brand value.

Related topics

Marketing mix productivity is a closely associated topic, where budgets are being related to the actual activities they support. Both should be reviewed together. Marketing waste is another related measure.

Selected references

Accountants and marketers both write on this fashionable topic. The accounting texts can be divided into standard textbooks, most of which have a section on sales and marketing, and newer performance measurement studies. A good example of the former would be Kaplan and Atkinson; Kaplan and Cooper provide a more modern approach. The annual survey of City analysts' views on the need for disclosure of marketing information, published by Brand Finance, also makes interesting reading.

Kotler sets out many of the key issues in his marketing "bible". For more specific problems, Broadbent has written an excellent account of advertising budgeting, which also illuminates some of the broader marketing budget issues, and Piercy has written about the practical problems inherent in setting marketing budgets.

R. Kaplan and A. Atkinson, *Advanced Managerial Accounting*, Prentice Hall, 1989.

R. Kaplan and R. Cooper, *Cost and Effect*, HBS Press, 1998.

D. Haigh, *The Brand Finance Report*, Brand Finance, 1998.

S. Broadbent, *The Advertising Budget*, NTC/IPA Publications, 1989.

N. Piercy, *Market-led Strategic Change*, Butterworth-Heinemann, 1992.

MARKETING MIX PRODUCTIVITY

Focus on: Marketing inputs

Measures: Quantity indicators for mix activities

Advertising activity (eg, TVRS, share of voice

Sales activity quantity (eg, call rate)

New product launches per year

Unit costs (per activity)

Quality indicators (see previous section)

Presented as: Activity rates (per month/year), ratios (per employee) and unit costs

Quality index on a multipoint scale

Yardstick: Competitive benchmarking of mix activity

Models of activity yields (eg, advertising models)

Significance: Low productivity relative to competition may indicate poor management of budget expenditure or bad resource management

Released: Internal measures may be monthly or quarterly

Competitive comparisons are generally annual or ad hoc

Description and methodology

Marketing mix productivity shows the total marketing activity associated with each element of the marketing mix, in terms of quantity of activity and unit costs. These are then expressed as productivity indices, as rates such as sales calls per day, and ratios such as customers per sales representative. Most activity information is collected from internal transaction systems. Competitive data are gathered by competitive intelligence surveys, either as an annual exercise or ad hoc.

Common uses and interpretations

Marketing activity indicators are used to check that the marketing budget is resulting in an appropriate level of activity, and that the quantity and quality of activities address customer needs.

Competitive benchmarking is the most common yardstick for evaluating productivity. For example, competitor call rate is used as a yardstick for sales activity, and share of voice is often used as a key indicator for advertising activity. Unit costs are being scrutinised as marketing departments adopt professional purchasing practices. It is increasingly common for the marketing team to include a purchasing officer.

Conformance quality and customer perceived quality measures are also being adopted by marketing departments. Quality represents the hidden side of the marketing mix, and it is often forgotten in financial evaluations which focus on transaction volumes.

Causes and theory

The concept of productivity, especially productivity benchmarking, is increasingly being questioned. Brands are often so different that comparision is meaningless. Models can help make comparisons more realistic, and their use is on the increase. They work by linking marketing activities to customer responses. Models can provide better yardsticks than the simple competitive comparisons, since they can take account of the different circumstances affecting each brand and its competitors.

For example, Andrex, a UK maker of toilet tissue, has been working for many years with models from OHAL, using the proprietary Brandpac model to optimise the marketing mix. The company recently won an IPA effectiveness award for its use of the model to win consistently in a highly competitive market. Bass, a brewer, optimises its sales activity using models created by SPA, which allow sales journey times to be optimised. Catalogue companies in the United States can optimise the frequency of mailing to customers using models developed by Kestnbaum & Co, a consulting firm, to select contact rates that will optimise the sales yield.

Process measures are replacing departmental measures of marketing activity. Activity-based costing systems are becoming important in this regard.

Problems and cautions

There are so many dimensions of marketing mix activity to monitor that the danger is that managers focus too much on inputs and too little on important customer and output measures. Benchmarking can be pointless, particularly when all competitors in a market copy one another.

Modelling, whose adoption has been slow, can help establish a link between marketing mix activities and customer outputs.

Selected references

One book reviews mix productivity and the associated models, as well as providing a valuable source of references to the extensive journal literature on this subject.

G. Lilien, P. Kotler and K. S. Moorthy, *Marketing Models*, Prentice Hall, 1992.

INNOVATION BENCHMARKS

Focus on: Marketing inputs

Measures: Order of market entry (pioneer, early follower, later entrant)

Percentage of sales from new products

Development time for new products

Response time to competitive threats

Response time to changes in customer needs

Effect of new products on relative quality and relative price

Failure rate and cost for new product responses

Presented as: Various measures of innovation and speed

Yardstick: Competitor process measures

Significance: Competitive factors that may be overlooked when routinely monitoring competitive performance

Released: Annual or ad hoc audit

Description and methodology

Innovation benchmarks measure dimensions such as the degree and speed of innovation. These are then benchmarked against similar measures for competitors.

Common uses and interpretations

Managers use these indicators to assess whether their competitive challenge lies in the speed or degree of innovation (consultants will often say both are crucial). Competitive benchmarking is a service offered by consulting firms, and it often encompasses benchmarks of marketing mix productivity as well as strategic processes.

Causes and theory

Business history is full of firms that have innovated but failed. The PIMS database is a useful source of such data. It has several indicators of innovation and speed. Customised measures can be overlaid on the basic PIMS data.

Studying new innovations is important. For one success there are about ten failures. The failure rate increases the more new products differ from existing ones. This is why successfully innovative managers favour minor innovations, not radical ones.

In Detroit's heyday the products barely changed. Only the outer skin, the packaging, was changed annually at an alarming cost, which was built into the price of the vehicle. This built-in obsolescence opened the doors to competitors who varied the core product. What mattered was not the amount of (trivial) innovation, but its quality. For this reason it is good practice to include quality measures for innovation as well as quantity. This also applies to responses to changes in the marketplace. They should include the effect of innovation on perceived quality and price, and the failure rate and cost of new product responses.

Problems and cautions

Innovation is not necessarily a recipe for success, and it can be a costly route to failure. The Mars Bar, Vaseline, Kleenex, Levis and Nivea all testify to the benefits of making only finely judged, hardly noticeable changes to established products in markets where others waste money on large-scale innovation.

In many markets new standards are established through innovation, such as VHS for video-recorders and Windows for PCS. Being first or second into the market does not guarantee success in a standards battle, unless the standard is one where patents or other intellectual property rights can be established to exclude later entrants.

Copying new ideas is now common. Benchmarking has made it into a routine process. Imitators who enter a market late can still take a significant share in many categories, especially where they have more significant financial backing than the early entrants.

Responding fast to customers also causes problems. It is fashionable to be customer-led, but customers are notoriously lacking in foresight. They will tick a box in an ill-conceived customer-response questionnaire with sometimes disastrous results. This is not to say that customers cannot play a role in helping a firm stretch its boundaries. However, too often the questions asked by market researchers – "Do you prefer a red button or a green one?" – provide little scope for fundamentally challenging traditional category concepts.

It is essential to measure the quality of innovations and responses, as well as the quantity, if firms are to be truly innovative and responsive.

Related topics

These process benchmarks should be reviewed alongside the more conventional strategic measures: category health; category potential; and competitive threats.

Selected references

Heller provides a wealth of case examples about the risks of innovation and speed. Utterbach provides a more serious, but no less cautionary, study of innovation. Cooper has written an excellent book on new product development. Schnaars, however, highlights successful imitation strategies.

R. Heller, *The Naked Manager for the Nineties*, 1996 Warner Books
J.M. Utterbach, *Mastering the Dynamics of Innovation*, HBS Press, 1996.
R. Cooper, *Winning at New Products*, Addison Wesley , 1993.
S.P. Schnaars, *Managing Imitation Strategies*, Free Press, 1994.

MARKETING WASTE

Focus on: Marketing inputs
Measures: Total marketing expenses to budget variance
                  Customer profit and loss reporting
                  Product profit and loss reporting
                  Cost of cancelled campaigns
                  Cost of failed new product development projects
Presented as: Budget variance reports by cost centre
                  Activity-based costing reports on unprofitable customers
                  and products
                  Total quality management (TQM) reports on marketing
                  waste
                  Re-engineering reports on non-value-creating processes
Yardstick: Value creation
Significance: Activities and processes that do not create value are
                  eliminated or changed
Released: Monthy reports and ad hoc studies

Description and methodology

Marketing waste is measured in terms of the money wasted by certain activities or processes.

Common uses and interpretations

Waste measures are used to highlight processes and activities that need changing to save money and resources.

Causes and theory

The budget variance report helps show spending which has exceeded the official limits, but it exists in isolation and gives no insight into the context and circumstances that caused the variance. New approaches have been developed for some years, and significant progress has been made in implementing these and reducing the amount of non-value-adding work. TQM, re-engineering and activity-based management have all attacked the problem in different ways, and all can claim successes. At best these techniques offer signposts to waste, which can then be dealt with on an ad hoc, project-by-project basis. A structured measurement approach has not yet been developed.

Customer profitability reporting has had some notable successes. All customers are not equally, or even positively, profitable. Use of activity-based costing has allowed firms to change their terms of business with customers and hence cut down on waste. Product profitability exercises highlight waste in terms of unprofitable brands, product lines and other clutter. This has led to significant product pruning. Re-engineering often highlights marketing processes which are wasteful and can be stream-lined. TQM exercises also highlight marketing waste. The task for managers is to learn how to separate the waste from the worthwhile. Project management disciplines, with a series of quality gates throughout the project, can dramatically reduce waste, but managers must accept that high levels of waste are inevitable in such areas as new product development or advertising.

Hewlett-Packard conducted a survey of the non-value-adding activity of one of its sales regions in 1992. Its aim was not cost-cutting but to eliminate wasteful bottlenecks. The project produced a list of waste areas, where non-value-adding work accounted for 35% of expenditure. By March 1994 more than half the waste was eliminated, sales were not reduced and profits significantly increased. John Golding, UK managing director, commented: "The company's performance was the result of quality programmes, eliminating waste, consolidating operations and keeping expenses under control."

British Telecom studied waste levels in its advertising process in the mid-1980s. As a result of the high levels of waste, in particular campaign cancellations, a project management approach was introduced. This cut waste significantly and provided a continuous monitor of the problem.

Problems and cautions

The passion for eliminating budget variances is often counterproductive, causing waste rather than eliminating it. It is common for a manager to embark on a spending binge simply to use up the budget before it can be clawed back in a periodic budget adjustment. It is also common for savings through buying low-quality items, such as promotional gifts, to lead to massive waste later; and hiring external staff who do not appear on the marketing department's headcount simply pushes their excessive costs on to the human resources department.

Spending variances are often misused. Hundreds of budget games are played by sales and marketing departments. Managers rarely have an incentive to eliminate waste this year, because it is likely to result in cuts to next year's budget. Most successful waste elimination is project-based, where teams of managers, often driven by external consultants, have identified and tackled particular trouble spots.

To avoid a lack of commitment to or know-how in the arts of waste elimination when consultants leave, it is important that employees are involved in creating, implementing, managing and continuously improving the waste measurement process.

Selected references

There is extensive literature on TQM and waste control. Perhaps the most relevant to marketing is Hope and Hope.

T. Hope and J. Hope, *Transforming the Bottom Line*, Nicholas Brealey, 1995.

APPENDICES

1 Notes

Chapter 1

1 Philip Kotler reserved these specialist tools for another book, *Marketing Models* (which is highly recommended to those who wish to dig deeper). P. Kotler and G. Lilien, *Marketing Models*, Prentice Hall International Inc, 1992.

2 Sir George Bull, "Brands in the Boardroom", *Journal of the Marketing Society*, spring 1998.

3 Sir Alistair Grant, "Marketing Redesign", The Marketing Council, May 1996.

4 Sir Colin Marshall, "Creating Wealth for Britain through Marketing", The Marketing Council, 1996.

5 Sir George Bull, op. cit.

6 Quoted in *Customer Service Management Journal*, Issue 15, June 1997, p. 7.

7 A Report of the Research and Findings of the CAM-I Advanced Budgeting Group, CAM-I Inc, September 1994.

8 T. Hope and J. Hope, *Transforming the Bottom Line*, Nicholas Brealey, 1995.

9 R. Shaw and L. Mazur, *Marketing Accountability*, FT Reports, 1997.

10 *Financial Times*, October 25th 1995.

11 "Creating Wealth for Britain through Marketing", The Marketing Council, 1996.

12 G. Hamel and C.K. Prahalad, *Competing for the Future*, HBS Press, 1994, p. 24.

Chapter 2

1 R.J. Howe, D. Gaeddert and M.A. Howe, *Quality on Trial*, West Publishing Company, 1992, p. 31.

2 R.J. Howe *et al*, op. cit. p. 3.

3 *Business Week Quality Issue*, 1991.

4 R.C. Buetow, "A statement regarding ISO 9000", reproduced in B. Gale, *Managing Customer Value*, Free Press, 1994.

5 R. Shaw and L. Mazur, *Marketing Accountability*, FT Reports, 1997.

6 B. Gale, op. cit., p. 308.

7 J. Ozment and E. Morash, "The Augmented Service offering for perceived and actual service", *Journal of the Academy of Marketing*

Science, 22, Fall 1994, pp. 352–363.
8 R.E. Kordupleski, R.T. Rust and A.J. Zahoric, "Marketing: the missing dimension of quality management", *California Management Review*, Spring 1993.
9 R. Kordupleski and W. Vogel, "The Right Choice – What Does it Mean?", AT&T *White Paper*, October 24th 1988.
10 W. Hewlett, April 20th 1977, courtesy HP company archives (no. 56).
11 D. Packard, Speech 1974, courtesy HP archives (no. 68).
12 R.J. Howe *et al*, op. cit., p. 44.

Chapter 3
1 F. Reichheld, *The Loyalty Effect*, HBS Press, 1996.
2 M. Porter, "How competitive forces shape strategy", *Harvard Business Review*, March-April 1979.
3 T. Peters and R. Waterman, *In Search of Excellence*, Harper and Row, 1982.
4 T. Peters, *Thriving on Chaos*, Pan, 1989.
5 T. Levitt, "Marketing Myopia", *Harvard Business Review*, July-August 1960.
6 T. Levitt, *The Marketing Imagination*, Free Press, 1986.
7 A. Jenkinson, *Valuing Your Customers*, McGraw Hill, 1995, pp. 16, 71.
8 S. Rapp & T. Collins, *The New Maximarketing*, McGraw Hill, 1996, pp. 6 and 286.
9 W.E. Sasser and L.A. Schlessinger, *The Service Profit Chain*, Free Press, 1997, p. 3.
10 W.H. Davidow and B. Uttal, *Total Customer Service – The Ultimate Weapon*, Harper Perennial, 1989, p. 86.
11 T. Peters, *Thriving on Chaos*, Pan, 1989.
12 T. Levitt, "Marketing Myopia 1975: A Retrospective Commentary", *Harvard Business Review*, September-October 1975.
13 J. Carlzon, *Moments of Truth*, Ballinger, 1987.
14 C. Coulson-Thomas, *Transforming the Company*, Kogan Page, 1993.
15 T.O. Jones and W.E. Sasser, "Why satisfied customers defect", *Harvard Business Review*, November-December 1995.
16 M. Stone, "Second-Rate Customer Service", *Customer Service Management Journal*, Issue 19, May 1998, pp. 38–40.
17 D. Peppers and M. Rogers, *The One-to-one Future – Building Relationships One Customer at a Time*, Bantam Doubleday, 1993.
18 L. O'Brien and C. Jones, "Do rewards really create loyalty?", *Harvard Business Review*, May–June 1995.

19 A. Ehrenberg and J. Scriven, "Brand Loyalty under the Microscope", *Economics and Business Education*, Vol. 4, Part 4, No. 16, Winter 1996.

20 M. Fishbein and I. Azjen, *Belief, Attitude, Intention and Behaviour*, Addison Wesley, 1975.

21 R. Oliver, *Satisfaction*, McGraw Hill, 1998, p. 34.

22 H. Assael, *Consumer Behaviour and Marketing Action*, South Western, 1995, p. 148.

23 R. Oliver, op. cit.

24 H. Assael, op. cit., p. 148.

25 R. East, *Consumer Behaviour*, Prentice Hall, 1997.

26 T.O. Jones and W.E. Sasser, op. cit.

27 F. Reichheld, op. cit., pp. 260, 14, 266.

28 Customer Satisfaction Index, *What Car*, July 1994.

29 T. Ambler, *Marketing from Advertising to Zen*, FT Pitman, 1996, p. 34.

30 A. Ehrenberg and J. Scriven, op. cit.

31 S. Rapp and T. Collins, op. cit., pp. 231, 261.

32 F. Reichheld, op. cit., p. 19.

33 J.F. Engel, R.D. Blackwell and P.W. Miniard, *Consumer Behaviour*, 8th edition, The Dryden Press, 1995.

34 R. East, op. cit., pp. 91–102.

Chapter 4

1   R. Cooper, *Winning at New Products*, Addison Wesley, 1993.

2   D. Aaker, *Managing Brand Equity*, Free Press, 1991.

3   R.C. Bennett and R.C. Cooper, "The Misuse of the Marketing Concept: An American Tragedy", *Business Horizons*, November-December 1981.

4   M. Hammer and J. Champy, *Re-engineering the Corporation*, Nicholas Brealey, 1994, pp. 15, 18, 65.

5   G. Hamel and C.K. Prahalad, *Competing for the Future*, HBS Press, 1996, p. 108.

6   T. Peters, *Thriving on Chaos*, Pan, 1989, p. 50.

7   C.A. Bartlett and S. Ghoshal, *Managing Across Borders*, Century, 1989, pp. 119–21

8   N. Bunten and S. Simmons, "Brand Extensions: Lessons of Success and Failure", *Brandweek*, June 28th 1993.

9   R. Cooper, op. cit.

10 T. Ambler, *Marketing from Advertising to Zen*, FT Pitman, 1996, p. 311.

11 R. Cooper, op. cit.
12 T. Ambler, op. cit.
13 M. Fishbein and I. Azjen, *Belief, Attitude, Intention and Behaviour,* Addison Wesley, 1975.
14 I. Ajzen and M. Fishbein, "Attitude-behaviour relations", *Psychological Bulletin,* 84, 1977, pp. 888–918.
15 I. Ajzen, *Attitudes, Personality and Behaviour,* Dorsey Press, 1988.
16 J. Wallace, *Overdrive,* Wiley, 1997.

Chapter 5
1 R. Shaw and L. Mazur, *Marketing Accountability,* FT Reports, 1998.
2 B. Carlsberg, January 1998.
3 D. Aaker, *Building Strong Brands,* Free Press, 1996, pp. 303–338.
4 K.J. Clancy and R.S. Shulman, *Marketing Myths that are Killing Business,* McGraw Hill, 1994.

Chapter 6
1 H. Wilson, interview with Kit Grindley, Cranfield School of Management working paper, January 1998.
2 I. Hugo, *Marketing and the Computer,* Pergamon Press, 1967.
3 P. Kotler, *Marketing Information Systems,* Houghton Mifflin, Boston, 1968, A design for the firm's marketing nerve center, pp. 14–29.
4 IT Directors' Forum, Richmond Events, 1997.
5 K. Shaffir and G. Trentin, *Marketing Information Systems,* Amacom, New York, 1973.
6 F. Graf, "Information systems for marketing", *Marketing Trends,* 2, 1979, pp. 1–3.
7 "The View from IBM", *Business Week,* October 30th 1995.
8 G. Hallberg, *All Consumers Are Not Created Equal,* Wiley, 1995, p. 193.
9 D. Pringle, "Dicing with data, Bounty Hunters – how smart companies seek to exploit business intelligence and delight their customers", *Information Strategy* (Executive Briefing), January 1998.
10 Julia Vowler, "Has data warehousing had its day?", *Computer Weekly,* February 27th 1997.
11 M. Evans, M. Patterson and L. O'Malley, "Database marketing: investigating privacy concerns", *Journal of Marketing Communications,* 3, 1997, pp. 151–174.
12 D. Peppers and M. Rogers, *The One-to-One Future,* Doubleday, 1993, pp. 102–103.

13 F. V. Cespedes and H.H. Smith, "Database Marketing: New Rules for Policy and Practice", *Sloan Management Review*, Summer 1993.
14 S. Fournier, S. Dobscha and D.G. Mick, "Preventing the Premature Death of Relationship Marketing", *Harvard Business Review*, January-February 1998.
15 W. Rees-Mogg, 1997.

Chapter 7
1 N.H. Borden, The Concept of the Marketing Mix, *Journal of Advertising Research*, June 1964, pp. 2–7.
2 PIMS Principles, p. 340.
3 Max Burt, "It's good to talk", IPA Advertising Effectiveness Paper, June 10th 1996.
4 For full analysis of the MSAT findings see the forthcoming publication: R. Shaw, *Customer Relationship Management – Tools and Techniques*, Business Intelligence, Autumn 1998.

Chapter 8
1 R. Shaw and L. Mazur, *Marketing Accountability*, FT Reports, 1997.
2 A. Ehrenberg, *The R&D Initiative*, South Bank University Working Paper, 1998.
3 R. Shaw and L. Mazur, op. cit.
4 D.L. Madison, "Organisational Politics: A Study of Management Perceptions", *Human Relations*, 33, 1980, pp. 79–100.
5 R. Cooper, *Winning at New Products*, Addison Wesley, 1993.
6 T. Hope and J. Hope, *Transforming the Bottom Line*, Nicholas Brealey, 1995.
7 R. Kaplan and D. Norton, *The Balanced Scorecard*, HBS Press, 1996.
8 Ibid, p. 67.
9 Ibid, p. 70.
10 Ibid, p. 70.
11 Ibid, p. 68.

2 Definitions used in the MSAT survey

The Measurement Systems Assessment Tool (MSAT) Framework, developed by the author in 1997, aims to offer an objective assessment of how managers choose tools, what they use, and how satisfied they are with them. MSAT assesses 30 of the most widely used tools.

CONSUMER MEASURES

Attitudes, interests and opinions tracking
Market research studies which categorise consumers into segments on the basis of attitudes, interests and opinions, and track the segment trends.

Complaints tracking
Recording of consumer complaints, tracking them until resolved, and analysing the causes and resolutions of complaints.

Customer profitability tracking
Tracking of the profits that an individual customer generates. To calculate it requires the allocation of costs to the customer. This usually depends on the use of activity-based costing.

Customer satisfaction tracking
Tracking of customers' satisfaction with the product or service, and its features.

Dissatisfaction Tracking
Tracking of dissatisfaction and eliciting comments on reasons for dissatisfaction.

Lost or dormant customer analysis
Recording of lost or dormant customers and analysis of the reasons for loss or inactivity.

Loyalty reward programme
Recording of customer loyalty levels and rewarding of loyal behaviour.

Market share tracking
Tracking of brand sales in a category and total category sales, and plotting trends in the ratio.

Needs and wants segmentation
Market research studies which categorise consumers into segments on the basis of perceived needs and wants, and track the segment trends.

New product adoption/diffusion tracking
Identification of early adopters and late adopters, and tracking of their behaviour as the new product enters the market.

Perceived quality/value tracking
Market research to identify customer perceptions of product quality, or value, or both, and tracking changes over time.

Perceived service tracking
Market research to identify customer perceptions of service, and tracking changes over time.

Perceptual mapping (positioning)
A graphic representation of the positions of brands within a market based on consumer perceptions gathered through market research.

Promotion/advertising effectiveness tracking
Tracking of advertising and promotion effects, expressed in terms of return on investment of the advertising and promotion expenditure, or other measures of effectiveness.

Repeat purchase/retention tracking
Tracking of repeat purchases from individual customers. In the case of infrequent purchases, this is represented as customer retention, or attrition.

TRADE MEASURES
Attitudes, interests and opinions tracking
Market research studies which categorise trade customers into segments on the basis of attitudes, interests and opinions, and track the segment trends.

Channel/trade profitability reporting
Tracking of the profits that an individual channel or trade customer generates.

Channel/trade customer satisfaction tracking
Tracking of customers' satisfaction with the product or service, and its features.

Distribution: availability, share of shelf, pipeline
Tracking of the product distribution in the supply chain, including availability, share of shelf, etc. Usually analysed down to individual store unit.

Efficient consumer response
Organisation of the supply chain, by sharing information between the supplier and trade customer, in order to improve efficiency. This often involves electronic data interchange (EDI) and other computer methods.

Win/loss analysis
Tracking of new accounts won, or bids lost, along with reasons given by the customer.

GENERAL TOOLS

Activity-based costing (ABC)
A system that accumulates costs for each of the activities of an organisation, and then assigns these costs to the products, services, or other items that caused the activity. ABC methods take into account the actual activities, cost drivers and processes required to generate products or services. Traditional methods of cost allocation typically rely on volume-based allocation using labour or machine hours.

Balanced scorecard
A performance measurement system that strikes a balance between financial and operating measures, links performance to rewards, and explicitly recognises the diversity of stakeholder interests.

Brand equity financial valuation
The goodwill that exists in the market towards a brand. A financial estimate of this value may sometimes be included on the balance sheet.

Competitive benchmarking
Comparing performance to the best achieved by competitors. Comparisons are made on the basis of performance ratios and unit costs.

Employee attitudes, interests and opinions
Market research studies which categorise employees into segments on the basis of attitudes, interests and opinions. Tracking of segment trends.

New product/brand portfolio strategy models
A system of grading new products and brands by reference to market share, market growth, or similar variables. Used in planning. Methods include the BCG matrix (see glossary).

Quality (actual) tracking
Technical measurement of quality against conformance standards. Widely used in total quality management (TQM).

Relative price tracking
Tracking of prices relative to those of competitors. Usually analysed by outlet (eg, retailer).

Service (actual) tracking
Technical measurement of service against conformance standards. Widely used in TQM.

3 Glossary

Here are brief explanations of terms used in this book and some others that are used in marketing measurement contexts. Many of the terms referred to in the entries have a separate entry.

A&P
Short for advertising and promotion, usually used to describe a department in a company or a budget.

Above the line
Promotional activities which use mass media and are traditionally paid for by commission on usage; for normal purposes, the term means advertising.

Account management
The process of building and maintaining systematic and multilevel contacts with a customer. The customer is often referred to as an account.

Activity analysis
The process of identifying appropriate cost drivers and their effects on the cost of a product or service.

Activity-based costing (ABC)
See definition in Appendix 2.

Added value
The difference between the market value of a firm's output and the value its inputs would have in comparable activities undertaken by other firms.

Adstock
The cumulative effect in the market of previous advertising, based on the fact that advertising may continue to have an effect on consumer perception for some time after it is shown. It is often calculated by applying a gradual decay rate to the rating points accumulated during campaigns.

Advertising awareness
The ability of a consumer to remember a particular advertisement, either

spontaneously or prompted. Widely used as a key indicator of advertising effectiveness.

Advertising coverage
The percentage of the target market who have at least one opportunity to see an advertisement during a campaign.

Advertising effectiveness
The effectiveness of advertising is expressed in terms of its ability to meet its objectives. If sales increases are the aim, advertising effectiveness is measured in terms of the return on investment (ROI) of the advertising expenditure. If competitive defence is the aim (particularly in mature markets), it is measured in terms of maintenance or improvement in competitive position indicators.

Advertising share of voice (SOV)
The proportion of the overall advertising in a market accounted for by a brand or company.

Advertising testing
Research undertaken before an advertising campaign to forecast its likely effectiveness, and to identify changes that are likely to improve its effectiveness.

Advertising-to-sales ratio (A/S)
Expenditure on advertising expressed as a proportion of sales (of a brand, company or industry).

AIO
Short for attitudes, interests and opinions, the name for market research studies which categorise consumers into segments on the basis of these variables. Similar to lifestyle schemes.

Ansoff matrix
This looks at marketing objectives solely in terms of what is sold to whom. Within this framework, Ansoff identifies four courses of action: sell existing products to existing markets; extend existing products to new markets; develop new products for existing markets; and develop new products for new markets.

Assets
Economic resources that are expected to benefit future activities.

Assets, tangible or fixed
Physical items that can be seen and touched, such as property, plant and equipment.

Assets, intangible
Long-lived assets that are not physical in nature, such as goodwill, franchises, patents, trademarks and copyrights.

Attention-directing report
Reporting and interpreting information that helps managers to focus on operating problems, imperfections, inefficiencies and opportunities.

Attitude
What people feel about something, which may be a brand, a category, a person, an ideology or any other entity about which people think and to which they can attach feeling. Attitudes are thus positive-negative feelings, taking the form of a liking or disliking and based on many separate evaluations of product or service features. They are not like mood, which is a generalised state of feeling without focus, and they are not thought structures with no feelings attached.

Attitudinal survey
A market research survey of customers' attitudes.

Audience research
Data on the number and categories of people who read, watch or listen to various media. Used as the basis for measuring the number of people who are exposed to an advertisement.

Awareness
See Advertising awareness.

Balanced scorecard
See definition in Appendix 2.

BCG grid
A 2 × 2 matrix developed by Boston Consulting Group in the early 1970s,

which divides brands (products) into stars, cows, dogs and question marks according to their ranking on growth and market share dimensions. Stars = high on both; dogs = low on both; cows = high shares, low growth; and question marks = unknowns (high growth, not much share yet). Portfolio management requires firms to support stars, cull dogs and milk cows.

Behaviour
Observable actions by consumers, as distinct from the attitudes which lie behind the behaviours.

Behavioural list
Data collected through questionnaires about likes, dislikes, hobbies, etc. (See also list brokers.)

Below the line
Promotional activities directed at targeted individuals or objectives, and traditionally paid for by fee. The term covers most non-advertising expenditure, such as that on sales promotions and direct mail.

Benchmark
A general rule of thumb specifying an appropriate level for a business performance ratio.

Best-practice benchmarking
Comparing performance of a process to the best performance standard. This approach to benchmarking has become popular as a result of criticism of competitive benchmarking (see below).

Blind test
A product test where consumers do not know the identity of the product, thus ensuring that they judge it solely on the basis of its attributes without any influence from advertising, packaging, etc.

Bottom-up plan
A plan prepared by operational functional staff within a framework set for the business as a whole.

Brand
A name, term, sign, symbol, or combination of these intended to identify the goods or services of one seller or group of sellers and to differentiate

them from those of competitors.

Brand awareness
The ability of a consumer to remember a brand, either spontaneously or prompted. Widely used as a key indicator of brand management effectiveness.

Brand association
Components of brand image, usually assessed by qualitative research methods: free association (what comes into your mind when?); describe user; project on to picture or place or animal; analysis of choice. Can also be assessed quantitatively.

Brand equity
The accumulated goodwill that exists in the market towards a brand, which gives the brand added value over similar unbranded products.

Brand extension
The extension of products that bear a brand identity. Such extensions can include line extensions within the category (eg, when Persil offered a clothes washing detergent in liquid form) or category extensions to product fields which are new to the brand name (eg, when a Persil washing up liquid was offered for the first time).

Brand image
How consumers perceive a brand. This often goes beyond a brand's physical properties and includes a range of associated feelings and meanings. It is often quantified in a survey, and also tracked over time.

Brand image endorsement
How consumers feel about a brand, in terms of liking or disliking it, based on many separate evaluations of the brand's characteristics.

Brand map
A graphic representation of the relative positions of a number of brands in the market, mapped against the main dimensions of consumer perception in that market.

Brand recall
The extent to which a consumer can recall the names of brands when a

category is named. Certain types of purchasing decisions require recall, eg, when the category is known and the consumer deliberately seeks a supplier.

Brand recognition
The extent to which a consumer can recognise a brand from cues, particularly visual cues. Certain purchasing situations require recognition, eg, when shopping in a supermarket visual recognition of the brand may trigger purchase.

Brand switching
Changes in customers' brand preferences which can be tracked to see if customers make repeat purchases.

Brand valuation
What a brand would fetch if it were up for sale.

Budget
A quantitative financial expression of a plan of action, and an aid to co-ordinating and implementing the plan.

Budget, capital
A budget that details the planned expenditure for new products and other long-term investments.

Budget, flexible or variable
A budget that adjusts for changes in sales volume and other cost-driver activities.

Burst
An advertising campaign where the advertisements are shown intensively over a short period of time.

Buying cycle
The period of time between repeat purchases, ie, the buying cycle for sugar is much shorter than that for cars.

Call logging or scripting
The automatic capture of telephone call (including e-mail) results and history against prospect, customer, campaign and operator records.

Scripts are maintained in a library and may be modified as more is learned during a campaign.

Capital asset pricing model (CAPM)
A theory of capital markets in which the returns to risk are based on the relationship between the risk of particular investments and overall market volatility.

Category
A group of products or services which compete directly with each other to satisfy the same consumer needs. Also known as a "needs market" or "needs segment". (See also Strategic group.)

Category health
The attractiveness of a category. Investors, in particular, will compare the health of different categories when deciding in which category to invest.

Category potential
The forecast potential of a category.

CATI
Short for computer aided telephone interviewing. Market research based on telephone interviews where results are fed into a computer for collation and analysis. The questionnaire appears on the computer screen, and the responses to questions are keyed directly into the computer. This speeds up the process, ensuring quicker and more efficient results.

Channel
The intermediaries between a supplier and the ultimate end user, eg, retailers and wholesalers.

Churn
The rate at which customers are gained and lost. Some categories have rapid churn, others do not.

Cleaning a list
An updating process involving the removal of names or addresses that are no longer valid.

Cluster analysis
A statistical technique which groups a large number of objects into a few clusters with similar characteristics. There should be fewer differences within individual groups than among groups. It is used commonly with census data to group neighbourhoods by type and to group customers into segments. (See also Factor analysis.)

Cold list
A list bought from a list broker or third party.

Competitive advantage
An aspect of a brand or product which meets customer needs better than the alternatives in the market.

Competitive benchmarking
Comparing performance to the best achieved by competitors – an approach criticised in industries where even the best competitor is still considered to perform badly. (See also Best practice benchmarking.)

Competitive intelligence (CI)
Collection of information about competitors, sometimes referred to as industrial espionage. Business history is littered with instances of CI that have been in breach of the law. IT has become an important CI tool, with hacking an increasingly serious threat.

Competitive threat
The ability of competitors to improve their competitive advantage in a category.

Concept
A term widely used for the basic idea behind a brand or an advertising campaign, rather like the USP or the proposition. Market research to test consumer reaction is therefore known as a concept test.

Conjoint analysis (or trade-off)
A research technique which reveals how people make purchase decisions. It assumes that, in a real situation, such decisions are based upon a range of factors considered jointly, hence the term conjoint. It therefore emulates this situation by creating an interview format which forces respondents to make trade-off decisions similar to those in real life.

Conservatism convention
Selecting the method of measurement that yields the gloomiest immediate results.

Contact management system
A system that keeps track of customers' dealings with an organisation, the sales activity involved, communications from customers, as well as a history of sales, returns, bad debts and complaints. Depending on the type of industry the underlying customer/prospect database is designed for, the system might hold detailed or simple customer and contact profile data. This function applies to office-based, telesales staff as well as field sales.

Continuous improvement
Efforts to make incremental improvements in performance.

Continuous research
Regular interviewing using the same questionnaire so results can be tracked and forecast. It can include the use of panels, retail audits and television viewer panels.

Conversion rate
The percentage of prospects converting into a lead; or leads into a buyer.

Copy test
A technique to evaluate the impact of the written copy in an advertisement on recall, comprehension, attention, arousal, interest, intention to buy or actual purchase.

Correlation
Most statistical techniques simply demonstrate that two activities appear to be connected, eg, if A goes up so does B, and when B goes down so does A. The most common error is to conclude that A causes B or vice versa. Suppose A is sales and B is advertising. Economists generally apply the rule that if time series analysis indicates A happens before B, A is presumed to cause B.

Correspondence mapping
A form of brand mapping showing the relative positions of brands within a market, or the relative importance of aspects of a brand to dif-

ferent segments of the market.

Cost accounting system
The part of the accounting system that measures costs for the purposes of management decision making and financial reporting. It uses special techniques to determine the cost of a product, service, or other cost objective by collecting and classifying costs and assigning them to cost objects. Important as a basis for product line profitability decisions, pricing, private label and make-versus-buy.

Cost centre
A responsibility centre for which costs are accumulated.

Cost driver
An activity that affects costs.

Cost of quality
All costs (labour, materials, overhead) attributed to preventing non-conformance to quality standards, appraising or checking output to ensure conformance to requirements, and correcting internal and external failures. Cost of quality is not a manufacturing term. It also refers to the quality of administrative work-flows. For example, the salesperson who books an incorrect order, the clerk who has to make sure the order is clean and the person who reworks the order are all examples of costs of quality.

Cost per hundred (CPH)
The cost of achieving 100 rating points during an advertising campaign.

Cost per thousand (CPT)
The cost of advertising to 1,000 consumers through a given media, used to judge the relative cost-effectiveness of the media. Commonly applied by list brokers.

Cost recovery
A concept in which assets such as inventories (stocks), prepayments and equipment are carried forward as assets because their costs are expected to be recovered in the form of cash inflows (or reduced cash outflows) in future periods.

Cost, direct
The cost of labour and materials in making a product and getting it to market, but not including any overhead costs.

Cost, fixed
A cost that is not immediately affected by changes in the cost driver. In a brand's budget, the total of those costs which do not change if the amount sold varies (within limits).

Cost, incremental or marginal
The cost of undertaking an additional activity or producing an additional unit of output. Important when there are economies of scope or scale.

Cost, indirect or overhead
A cost that cannot readily be attributed to a particular product, eg, the board, the canteen, the finance department. The term can be imprecise, especially when product profitability calculations attempt to allocate all such costs.

Cost, non-value-added
A cost that can be eliminated without affecting a product's value to the customer.

Cost, standard
A cost per unit calculated for management accountants to apply in other cost calculations.

Cost, value-added
The cost of an activity that cannot be eliminated without affecting a product's value to the customer.

Cost, variable
A cost that changes in direct proportion to changes in the cost driver. In a brand's budget, the average cost of raw materials will often depend on the quantity bought.

Cost-management system
A system that identifies how management's decisions affect costs by first measuring the resources used in performing the organisation's activities

and then assessing the effects on costs of changes in those activities.

Critical success factor (CSF)

A term popularised by John Rockart of MIT's Sloan Management School based on his research into what information executives need. In his words, csfs are "those few critical areas where things must go right for the business to flourish".

Customer loyalty

Loyalty is measured in several different, and potentially contradictory, ways. It can be an attitude. It can be a repeat purchase measure (which further splits into purchase-to-purchase, or period-to-period, or average purchases per buyer). It can also be measured as share of category requirements (scr).

Customer needs and values

These are likely to influence the purchase behaviour and choice of rational customers. Market research techniques can help identify these needs and values. Care should be taken to ensure that emotional needs are included.

Customer profitability

The profits that an individual customer generates; often more interesting for channel customers than for end consumers. To calculate it requires the allocation of costs to the customer, which usually depends on the use of activity-based costing.

Customer retention

This is measured in several different ways, depending on circumstances. For long-term contracts (eg, insurance, or bank accounts) it is measured by renewals. For transactions the term is often used synonymously with customer loyalty.

Customer satisfaction survey

An expanding area of market research, which attempts to assess the quality of service offered by a particular organisation, and thus define consumer perceptions of that company's brands or services. This is a good indicator of how likely customers are to re-buy and stay loyal to the brand.

Customer switching cost
The cost to a customer of switching from using one product or service to using another. It is a deterrent to customers who want to switch. It may also be a deterrent to potential customers, wary of the cost of switching if they are dissatisfied.

DAGMAR
Short for Defining Advertising Goals for Measured Advertising Results, a conceptual approach to advertising management arguing that a specific communications objective can be set for any promotional activity, thus enabling expenditure to be evaluated.

Data warehouse
A way of combining and holding data from many corporate systems and external sources in a new database or warehouse, sometimes known as a mirror database. The data can then be accessed by end-users using online analytical processing (OLAP) tools.

Database management system (DBMS)
A type of software used for structuring, organising and managing databases. A DBMS can attach data together in structures which permit the fast, efficient access or particular elements.

Day-after-recall (DAR)
A method of evaluating an advertisement based on surveying consumers to see how many can recall an advertisement shown the previous day.

Diary panel
Diaries are used as an alternative to questionnaires to record consumer behaviour on or between specific dates, perhaps at specific times of day. They require a panel member to complete the diary at the time that behaviour occurs. They are used to record behaviour that repeats at fairly frequent intervals. Three types are common: product diaries that record product purchasing or usage; media diaries that record viewing or listening to broadcast media; and diaries which record face-to-face, telephone or mail contacts.

Decision support system (DSS)
An integrated management information and planning system that provides users with the ability to: query databases and information systems;

analyse the information in various ways; predict the impact of decisions before they are made.

Deduplication
The removal of duplicate records from an in-house customer database.

Delphi technique
A method of expert judgment without adequate hard data, eg, long-term forecasting. Stage 1 is to poll experts, anonymously and separately. In Stage 2 the results are consolidated and fed back to the experts as a group. Stage 3 polls them individually again, in the light of peer group opinion. In theory, the process continues until consensus arrives. In practice, ennui arrives faster. Often the differences of opinions are more enlightening than the consensus.

Demographics
Social and economic information about people or groups of people, including age, income, educational level, etc.

Depth
An unstructured one-to-one market research interview designed to encourage exploratory discussion.

Directional policy matrix (DPM)
Works on the assumption that products will make money for businesses if they are sold into markets with the potential to generate high profits, and the business is competitively positioned to meet the needs of those markets. Product markets are scored according to the attractiveness of the product market and the strength of the business in that market.

Discriminatory pricing
Charging different prices to different customers for the same product or service.

Distribution coverage
The percentage of the target distribution channels which list the product or brand.

Distribution effectiveness
There are different ways of measuring this. For groceries, it is usually list-

ings – the percentage of outlets or shops (weighted by the total turnover through each outlet) which have agreed to stock the brand. It may mean this figure modified in various ways to make it closer to availability by: subtracting out-of-stocks (the percentage of outlets which temporarily did not carry the brand); or measuring front of shop, which means actually on the shelf, excluding times when the brand was officially in stock but only in the storeroom. Also the quality of distribution may be measured by: position in store; the number of facings; length of shelf occupied; or percentage of the chiller cabinet occupied.

Distribution leadership
An assessment of the brand's occupation of distribution channels relative to competing brands.

Drip
An advertising campaign where the advertisements are shown at intervals over a longer period of time.

Dynamic difference model
A method of evaluating advertising effectiveness by tracking the relationship between promotional expenditure and market share.

EVA
Short for economic value added, a method of profit and cost analysis that can be used to calculate the return on net assets (RONA) of any product line by imputing a capital cost to it. EVA is calculated as the normal operating profit on a product minus the imputed cost of capital. Its aim is to focus managers on the cost of capital.

EDI
Short for electronic data interchange, the transfer of structured data between computers using agreed communications standards.

EFTPOS
Short for electronic funds transfer at point of sale. Payment is made at the time of purchase by presentation of a card, and EFTPOS immediately debits the relevant bank account.

Enduring involvement
The long-term personal involvement of consumers with a particular cat-

egory or brand. (See also Situational involvement and Involvement).

EPOS
Short for electronic point of sale, which allows transactions to be linked to planning, ordering, stock control systems, etc.

Exponential smoothing (ES)
A forecasting technique for extrapolating historic data into the future. The more complex version, time series analysis, extrapolates sales by decomposing them into the basic trend, short-term cycles/seasonality and random variations. Some fancy weightings and arithmetic apart, ES simply tells you that whatever happened yesterday is likely to happen tomorrow.

Extended problem solving (EPS)
A decision process which includes: problem recognition; extensive search for alternative solutions; extensive search for information about each solution; extensive evaluation of alternatives; purchase; post-purchase activities, such as recommending to others. This is one of three approaches to decision making described by Engel, Blackwell and Miniard (*Consumer Behaviour*, 8th edition, The Dryden Press, New York, 1995). It is commonest when customers are unfamiliar with the category and brands, and have high involvement.

Factor analysis
Reducing the many rating scales used by the researcher to the minimum (probably 3–4) independent dimensions supposedly forming the consumers' unconscious model. Mathematically, this is fine, but usually it involves a ragbag of rating scales to which researchers apply their creativity.

Fast-moving consumer goods (FMCG)
Goods bought frequently by consumers, such as food and drink.

FCB grid
One of the better pieces of "how advertising works" research done for the Foote Cone and Belding agency. Not all advertisements work the same way. The FCB grid groups them into four. The 2 × 2 matrix is high/low involvement and think/feel, depending on whether the product category is one the consumer gets involved with (eg, cars) or not (eg, flour), and whether the purchase is driven more by cognitive or by emotional factors.

First brand loyalty
The proportion of purchase devoted to a consumer's most popular brand over a period.

Fishbein
The best-known (cognitively biased) modeller of consumer attitudes. Pioneer or expectancy-value (EV) models which break attitudes into two components: the attributes of a brand; and how much these are worth to the consumer. Consumer actions are consistent with these expectations and values, although some rapid post hoc shifting may go on.

FMCG
See Fast-moving consumer goods.

Focus group
A market research discussion group, with a researcher chairing a group of consumers.

Frequency
The number of times within a given period that a consumer has the opportunity to see an advertisement.

Geographic information system (GIS)
A system that takes data relating to physical location from different sources, combines them together and presents them as a colour-coded map.

Gross rating point (GRP)
The total rating achieved by an advertising campaign, ie, the sum of the ratings achieved by each individual exposure of the advertisement.

Hall tests
Tests normally carried out in hired rooms in pubs, clubs, hotels or shopping centres. Following specific recruitment criteria, field workers invite relevant passing respondents to be interviewed for about 30 minutes on a specific topic.

Independent variable
One key, but much abused, requirement of many statistical techniques, such as regression, is that the variables used for prediction or explanation

should be independent or completely uninfluenced by each other. The trick is to determine whether they really are. For example, if one variable is rainfall and another temperature, they are not truly independent; the temperature in summer will usually be lower when it is raining.

Inertia
The propensity of a consumer to continue to behave in the same way, even when there are good reasons for changing.

Innovation
New products or processes, or styles or relationship. Innovation is often used mainly to refer to technological innovations, but it should really be used in a much more general sense to identify a distinctive capability.

Internal control system
Methods and procedures to prevent errors and irregularities, detect errors and irregularities, and promote operating efficiency.

Internal customer
The next operation, department, or user in an organisation in the value-added chain.

Involvement
A focused orientation towards specific products and services of a more intense nature, consisting of greater pre-purchase behaviour (eg, search), greater attention to consumption and greater processing of consumption outcomes.

Lead
Relates to information that can help track and secure a sales opportunity.

Lead qualification
The process of finding out more about leads, to determine whether it is worthwhile (according to the qualifying criteria) visiting or calling them.

Lead tracking system
Software that supports the routing of leads to the most appropriate handler, and controlling and monitoring their progress from capture to conclusion. Lead tracking may include adding response (coupons, telephone calls) and enquiry data or records linked to customer details. It may also

include rules for scoring enquiries according to their likelihood of leading to a sale, either manually or automatically. When leads are passed around different parts of the organisation, integration of field and telesales systems is important.

Lifestyle
A set of consumer behaviours uncovered by market research which are taken to indicate a particular set of social values and attitudes. Used as a label for a segment.

Likert scale
See Semantic differential scale.

Limited problem solving (LPS)
A decision process which includes: semi-automatic problem recognition; limited search for alternative solutions; limited search for information about each solution; limited evaluation of alternatives; purchase; post-purchase activities, such as recommending to others. It is commonest when customers are familiar with the category but unfamiliar with the brand and have medium involvement. (See also Extensive problem solving and Routine problem solving.)

Line extension
The addition of a new variant to an existing brand.

List
A list of customers, such as a mailing list of all subscribers to *The Economist*.

List broker
Someone who helps list seekers acquire lists from list owners and list owners sell their lists to list seekers.

Logit model
A version of regression analysis using an S-shaped curve instead of a straight line. Used when responses are binary, eg, yes/no, rather than continuous numbers.

Management accounting
The process of identifying, measuring, accumulating, analysing, prepar-

ing, interpreting and communicating information that helps managers
fulfil organisational objectives.

Management control system
A logical integration of management accounting tools to gather and
report data and evaluate performance.

Market
Economists use the term to refer to a collection of buyers and sellers who
trade in a category of products and services. Marketers see customers as
constituting the market and sellers as constituting the industry. Business
people use the term to cover various groupings of customer transactions.
They talk about need markets (such as diet-seeking); product markets (such
as frozen foods); demographic markets (such as young people aged 18–25);
and geographic markets (such as Western Australia).

Market modelling
Conjoint analysis produces output which makes it possible to build a
model which can predict a product's attractiveness when placed alongside a range of products already available. "What if?" modelling can be
used to identify optimum product profiles for any given market segment.
Other forms of market modelling are also available.

Market segment
A subdivision of a market. These subdivisions can include need segments, product segments, demographic segments and geographic segments.

Market share
The percentage of the market represented by a company's sales in relation to total sales. Some marketing theorists argue that the term is misleading since the market may be considerably larger than that revealed
by total sales.

Marketing mix
The mix of marketing inputs that affect customer motivation and
behaviour; traditionally the "four Ps" of product, price, promotion and
place (distribution). More recently process, policy and people have been
recognised as additional key factors.

Marketing mix productivity
Indicators of different types of marketing productivity, such as sales calls per day, unit costs per mailshot, etc.

Marketing waste
Unproductive marketing costs, resources and activities. Pure waste consists of activities and expenses that are unnecessary, such as scrap and rework. Hidden waste comprises costs associated with activities that do not add value, such as inspection and storage. Such wasteful activities are typically necessary because of existing operating conditions and strategies.

Markov model
Sets out in a matrix the probability that the user of a brand in a category will switch to another brand in the category. Mathematically sound and now measurable through scanners. Follows the Dirichlet expectation.

Merge-purge
A computer process whereby postal lists may be merged to facilitate postal/zip code sequencing and purged of duplicate and undesirable names.

Model
Anything from a set of equations to a simple diagram that helps a group of people represent reality is a simple way to share understanding. A model is no more reliable than the assumptions on which it is based.

Multiple regression analysis
See Regression analysis.

Mystery shopping
A popular form of research among large organisations such as supermarkets and banks to discover how their staff treat their customers. A mystery shopper is a trained researcher who goes through the normal buying process and reports on the experience.

Normal costing system
A system that applies actual direct materials and labour costs to products or services but uses standards for applying overhead.

Observational research
Research where interviewers are required to report on activity they observe, rather than asking questions; it includes mystery shopping and customer behaviour studies.

Omnibus survey
A form of market research whereby the same audience group is surveyed periodically, and various companies may buy into the survey with one or two questions. Clients benefit from sharing the cost of the survey and gain information which can be analysed on a regional, class or age basis.

Online analytical processing (OLAP)
A technology which enables end-users to analyse and manipulate data from many corporate systems using a series of end-user tools. It requires the use of a data warehouse.

Organisational knowledge
Systems, routines or data within an organisation which are only imperfectly understood by any individual. Their value is therefore partly appropriable by the organisation.

Opportunity to see (OTS)
Used to describe the level of advertising exposure. The measure is generally used to show the fraction of the population reaching a given OTS. Loosely, a person who is in the room when a TV commercial is on is said to have had an OTS. Other media have equivalent definitions.

Panel
A group of consumers who record their purchases to help market researchers identify consumption patterns.

Penetration
The percentage of a target market who have bought a particular brand at least once.

Perceived price
Price is perceived not only in terms of what things actually cost to buy, but also in terms of customers' expectations and perceptions of price-related items. For example, telephone users often have poor knowledge of the actual price of a telephone call, and their perceptions of the unit price

are influenced by their expectations and their recall of previous telephone bills (which therefore also reflects total numbers and length of calls).

Perceived quality
Quality is perceived not only in terms of technical specifications, but also in terms of customers' perceptions of its match with their expectations.

Perceived value
Value is perceived in terms of both perceived price and perceived quality. Value perceptions may also be significantly influenced by the views of the media, and friends and colleagues.

Perceptual mapping
See definition in Appendix 2.

Performance management system
A systematic approach to developing, strengthening and reinforcing the right actions to maximise performance and organisation learning.

Pilot study
Once a preliminary questionnaire has been designed, a subsample should be used to pilot (test) the validity and efficiency of the questions, and thereby ensure that the questionnaire meets the required standard before it is commissioned in the field.

PIMS
Short for profit impact of market strategy, an extensive database on the market performance and other characteristics of business units supplied anonymously by 7,000 companies. Now a consultancy spin-off from academia and the Marketing Science Institute in Cambridge, MA, set up to gather and analyse company data. Mainly known for suggesting that market share drove profit. Now (and more likely) the perception is that perceived quality drives long-term profit.

Placement test
A technique to gain a thorough understanding of consumer attitudes to new or existing products by asking a selected sample to use a particular product in their home, and complete a questionnaire at the end of the process.

Portfolio planning
A system of grading business units with reference to market share, market growth, or similar variables.

Positioning
There are three related meanings. (1) Product positioning is the relationship between a firm's products and those of its competitors. (2) Corporate positioning refers to a firm's overall strategy relative to its competitors. (3) Image positioning refers to influencing the consumers' perception of a brand through the use of advertising. All techniques apply a process of selecting, delineating and matching the segment of the market with which a product, company or image will be the most compatible.

Predictive dialling
Systems used in telemarketing to ensure that representatives always get through to potential customers. The systems involve the maintenance of call lists, scheduling call-backs and automatically dialling the next person on the list.

Price premium
The amount that a customer is prepared to pay above the average price in a category. Price premiums are often dependent on perceived quality and brand image endorsement.

Product adoption
The process whereby customers choose new products with which they are unfamiliar. Some customers (early adopters) are more willing to take a risk to gain the promised benefits of the new product; others (late adopters) are more risk averse and wait until the product has been widely adopted.

Product differentiation
Differences between related products on the basis of such features as performance, durability, reliability, repairability, design and style.

Product life cycle
Charts how the sales revenue, sales costs and volumes of a product are likely to grow and then decline over time. This pattern is typically divided into four stages: growth; maturity; saturation; and decline.

Productivity
Relates to how resources (including time) are managed. Emphasis on waste reduction and faster process times improves productivity.

Profit centre
A responsibility centre for controlling revenue as well as costs, ie, profitability.

Projective technique
A qualitative market research technique used to investigate attitudes and perceptions not described by verbal answers.

Psychographic segmentation
Grouping people according to their personality and lifestyle characteristics, which influence their purchasing decisions. These continue to evolve as society changes. Brand choice is often a public statement about the purchaser, and this makes lifestyle segmentation (trendsetter, pleasurist, homebody, traditionalist, etc) a useful tool for marketing personnel.

Qualitative research
This usually takes the form of in-depth interviewing (one-to-one) or group discussions (sometimes called focus groups) led by a moderator. It is used to explore respondents' motives for their purchasing decisions in some detail, using small samples.

Quality
Consistent conformance to customer expectations, 100% of the time, through the delivery of a defect-free product or service.

Quality assurance
The planned or systematic actions necessary to ensure that the product or service will satisfy the customer.

Quality control
Operational techniques and activities to sustain the quality of a product or service. A regulatory process to measure actual quality performance.

Quality function deployment (QFD)
A system for designing products or services based on customer demands and involving all members of the producer or supplier organisation.

Quality management
Eliminating production faults through a management-led philosophy of continuous improvement in every process of planning, production and service. W. Edwards Deming laid down the principle that all processes are vulnerable to loss of quality through variations but that the levels of variation can be managed in order to raise quality consistency. Both Deming and Joseph Juran insist that quality control starts at the top; Deming believes that 85% of production faults are the responsibility of management.

Quantitative research
This involves large samples and the use of closed and structured techniques, such as questionnaires, which must be carefully designed to ensure the questions are not ambiguous, leading or difficult to comprehend (see Pilot survey). The results will have more statistical validity than those from qualitative research.

Quarterly repeat purchase
The percentage of people that bought a brand in successive quarters.

Quota sampling
Used where a list of the specifically chosen part of the population (a sampling frame) is not available. It can be used where the percentage of the population that should be allocated to the required grouping is known, such as social class. This sample is then found by requesting interviewers to find individuals on the basis of these percentages, eg, 52% female, 48% male. This is defined as non-random sampling, as not everybody has an equal chance of being chosen.

Quotation generation system
A system that generates sales quotations by referring to a library of standard quotes or by the creation of a customer quote.

Random sampling
Everyone (be it companies or individuals) in the sampling frame is allocated a number and then numbers are selected randomly until the total sample required is reached. Everyone has an equal chance of being selected. Useful when trying to eliminate bias from research.

Reach
The proportion of a target population exposed to an advertisement at least once in a period.

Recall
The extent to which something can be remembered; often used as a measure of the effectiveness of advertising.

Regression analysis
Rejected by some academics and adored by others, the full title is multivariate linear regression model, a basic tool of econometricians. Regression is needed to "fit" a "dependent" variable (eg, sales share) by one or more "explanatory" variables (eg, price). The fit is by an equation (eg, sales share = A + B × price). The result is that the "parameters" (eg, A and B) are chosen so that the "residuals" (differences between the original values of the dependent variable and the fitted values) are as small as possible. Used for forecasting on the dubious assumption that what fitted before will fit again. Powerful but dangerous in the wrong hands.

Relational database management system (RDBMS)
A system based on tables of data and the relational algebra devised by Ted Codd. Popular in IT circles, its main benefit is that programming costs are generally lower than for other types of databases.

Relative market share
An organisation's share of the market relative to its largest competitor.

Relative purchase penetration
An organisation's purchase penetration relative to its largest competitor.

Repertoire
The group of brands within a product category which a consumer regards as acceptable. In many markets exclusive brand loyalty is rare, and consumers switch within their repertoire.

Repertory grid
A research technique which investigates the variables used by consumers to distinguish between brands within a market. Sometimes referred to as a Kelly after the founder of the technique.

Research brief
Your research will only be as good as your brief. This should include the product's current positioning in the market, its full history and competitor activity, the potential target audience, the overall aim of the research, as well as the time scales involved and the allocated budget.

Residual error
What still cannot be explained, after estimating the coefficients of the independent variables. Usually blamed on measurement or omissions by analysts who, naturally, claim their model cannot possibly be wrong.

Response rate
The number of responses per thousand contacted.

Responsibility accounting
Identifying what parts of the organisation have primary responsibility for each objective; developing measures of achievement of objectives; and creating reports of these measures by organisation subunit or responsibility centre.

Restructuring
The redesign of organisational structure and management reporting relationships.

Retail audit
A form of continuous research, whereby sales of products can be measured, in co-operation with retail outlets, by laser scanning of the barcodes featured on packaging as the goods are purchased. Audits are run by sophisticated specialist companies of which the largest is Nielsen, after whom audits are sometimes named. Widely used as the basis for market share calculations.

Rollout
A large campaign carried out if a test is successful.

Routine problem solving (RPS)
The decision process which mainly includes purchase and post-purchase activities. It is most common when customers are familiar with the category and brands, and have low involvement. (See also Limited problem solving and Extensive problem solving.)

Sales-activity variance
A variance that measures how effective managers have been in meeting the planned sales objective, calculated as actual unit sales minus master budget unit sales times the budgeted unit contribution margin.

Salient attribute
The aspect of a brand most noticeable to consumers, and by which they generally remember and judge the brand.

Sampling
Usually assumed to be random but for convenience is more likely to be pseudo-random (eg, every tenth person) or stratified (categorised by some variable such as age group) to try to ensure the sample mirrors the total population. Convenience sampling is a polite expression for including just those you come across.

Sampling error
When interpreting market research results given in percentages, beware of sampling errors. Always consider whether differences apparent in sample behaviour are likely to be real, or merely the result of interviewing only a sample.

SBU
See Strategic business unit.

Score
A value calculated for an individual, which assesses propensity such as purchasing or creditworthiness. Often calculated using a multiple regression formula.

Segment
A subdivision of a market, consisting of a group of consumers with similar requirements of the product category, which are significantly different from the requirements of other consumers in the market.

Semantic differential scale
Typically, a five-point scale from a superlative (eg, very much) to its equal and opposite (eg, very much not). Used for measuring attitudes or perceptions. One form was popularised by R. Likert in 1932 and asks the extent to which the respondent agrees or disagrees with a statement.

Served market
The part of a market which a particular brand or company is targeting.

Share
The proportion of overall sales in a market accounted for by a particular brand or company. It may be expressed as value share (when the calculations are based on expenditure in the market) or volume share (when the calculations are based on units sold in the market).

Share of market surplus
The share that a supplier, or its channels, appropriates of the total value added in the value chain (ie, total value added by supplier plus the channels).

Shareholder value
An approach to business planning which stresses maximisation of the value of shareholders' equity and discounted cash flow methods of investment appraisal.

Shopper panel
Market research using a representative sample of shoppers whose purchasing behaviour for a defined category of products is tracked continuously or at regular intervals over a long period.

Situational involvement
Temporary involvement with a product or service only in certain situations, such as when a purchase decision is required.

Smart card
A device the size of a credit card with an embedded computer chip.

SOM
Short for share of market

SQL
Short for structured query language, a database enquiry and update language used to operate relational database management systems. SQL enables the extraction, update, deletion and manipulation of data as well as creation and management of the databases.

Standard cost system
An accounting system that values products according to standard costs only.

Stochastic
Fancy word for random or chance.

Strategic business unit (SBU)
A separate business in a large, usually diversified company, first used in the United States by General Electric as a concept for product classification. This form of organisation makes it easier to make independent decisions regarding, for example, market share and cost structure. SBUs make sense when the following criteria are met: units have distinct business concepts and missions; units have their own competitors; units' competitors are external; units are better off managing their strategies independently.

Strategic group
Organisations which adopt similar strategies and hence see themselves as in direct competition (see also Category).

Stratified random sampling
A more sophisticated way of eliminating bias than random sampling. The population is split into sections, eg, by company size or type, and then the random sampling process is applied to make sure each section is represented.

Switching matrix
A matrix, or table, which plots the rate at which customers switch from one supplier (in rows) to a new supplier (in columns).

SWOT analysis
The discussion of an organisation's prospects by reference to an evaluation of internal strengths and weaknesses relative to competitors as well as key external opportunities and threats.

Target costing
A strategy in which companies first determine the price at which they can sell a new product or service and then design a product or service that can be produced at low enough cost to provide an adequate profit mar-

gin. Made popular when Japanese firms were discovered to be using it.

Television rating
See TVR.

Territory management system
Software that provides analyses of sales territories by number and type of customers and prospects, historic and potential sales and geographical location. Enables territories to be designed with fair and equal workloads, targets to be set by territory and performance to be evaluated. Sophisticated territory management systems will include a database of journey times.

Testing
Preliminary campaign to evaluate a product, advertisement or other element of the marketing mix.

Total quality management (TQM)
A structured system for meeting and exceeding customer needs and expectations through organisation-wide participation in the planning and implementation of breakthrough and continuous improvement processes (see also Quality management).

Tracking study
Market research to measure brand positions and the long-term effects of marketing activity. Usually consisting of a regularly repeated survey, a tracking study measures awareness and attitudes, which can then be compared with the patterns of marketing activities.

Trial purchase
The first purchase of a brand.

TVR
Short for television rating (point), a measurement used to accumulate total television exposure in a period. One TVR is 1% of the target population having one opportunity to see the advertisement. A campaign may be credited with 200 TVRs derived from 20 different showings of the advertisement at an average rating of 10.

U&A
Short for usage and attitude, the name given to a comprehensive research study of a market which includes both quantitative measures of consumer behaviour and qualitative information on attitudes and consumer perceptions.

USP
Short for unique selling point or unique selling proposition, a phrase used to describe the thing about a brand which is unique and motivating to consumers, and is thus its main appeal to the market.

Value positioning
A position in the market where products are perceived to provide good value for money. This often results from a combination of good perceived price and good perceived quality.

Vertical integration
The system favoured by some large corporations for integrating a number of companies down to supplier level to act as an in-house chain of manufacture. Once an established and successful strategy of the American automobile industry, its weaknesses are now more clearly seen as companies have learned that they cannot be equally good at a variety of activities. Forming alliances with suppliers rather than integrating them is now fashionable.

Viewing studio
Allows clients to observe group discussions through a one-way mirror and to hear the target audience's reactions to their products first-hand, as well as allowing the discussion to be discreetly videotaped.

Volume
A measure of how much of a product is sold. The units depend on the nature of the product and are not restricted to the literal sense, eg, litres or gallons. Weight (kilograms and tonnes) and numbers (of standard cases) are included. The number of packs is rarely used, because packs vary in size.

Weight
Weight of advertising is the number of exposures in a period.

Weight test
Measures the impact on sales of changes in the weight of advertising.

Win/loss analysis
Analysis of the underlying reasons for customer purchases being won and lost against competition.